D0277626

ADVANCES IN
SOCIAL SCIENCE
METHODOLOGY

Volume 1 . 1989

EDITORIAL BOARD

ADVANCES IN SOCIAL SCIENCE METHODOLOGY

A Research Annual

Editor: BRUCE THOMPSON
College of Education
University of New Orleans

VOLUME 1 . 1989

JAI PRESS INC.

Greenwich, Connecticut *London, England*

55 Old Post Road, No. 2
Greenwich, Connecticut 06836

JAI PRESS LTD.
3 Henrietta Street
London WC2E 8LU
England

ISBN: 0-89232-736-7

Manufactured in the United States of America

CONTENTS

LIST OF CONTRIBUTORS

James Algina — College of Education, University of Florida

Carl Huberty — College of Education, University of Georgia

Richard Lomax — College of Education, Louisiana State University

Robert McKinley — Educational Testing, Princeton, NJ

Craig N. Mills — Educational Testing, Princeton, NJ

Hari Swaminathan — School of Education, University of Massachusetts

Bruce Thompson — College of Education, University of New Orleans

FOREWORD

The inaugural volume in the new series, *Advances in Social Science Methodology,* includes chapters discussing a wide range of research methods employed by social and behavioral scientists. Some of the chapters emphasize discussion of recent extensions of methods that have been available to researchers for some time; other chapters present methods that have been developed more recently, but which seem to have great potential for yielding more accurate or complete understanding of the phenomena that social scientists investigate. All of the chapters bring to the reader the most current thinking and findings regarding the methods under consideration.

The first chapter considers in detail the conflict between the quantitative and the qualitative research paradigms, a conflict that is provoking considerable discussion among social scientists today. Bruce Thompson suggests that practitioners of both paradigms have at times violated the premises underlying their methods. It is suggested that social science would be more productive if researchers were more able to recognize the philosophical assumptions underlying methods, and if the paradigm pressure to consider some issues not worthy of reflection could be overcome more readily. The limits and advantages of various paradigms are considered.

Carl J Huberty notes that many social scientists employ stepwise regression and discriminant analysis methods. It is argued that conventional stepwise methods are generally inappropriate for either variable selection or interpretation of the importance of different variables. A variety of better alternatives are cited, and computer software that implements some methods is discussed.

A fairly recently developed theory of measurement, item response theory, offers very noteworthy advantages in constructing and analyzing both achievement and attitude measures. Robert L. McKinley and Craig N. Mills discuss the various item response theory models available to social scientists, including one-, two-, and three-parameter models. The chapter is replete with examples, discusses the merits of various models, and discusses computer software that can be used to implement various analyses.

Most social scientists have been trained to evaluate the reliability of their measures using what has come to be called classical measurement theory. However, a more general measurement theory, generalizability theory, has been available to researchers for ten to twenty years. James Algina compares classical measurement theory with generalizability theory. Advantages and uses of generalizability theory are elaborated. Example analyses are reported, and various computer programs that can implement the methods are discussed.

Richard G. Lomax argues that the development of methods to test hypotheses using covariance structure analysis "appears to be the single-most important contribution to the social and behavioral sciences during the past twenty years." One increasingly popular method of such analysis is the general structural relationship (LISREL) model developed by Joreskog, but Lomax discusses alternative models as well. Again, computer programs that implement these analyses are noted.

Multivariate methods have become increasingly popular as sophisticated computer programs have become more available to social scientists. Multivariate analysis of variance (MANOVA), the more general case of popular univariate analysis of variance methods, have become increasingly popular on this basis. H. Swaminathan notes that MANOVA, unlike ANOVA, provides several tests statistics to evaluate given hypotheses, and that different test statistics can yield conflicting results even for a given hypothesis and the same data. The four alternatives are explained and situations in which each test statistic should be selected are detailed. A summary of comparison procedures for evaluating more specific hypotheses in a multivariate context is presented.

Most social scientists will find several of the chapters in this volume to be of interest, though interest may vary across individual background or discipline. However, the chapters present lucid and informed treatments of their respective topics, and should stimulate discussion and insight regarding recent advances in the methods of our science.

Bruce Thompson
Series Editor

THE PLACE OF QUALITATIVE RESEARCH IN CONTEMPORARY SOCIAL SCIENCE:

THE IMPORTANCE OF POST-PARADIGMATIC THOUGHT

Bruce Thompson

For most of this century, behaviorist quantitative research traditions have constituted the dominant paradigm for social science research. The traditions have been regarded as

> the only means for settling disputes regarding educational practice, the only way of verifying educational improvements, and the only way of establishing a cumulative tradition in which improvements can be introduced without the danger of a faddish discard of old wisdom in favor of inferior novelties. (Campbell & Stanley, 1963, p. 2)

However, during the last 25 years criticisms of the quantitative research paradigm have been voiced more and more frequently. For example, with respect to psychology, Manicas and Secord (1983, p. 399) note that

> In the monumental *Psychology: A study of a science,* edited by Sigmund Koch (Volumes 1–6, 1959–1963), one eminent psychologist after another, after many years—or even a lifetime of

Advances in Social Science Methodology, Volume 1, pages 1–42.

ISBN: 0-89232-736-7

> research—admitted to strong doubts about where they had been and what had been achieved and some suggested that our most basic assumptions about the nature of psychology as a science and a method had to be questioned.

Similarly, Weimer (1979, p. ix) suggests that "Traditional conceptions of science and its methodology have been examined, found wanting, and are in large part being abandoned." With respect to educational research, MacMillan and Garrison (1984, p. 19) report that "No one, it seems, feels that the tradition of research on teaching is where it should be, given the resources put into it in the last 20 years or so."

Certain philosophers have concurred with this judgment:

> The bottom line is that social scientists have not been able to discover generalizations that are reliable enough, and about which there is enough professional consensus, to form the basis for social policy . . . So the wise educational practitioner ought not to hold his or her breath waiting for new, reliable, far-reaching breakthroughs by researchers. A skeptical, if not cynical, attitude toward research seems to be justified. (Phillips, 1980, p. 17)

Practitioners of the quantitative paradigm have concurred with at least aspects of these views:

> There would have been little discernable effect on educational practice if most of the studies reported in educational journals and dissertations had never been conducted. (Shaver, 1979, p. 3)
>
> On the basis of my experience in synthesizing research, I believe that we cannot now explain any appreciable portion of the variance in success of different methods of schooling implemented in different places. (Glass, 1979, p. 14)

Finally, representatives of an emergent research paradigm, the qualitative research paradigm, have also been critical of the traditions of quantitative research:

> The reaction of increasing numbers of researchers to the limitations of quantitative methods suggests that this method has approached its outer boundaries. (Rist, 1980, p. 8)
>
> Many researchers in education had come to feel that the years of promise for what quantitative research would be able to do (the problems it solved) had caught up with it. Quantitative methods, relying on the hard science paradigm, had not delivered. (Bogdan & Bilken, 1982, p. 21)
>
> We have gone through a period in which the strictures within the Campbell-Stanley monograph described *the* way of doing educational research. Yet who among us would say that such procedures have been a rousing success? Some of us have, understandably, looked elsewhere. (Eisner, 1983, p. 14)

Paradigms are fundamental to the research endeavor. As defined by Gage (1963, p. 95), "Paradigms are models, patterns, or schemata. Paradigms are not the theories; they are rather ways of thinking or patterns for research." Tuthill and Ashton (1983, p. 7) note that

> A scientific paradigm can be thought of as a socially shared cognitive schema. Just as our cognitive schema provides us, as individuals, with a way of making sense of the world around us, a scientific paradigm provides a group of scientists with a way of collectively making sense of their scientific world.

Two types of paradigms are relevant to the practice of science. Substantive or *ontological* paradigms guide expectations and thinking regarding the nature of the reality about which one inquires. For example, invoking a "restaurant" paradigm creates expectations that one will need to know about food, menus, tables, chairs, waiters, other diners, and checks. Methodological or *epistemological* paradigms govern thinking regarding the appropriate processes of inquiry. For example, invoking a "fairy-tale" schema tells one that there will be a story beginning with some variant of "Once upon a time," that there will be a hero or heroine, a villan, a happy ending, and presumably a moral.

It is difficult to consciously realize which thoughts are dictated by paradigms. As Lincoln and Guba (1985, pp. 19–20) note:

> If it is difficult for a fish to understand water because it has spent all of its life in it, so it is difficult for scientists . . . to understand what their basic axioms or assumptions might be and what impact those axioms and assumptions have upon everyday thinking and lifestyle.

Notwithstanding the fact that researchers are often unaware of the influence of their paradigms, paradigms are still potent influences indeed. We tend to let our paradigms tell us what to think, and *what not to think about.* As Patton (1975, p. 9) argues,

> Paradigms are normative, they tell the practitioner what to do without the necessity of long existential or epistemological consideration. But it is this aspect of a paradigm that constitutes both its strength *and* its weaknesses—its strength in that it makes action possible, its weakness in that the very reason for action is hidden in the unquestioned assumptions of the paradigm.

An example may illustrate the potency of our paradigms. Quantitative researchers take it as axiomatic that the residual variance (e.g., the error sum of squares in ANOVA, the residual sum of squares in regression analysis, the coefficient of alienation in canonical correlation analysis) should always be minimized. Many quantitative researchers unconsciously assume that "error" variance is simply a function of sampling and measurement inadequacy. For example, Kerlinger (1973, p. 307) advocates his "maxmincon" principle, indicating that one always wants to "*max*imize the systematic variance under study; *con*trol extraneous systematic variance; and *min*imize error variance."

Yet alternative views of "error" variance can be offered. For example, Shapiro (1984, p. 15) notes that "Econometricians view the residual [variance] as a reflection of the true nature of human behavior rather than the ignorance of the researcher, and often label it the disturbance rather than error term." Manicas and Secord (1983, p. 407) make a similar point:

> In effect, the statistically significant difference between the mean performance of two or more sets of individuals so common to experiments is a kind of probability usage. What it amounts to is making a crude generalization by attributing individual variances to ''error'' when, in fact, there are usually real differences between individuals.

One fundamental purpose of the present chapter is to argue that scientists will be able to do their best research only if they struggle to become and to remain ''post-paradigmatic.'' By post-paradigmatic I mean that researchers may continue to be guided by paradigm precepts but that they should struggle to be conscious of the restrictions on insight imposed by their paradigms. This is difficult at best, but as Kuhn (1962, 1970) has argued, may happen when different paradigms, such as the quantitative and qualitative epistemological paradigms, come into radical conflict. The effort to remain post-paradigmatic should be fruitful. As Soltis (1984, p. 9) has argued:

> There is a deeper level of ideological consciousness less easily brought to the surface for empirical, interpretative, and normative consideration but necessary to reach if we are to be able to emancipate ourselves and our fellow human beings from uncritical consciousness, from the unexamined life of social beings in a history.

A second purpose of the chapter is to discuss in detail a relatively new paradigm that may be inherently superior to its precursors. Finally, a third purpose of the chapter is to suggest appropriate ways that the methods of the previous paradigms might be incorporated into the new pardigm.

CRITERIA FOR PARADIGM EVALUATION

As MacMillan and Garrison (1984, p. 15) have suggested, ''any critic bears a heavy burden when approaching a new instance of the genre that is the center of critical attention. . . . In all cases critics must make their criteria as clear and perspicuous as possible.'' Paradigm evaluation is particularly difficult because, as Kuhn (1962, p. 93) has argued, ''When paradigms enter, as they must, into a debate about paradigmatic choice, their role is necessarily circular. Each group uses its own paradigm to argue in that's paradigm's defense.''

One fundamental error that must be avoided in evaluating paradigms is what Hume (1957) would call the ''is/ought'' error. The error is so fundamental and so easily made that the error has itself been the topic of extensive discussion (Hudson, 1969). As Strike (1979, p. 13) explains:

> To deduce a proposition with an ''ought'' in it from premises containing only ''is'' assertions is to get something in the conclusion not contained in the premises, something impossible in a valid deductive argument.

Arguing that something "ought" to be done in the future simply because something else "is" not being done now (ignoring whether it "ought" to be done now) is an example of this logical inconsistency. Consider Stake's (1978, p. 5) warrant for doing more case study research:

> I claim that case studies will often be the preferred method of research because they may be epistemologically in harmony with the reader's experience and thus to that person a natural basis for generalization . . . If the readers of our reports are the persons who populate our houses, schools, governments, and industries; and if we are to help them understand social problems and social programs, we must communicate in a way that accommodates their present understandings.

The implication of the "is/ought" fallacy is that a prima facia case for a paradigm shift is only established when two conditions are met. First, the flaws in a given paradigm must be shown be significant and inherent in the paradigm. As W. Thompson (1971, p. 82) explains,

> *Inherency* means inseperable. If an evil is inherent in a problem, then the only appropriate solution is one that alters the situation fundamentally. No lesser or limited remedy can suffice. A boil on the forearm does not constitute a need for amputation; the boil is not an inherent evil . . . The existence of radioactive fallout is not inherently a need for stopping nuclear tests, for a modification of the method of conducting such tests can prevent fallout.

For example, arguing that some quantitative research is poorly done is not sufficient reason to reject the quantitative paradigm unless it can be shown that the problem is inherent. It is well known that some quantitative research is poorly done.

> [Experimental treatments are often] so brief that the achievement of educationally significant results is highly unlikely. The median experimental treatment time for seven of the 15 experimental studies that reported experimental treatment time in Volume 18 of the *AERJ* is 1 hour and 15 minutes. I suppose that we should take some comfort in the fact that this represents a 66 percent increase over a 3-year period. In 1978 the median experimental treatment time per subject was 45 minutes. (Eisner, 1983, p. 14)

Similarly, noting that some qualitative research is poorly done (Rist, 1980, p. 9) does not seriously threaten the qualitative paradigm unless inherency can be established. It is well known that some qualitative research is poorly done. For example, Fetterman (1982, p. 17) notes that, "In one study, labeled 'An ethnographic study of . . . ,' observers were on site at only one point in time for 5 days. In a national study purporting to be ethnographic, once-a-week, on-site observations were made for 4 months."

The emphasis on inherency means that one must focus on features of the paradigm as against features of researcher practice. This is especially important since researchers often do not do all the things their paradigms may require. Thus, Manicas and Secord (1983, p. 412) note that "Scientists know that they do not follow rules in jumping from observations or empirical generalizations to theoretical propositions.'' Similarly, Miles and Huberman (1984, p. 21) note that

> It is typical for the hardest of hypothetico-deductive noses to engage in inductive sniffing in data sets; to acknowledge the imposition of the researcher's vision on a messy world; to launch into flights of inspired intuition when it comes to giving names to objectively-founded factors; and to give as much weight to what the subjects said after the experiment as to the type and frequency of buttons they pushed.

Thus, Soltis (1984, p. 6) refers to the researcher's ''logic-in-use'', meaning ''the basically reasonable, flexible, and intelligent ways scientists actually go about working on problems in contrast to the 'reconstructed' logical form in which they write up and justify their research findings, omitting much of what they actually did and thought during the research process.''

Culbertson (1983, p. 17) provides an example of a logically acceptable inherency argument, though the argument deals with movements rather than with paradigms per se.

> An alternative thesis is that significant intellectual movements typically create great expectations because the ideas that shape them inevitably contain hopes and promises for better futures . . . [Perhaps] inflated expectations are inherent in, and in a sense propel, all significant intellectual movements.

Second, an acceptable case in favor of a paradigm shift must show that the shift will correct the inherent problem upon which the shift was justified. In this respect it is intriguing to note that some researchers have justified the shift to the qualitative paradigm based on the perceived inadequacies of findings yielded by the quantitative paradigm.

> This surge of interest in qualitative methodology has been the result of a significant disillusionment with quantitative methods. This disillusionment also has extended to the use of experimental design. (Fetterman, 1982, p. 19)

> If quantitative research in the social areas had achieved an intellectual and material mastery of its subject matter similar to that of the physical sciences, there would probably be no concern over competing approaches. (J. Smith, 1983, p. 13)

NON-INHERENT FLAWS IN QUANTITATIVE PRACTICE

Three aspects of contemporary practice of the quantitative paradigm have caused significant problems, but are not inherent in the paradigm. Some of these practices have been the basis for ''is/ought'' arguments against the quantitative paradigm. The examples also offer persuasive testimony regarding the unfortunate effects that can originate in a paradigm's power to encourage scientists to *not* think. Thus, the examples offer some warrant for the importance of post-paradigmatic thought. As J. Smith (1983, p. 10) notes, the quantitative method can be "very significant in that it is adherence to a series of established procedures which prevent the self from disrupting or distorting this 'journey of the facts.'"

Significance versus Effect Size Interpretation

Some quantitative researchers have correctly argued that quantitative researchers are obsessed with testing and interpreting the statistical significance of their results. For example, Rist (1977, p. 45) notes that "for the quantitative researcher, working at the level of inductive statistics is intrinsically more interesting than working with descriptive statistics." The text by Blalock (1960) provides an example of this obsession:

> Statistical inference, as the process is called, involves much more complex reasoning than does descriptive statistics, but when properly used and understood becomes a very important tool in the development of a scientific discipline. Inductive statistics is based directly on probability theory, a branch of mathematics.

Unfortunately, "The emphasis on statistics and the 'test of significance' procedure has resulted in a methodological orientation toward establishing generalizability that has been deleterious in its effects on the scientific accumulation of knowledge in education" (Shaver, 1979, pp. 5–6). As Carver (1978, p. 378) argues:

> Statistical significance testing has involved more fantasy than fact. The emphasis on statistical significance in educational research represents a corrupt form of the scientific method. Educational research would be better off if it stopped testing its results for statistical significance.

Morrison and Henkel (1970) and others have presented similar arguments.

The problem with statistical significance testing is not that researchers do not randomly sample from defined populations, and therefore should not use the procedure. True, researchers rarely select their subjects randomly. As Shulman (1981a, p. 9) notes:

> Unfortunately, it is rarely the case that investigators truly sample randomly from a total population to which they might ultimately wish to generalize . . . We sample as best we can and then make a case for the subsequent claims of generalizability.

In his study of practices reflected in several volumes of a prominent research journal, Willson (1980, p. 8) reported that random selection occurred in only 15% of the reported studies.

Shaver and Norton (1980, p. 14) suggest that random sampling is frequently not possible:

> Despite its central position in statistical theory, random sampling does not seem to be a firmly established part of the operational research paradigm in education. Certainly the reality is that the random sampling of meaningful accessible populations is frequently not possible.

But post-paradigmatic thought suggests a solution to the problem. Significance testing assumes the product of representativeness independent of whether or not the process of random selection was employed. If researchers are unable to sample randomly, they can build a "bridge" (Cornfield & Tukey, 1956) from the sample to the population by comparing known sample characteristics with known population characteristics to build some warrant for an assumption of representativeness.

The inherent problem with statistical significance testing is that it is primarily an artifact of sample size. Many researchers try to employ large samples in order to "wash out" the effects of individual differences or outliers, or to invoke the central limit theorem to meet distribution assumptions of parametric tests (B. Thompson, 1984, p. 18), or to maximize generalization. Then, somewhat independently of obtained results, a "significant" effect is isolated as a function of sample size. The significant test often only confirms what the researcher already knew, that is, that he or she began the study with a large sample size.

Of course, the reciprocal case is equally damaging. If the population size itself is very small (e.g., children writing symphonies at age 5), or if the nature of the population means that only longitudinal observation of intensive interventions have any chance of detecting effects (e.g., interventions with autistic or catatonic persons), then researchers must employ smaller sample sizes. Again, the failure to detect "significant" effects only tells the researcher what the researcher already knew, that is, sample size was small.

Significance testing does inform scientific practice when a significant effect is detected given a small sample. The procedure also informs practice when sample size is large (i.e., there is good power against Type II and Type IV (Marascuilo & Levin, 1970) error) and a "significant" result is not realized. These are less likely occurences, and the researcher can persuasively argue, *a fortiori,* that the results are especially noteworthy.

The failure to think about statistical significance testing may be understandable, given the erudite logic inherent in the procedure. Thus, as Kaiser (1976) notes via examples involving two prominent statisticians known for their work in maximum likelihood factor analysis, even extremely bright people can misinterpret the logic.

It is widely recognized that researchers will resist giving up their current paradigms until they see viable alternatives (Kuhn, 1962, 1970). This notion is even represented in popular science fiction literature (Assimov, 1972). Question arises, then, regarding what social scientists should do to evaluate their results. It may not be necessary to completely abandon significance testing, as long as these results are interpreted in a more meaningful context.

Effect sizes represent an appropriate context for result interpretation. The context is more congruent with the quantitative paradigm view that both experimental and correlational studies are concerned with "the job of stating and testing more or less general relationships between properties of nature" (Homans, 1967, p. 7). This context is also congruent with the practice of computing comparable effect size estimates for both experimental and correlational studies in empirical research syntheses of previous research (Glass, McGaw, & Smith, 1981). Effect size estimates range in their sophistication from the fairly simple (Hays, 1963, p. 382) to the very complex (Tatsuoka, 1973, p. 30). A very simple effect size estimate is the sum of squares for an effect divided by the sum of squares total, which is analogous to the coefficient of determination.

Use of OVA versus General Linear Model Methods

Social scientists have historically been predisposed to employ analysis of variance (ANOVA) methods and their analogs (ANCOVA, MANOVA, and MANCOVA—collectively labelled here as OVA methods). For example, Edgington (1974) studied several volumes of several prominent journals of the American Psychological Association and reported that 71% of the articles used OVA methods. Willson (1980, p. 7) studied several volumes of a prominent educational research journal and reported that 41% of the articles used OVA methods. Goodwin and Goodwin (1985, pp. 8–9) studied several volumes of two prominent journals from two social science disciplines and found that OVA methods were employed in 37% of the articles they considered.

There is no question that OVA methods have been important in the development of insight in social science. For example, Kerlinger (1977, p. 9) notes that:

> Before the 1930's, for example, experiments were mostly two-variable affairs. After the invention of analysis of variance, however, more realistic and more theoretically interesting experiments could be done using two or more independent variables. Moreover, the important phenomenon of the interaction of two or more variables could be studied.

Kerlinger (1973, p. 216) has also noted that "the analysis of variance is not just a statistical method. It is an approach and a way of thinking." From a paradigm standpoint, OVA methods are also ways of *not* thinking.

However, the post-paradigmatic view recognizes that all univariate parametric methods are "Siamese twins" (Nunnally, 1975, p. 7), that is, special cases of multiple regression analysis. Cohen (1968) showed this in some detail. Moreover, Knapp (1978) has proven that both univariate and multivariate parametric methods are special cases of canonical analysis. B. Thompson (1985b, 1988) provides concrete heuristic examples in which a small data set is analyzed using a variety of parametric methods to illustrate these identities.

B. Thompson (1986, p. 918) notes that:

> Most variables other than experimental conditions are higher than nominally scaled. The most notable exception is biological sex of the subjects in a study. Although in atypical areas such as math anxiety (Aiken, 1976, p. 302) the use of sex as an independent variable may be warranted, as a general rule the use of even these variable may stem more from ease of measurement than from theoretical justification.

Many quantitative researchers prefer experimental designs because the designs allow somewhat more warranted confidence in the internal validity of conclusions about causality. The fact that OVA methods are appropriate when predictor variables such as experimental assignment naturally occur at the nominal level of scale has stimulated some researchers to unconsciously associate the consequences of experimental design selection with OVA methods. But as B. Thompson (1984, p. 56) notes:

> Yet it is the design *and not the analytic technique* that allows causal inferencing. Hicks (1973) provides a classic example of this confusion in his fine book, *Fundamental Concepts in the Design of Experiments*. The book is entirely about ANOVA techniques and does not touch at all upon experimental design issues.

Several aspects of the non-thoughtful use of OVA methods when some predictor variables are higher than nominally scaled are disturbing. First, the practice represents the "squandering [of] much information" (Cohen, 1968, p. 41). As B. Thompson (1981a, p. 8) suggests:

> When we reduce interval level of scale data to the nominal level of scale we are doing nothing less than thoughtlessly throwing away information which we previously went to some trouble to collect. If research is conducted for the purpose of acquiring knowledge, then is it consistent with our purpose to employ a method which "throws away" information which might provide a more refined understanding of the phenomena which we are studying?

Second, OVA methods distort the distribution shapes of and relationships among non-interval predictor variables. "Balanced" sample sizes distributed evenly across cells constituted by nominally scaled variables allow the predictors to be perfectly uncorrelated; for example, the sums of squares for all effects add exactly to the total sum of squares for the dependent variable. Cohen (1968, p. 440) noted that this "computational simplicity" may have been important in the era preceeding the widespread availability of computers. However, these distortions do not seem warranted in the contemporary analytic environment.

Third, OVA methods tend to reduce power against Type II error by reducing the reliability of interval predictor variables *as they are analyzed* (as opposed to as they were actually measured). Reliability is primarily a function of variance. By discarding information about predictor variable variance OVA methods tend to lessen reliability.

The fact that OVA methods lessen the reliability and validity (via distortion) of interval predictor variables suggests that alternative methods ought to be employed when some predictors are interval. For example, B. Thompson (1985a) provides a heuristic comparison of use of ANOVA, the regression approach to ANOVA using a priori contrasts, and regression utilizing all the predictors in their original levels of scale followed by a commonality analysis to investigate the unique and the shared portions of each effect size. Alternatively, in the univariate case, each variable's squared regression structure coefficient (Thompson & Borrello, 1985) could be taken as an effect size estimate.

The post-paradigm view thoughtfully recognizes the identities among analytic techniques and encourages selection of methods that do not distort representations of the reality to which scientists are trying to generalize. Until this view is adopted, some solace can be taken in Monte Carlo empirical findings that the magnitudes of OVA distortions may be small even though they seem to be systematic (B. Thompson, 1986). Furthermore, although OVA methods continue to be employed with great frequency,

> There is a marked decrease in the percentage of articles using ANOVA (one-way and factorial) and *t*-tests in *AERJ* between 1972 and 1982. A similar decrease in ANOVA usage was observed in APA journals versus *JEP* for the 10-year span. (Goodwin & Goodwin, 1985, p. 9)

Inappropriate Use of Statistical Control

Many "statistical controls" can be invoked to adjust findings when the quantitative researcher believes that random selection or random assignment or design selection have failed to create groups that were equivalent at the start of the experiment or quasi-experiment. For example, results can be adjusted for attenuation due to imperfect reliability of a variable or for attentuation due to restricted variance caused by sampling problems (e.g., Guilford, 1965, p. 480). These statistical controls are available throughout the entire gamut of quantitative methods. For example, Gorsuch (1983, pp. 89–90) notes that the first factor extracted in a factor analysis can be located to pass directly through a "covariate" variable in factor space. Since factors are uncorrelated, the effects of the first factor on all other factors will have been statistically controlled.

Though many of these statistical controls date back to the beginning of the century (Nunnally, 1975, p. 9), most of the controls have not enjoyed wide use. Analysis of covariance (ANCOVA), however, has been used in about four percent of the recently published research (Goodwin & Goodwin, 1985, pp. 8–9; Willson, 1980, p. 7). As explained by McGuigan (1983, p. 230):

> Briefly this technique enables you to obtain a measure of what you think is a particularly relevant extraneous variable that you are not controlling. This usually involves some characteristics of your participants. For instance, if you are conducting a study of the effect of certain psychological variables on weight, you might use as your measure the weight of your participants before you administer your experimental treatments. Through analysis of

covariance, you then can "statistically control" this variable—that is, you can remove the effect of initial weight from your dependent variable scores, thus decreasing your error variance.

One problem with statistical controls is that they assume very reliable measurement of the control variables. For example, Nunnally (1975, p. 10) notes that reliability will not usually have an appreciable influence on the substantive interpretation of results as long as reliability of measurement is at least .70, but that "Measurement reliability becomes crucial . . . in employing statistical partialling operations, as in the analysis of covariance or in the use of partial correlational analysis." Unfortunately, too many researchers may not consider and certainly do not report the measurement error of their variables. As Willson (1980, p. 9) comments, "That reliability of instruments is unreported in almost half the published research is likewise inexcusable at this late date."

Statistical control has been particularly appealing to some quantitative researchers when random assignment was not performed. These researchers expect the statistical adjustments of ANCOVA to magically make groups equivalent. This appeal could grow in an era of informed consent requirements:

> The notion of randomly assigning individuals to contrasting experimental treatment groups may seem far less acceptable a research strategy in these days of legislation requiring informed consent and protection of human subjects. (Shulman, 1981a, p. 12)

Gardner (1978) provides an example of some of the substantive distortions introduced by these requirements.

The situation may be unfortunate, because true experiments were already fairly rare in certain areas of inquiry. For example, Welch and Walberg (1974, p. 113) note that

> Although the need for true experiments on broadly defined populations has long been recognized, there are very few local experiments and no national experiments in curriculum research. For example, among 46 government-sponsored course development projects in science and mathematics, a few relied on teacher reports and classroom visits for evaluation, but only four used true experiments in their evaluation strategies.

It is ironic that education experiments are so rare in a country that participated in the longitudinal Tuskegee syphillis study (e.g., Hiltner, 1973).

However, the primary difficulty with statistical control in order to make groups equivalent involves the homogeneity of regression assumption of the methods. The methods assume that the relationship between the covariate and the dependent variable is equivalent in all experimental groups. This assumption is necessary because the statistical control procedures are implemented by adjusting the dependent variable to the extent that the covariate and the dependent variable are correlated *when group membership information is ignored.*

Campbell and Erlebacher (1975) present a concrete illustration of how the use of statistical controls can seriously distort findings when the homogeneity of regression assumption is not met. ANCOVA has been very appealing in research investigating the effects of compensatory education programs. In these cases the treatment intervention is made available to all or most children who are eligible. The control group usually consists of children who were not eligible for the treatment and, therefore, the group is inherently different in its character than the treatment group. In these analyses both the dependent variable and the covariate are cognitive variables. The statistical control procedure assumes that the relationship between the two variables is the same in both groups, that is, since correlation is a measure of the slope of the regression line for the two variables, that children who are eligible for and receive compensatory interventions *learn at the same rate* as children who are not eligible for the intervention. The decision to blithely use the statistical control in these cases leads to "tragically misleading analyses" that actually "can mistakenly make compensatory education look harmful"" (Campbell & Erlebacher, 1975, p. 597).

Persons who wish to use statistical controls of this type are usually trapped in a nasty dilemma. If the controls are not needed then they should not be used. For example, Carlberg and Kavale (1980, p. 303) found in their meta-analytic study that the presence or absence of random assignment makes virtually no difference in treatment effect sizes; this suggests that the failure to randomly assign is not sufficient to automatically warrant the use of statistical control. If statistical control is needed because the groups in a study are not equivalent, then often the homegeneity of regression assumption cannot be met and the use results in seriously distorted inferences. In this context it is ironic to note that the inappropriate use of statistical control in federal program evaluation may have resulted in the infusion of federal dollars into qualitative research efforts:

> A former federal official argues that the displeasure of policymakers with quantitative studies arose less from a concern about lack of richness of their findings as from a concern about the findings themselves, "few of which were liked by program advocates." To him qualitative studies were attractive because "case study approaches . . . tend to yield less controversial findings, ones with conclusions on both sides of a political decision". (Herriott & Firestone, 1983, p. 15)

The infusion of millions of dollars into dozens of longitudinal qualitative evaluation projects (Herriott & Firestone, 1983) tended to legitimize the qualitative paradigm in the minds of many researchers.

Post-paradigmatic thought would have recognized the fallacious use of statistical control in these ANCOVA applications, just as some researchers have long warned of these various dangers (Elashoff, 1969; Lord, 1960). ANCOVA is a special case of regression analysis, as noted previously. Consider the hypothetical data presented in Table 1. The hypothetical study involves four children from a compensatory program ("A") who have lower mean achievement (−.19)

Table 1. Hypothetical ANCOVA Data Set

Group	*ZY*	*ZX*	*ZYZX*	*YHAT*	*YE*
A	−.88	−1.68	1.48	−1.36	.48
A	−.44	−.68	.30	−.56	.11
A	.00	.31	.00	.25	−.25
A	.44	1.30	.57	1.06	−.62
B	−1.32	−.68	.90	−.56	−.77
B	−.44	−.19	.08	−.15	−.29
B	.88	.56	.49	.45	.43
B	1.76	1.06	1.86	.86	.91

Note: The beta weight for the covariance procedure (.813) equals the sum of the cross products (ZXxZY) of ZX and ZY divided by $n-1$ (5.694/n−1). The predicted posttest score (YHAT) is each child's pretest (ZX) multiplied by the beta weight. The error in each prediction (YE) is equal to ZY minus YHAT.

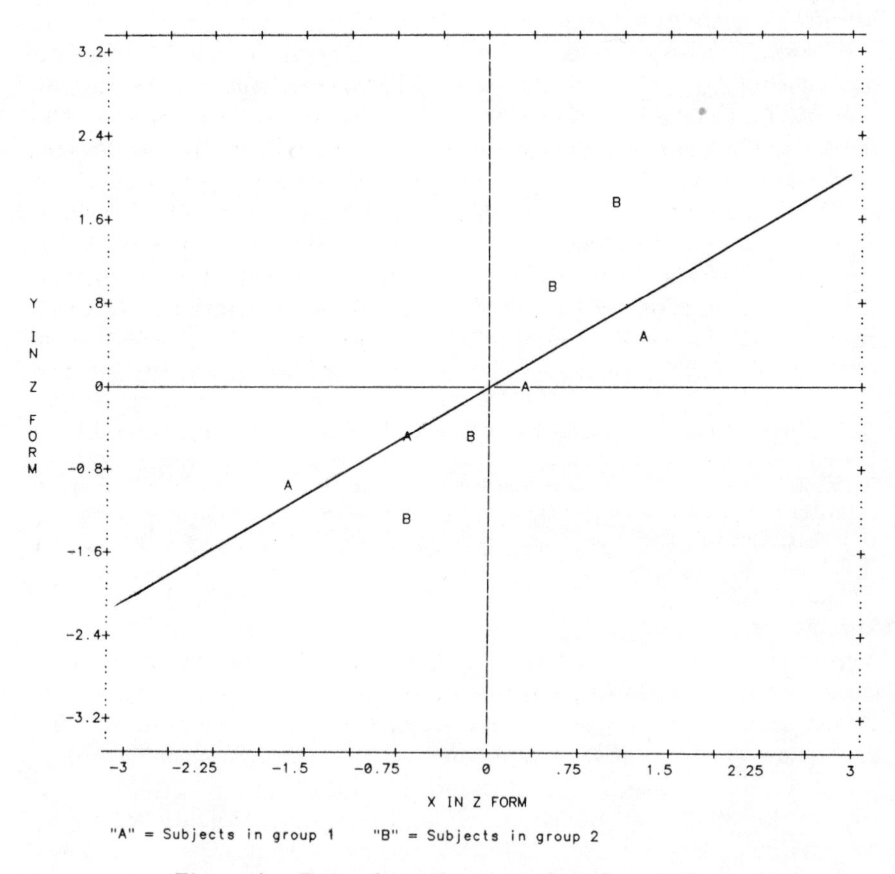

Figure 1. Example nonhomogeneity of regression

Table 2. ANCOVA Results

Source	*Sum of Squares*	*df*	*Mean Squares*	*F*	*Effect Size*
Covariate	4.63	1	4.63	9.95	.661
Treatment	.04	1	.04	.08	.006
"Error"	2.33	5	.47		
Total	7.00	7	1.00		

Note: Effect size is a *r* squared analog.

on the cognitive pretest (ZX) than do their peers (mean = .19) from the noncompensatory group. Furthermore, as one might expect, and as illustrated in Figure 1 which also presents the cognitive posttest (ZY) scores of the eight children, the children in the two groups are learning at different rates.

Nevertheless, the ANCOVA procedures employs the beta weight (r = beta weight for two variable case = .81) derived by ignoring the group membership (''A'' or ''B'') of the children, that is, derived by ignoring the fact that the children are learning at different rates. Table 2 presents conventional ANCOVA results for this data set. Table 3 presents an ANOVA performed on the residual raw scores (YE = ZY − YHAT).

The fact that ANCOVA is simply ANOVA on the residual raw scores is disturbing from a post-paradigm point of view. The researcher took a variable that presumably had some meaning (ZY), made an adjustment on it, and was left with an analysis of a residual raw score that, unlike the original dependent variable, has little intrinsic meaning. The result would be difficult to interpret even if the adjustment was reasonable, that is, if the homogeneity of regression assumption had been met. Post-paradigmatic insights may force researchers to think more about what they are doing. As McGuigan (1983, p. 231) has observed, ANCOVA

> can be seriously misused, and one cannot be assured that it can ''save'' a shoddy experiment. Some researchers overuse this method as in the instance of a person I once overheard asking of a researcher, ''Where is your analysis of covariance?''—the understanding in his department was that it is *always* used in experimentation.

Table 3. ANOVA Results Using YE as Dependent Variable

Source	*Sum of Squares*	*df*	*Mean Squares*	*F*	*Effect Size*
Treatment	.04	1	.04	.08	.006
"Error"	2.33	5	.47		
Total	2.37	6			

Of course, the preceeding discussion of the ANCOVA case generalizes to the various types of statistical control that are available to researchers.

BASIS FOR PARADIGM COMPARISON

The Dangers of Relativism

Relativism is a philosophical construct referring to thought presuming that inherently different paradigms are equally good or equally bad because the merits cannot be evaluated. In Donmoyer's (1985, p. 13) view, relativism is "the belief that judgments cannot be made about the adequacy of conflicting interpretations." Unfortunately, as Phillips (1983, p. 9) notes,

> Contemporary thinking is much taken with relativism, with the view that there are multiple realities or viewpoints or paradigms and that no one framework provides the royal road to truth. In fact, [the definition of] truth itself is relative to the framework that the investigator chooses to adopt.

With respect to the quantitative and qualitative research paradigms, Smith and Heshusius (1986, p. 4) note that

> Many educational inquirers now seem to think that the profession has reached a stage of, if not synthesis, then certainly compatibility and cooperation between the two approaches.

Both qualitative and quantitative researchers have participated in the supposed denouement. For example, Rist (1980, p. 10) speaks of "rapproachment" between the paradigms. Elsewhere he (Rist, 1977, p. 42) has argued:

> It is my view that with respect to the broad categories of quantitative and qualitative research, a situation of detente is rapidly evolving. This is due to at least two reasons. First, there is a general recognition among some researchers and even more among practitioners that no one methodology can answer all questions and provide insights on all issues . . . Second, the internal order and logic of each approach is sufficiently articulated that it is difficult if not impossible to foresee the time when they would merge under some broader, more eclectic research orientation.

Miles and Huberman (1984, p. 20, emphasis in original) have argued that "If one looks carefully at the research actually conducted in the name of one or another epistemology, it seems that few working researchers are *not* blending the two perspectives." Cooley (1978, p. 13) has suggested that "every research study is inevitably both qualitative and quantitative to some degree." Cronbach, Ambron, Dornbusch, Hess, Hornik, Phillips, Walker, and Weiner (1980, p. 223) have suggested that researchers ought to "draw on both styles at appropriate times and in appropriate amounts."

The conceptual confusion of assuming the quantitative and qualitative paradigms are compatible has originated for several reasons. For example, the fact that some *methods* are transportable across the two paradigms has lulled some researchers into presuming that therefore the paradigms themselves are compatible. But this is a non sequitur since the paradigms are more than their methods. It may be well to use methods that originated in the other paradigm. But whatever methods are employed in the quantitative paradigm, the paradigm remains quantitative, and vice versa. In effect, paradigms can sometimes suck in methods from other paradigms. As Smith and Heshusuis (1986, p. 8, emphasis in original) note, "Especially for qualitative inquiry, the logic of justification does not impose detailed boundaries that determine *every single aspect* of practice."

Another cause of the confusion has been the tendency of some paradigm representatives to explain or defend their paradigm by using the constructs inherent in the alternative paradigm. The tendency may arise from an effort to achieve credibility, but each paradigm must be judged on the basis of its own concepts. LeCompte and Goetz (1982, p. 33) provide an example. They argue that differences in the quantitative and the qualitative paradigms are due

> less to the initial formulation of a research question than to the stage of the research at which the use of theory becomes salient, the way theoretical considerations are integrated into the study, and the extent to which the goal of the study is to substantiate existing theory or to generate new theories.

As Smith and Heshusius (1986, p. 6, 8) argue, parallelism in communicating the primary elements of a paradigm, for example, linking qualitative credibility concerns with quantitative concern for internal validity,

> is sufficient to direct attention away from basic differences in the philosophical assumptions of the two perspectives. Thus, one can easily get the impression that the two approaches are variations in techniques within the same assumptive framework, to reach the same goals and solve the same problems . . . Given this situation, the claim of compatibility and the call for cooperation are not surprising; as presently conceptualized, the two perspectives do not differ in any important ways.

Furthermore, even if the paradigms were unique but complimentary, there would be an opportunity cost in selecting one paradigm over the other. As MacMillan and Garrison (1984, p. 16, emphasis in original) observe:

> The assessment of research traditions is always *comparative*. No theory or tradition can be viewed as existing in a vacuum; it is always seen as competing with other theories or traditions for the affections and attention of practicing scientists.

In Donmoyer's (1986, p. 27) view, "Even when researchers can see different conceptual orientations as complimentary rather than contradictory, they will still have to make choices."

However, the argument regarding opportunity costs forcing choices is contingent on the two paradigms being different but potentially complimentary. The methods may be, but the hypothetical contingency of compatibility was only hypothetical for the sake of argument since the two paradigms are inherently contradictory, as will be argued momentarily. Thus, Smith (1983, p. 12) notes that

> These positions do not seem to be compatible given our present state of thinking. This is not to say that the two approaches can never be reconciled, only that at the present time the actual divisions are more notable than the possibilities for unification.

The fact that the paradigms are different and contradictory compels some thought regarding which paradigm is most appropriate in service of science. As Shulman (1981a, p. 5) notes

> Scholars who agree on matters of method can pursue research questions in a parallel fashion and then argue over the results of their respective investigations. However, if they do not agree even on some matters of research method, then their findings are likely to be incommensurable.

Thus, Donmoyer (1985, p. 14) expresses the concern that

> The field of education has become a solipsistic morass where one researcher's conclusions must be judged as adequate as another's even when their findings conflict; where even the shoddiest of scholarship can be made impervious to criticism by the claim of paradigm difference.

Philosophical Origins of the Current Paradigm Conflict

Some researchers are not comfortable dealing with philosophical issues. They may feel poorly trained for the pursuit or may feel that philosophy is the practice of infinite regress. Thus, many scientists are discomforted by statements such as

> What counts as a gene is determined by current biological theories; furthermore, the sceptic can only be assured that what is being seen is not an artifact of the instrument by relying on the physical theories that explain the workings of the electron microscope. (Phillips, 1983, p. 10)

As Manicas and Secord (1983, p. 412) note:

> Philosophy of science has most commonly been the work of philosophers, not scientists . . . A few philosophically oriented scientists may perhaps be partly influenced in their choice of criteria by philosophical writings, but more commonly, scientists contrast with philosophers in generating their own criteria for validity out of their daily practice in scientific research.

But whether scientists like it or not, the current paradigm conflict had it historical roots in the reaction to the philosophical school called ''positivism'', and understanding the current conflict requires understanding of certain philosophical developments. As Smith and Heshusius (1986, p. 11) argue, "Moreover, since these issues are crucial to who we are and what we do as researchers, this is not something to be turned over to philosophers with the hope they will eventually solve our problems."

During the late nineteenth century and the early twentieth century, some dominant schools of philosophical thought in Europe became deeply interested in metaphysical issues. A group of philosophers associated with what has come to be called the "Vienna Circle" articulated their positivistic views partly in reaction this dominant interest in metaphysical issues. As Scriven (1969, p. 195) explains,

> The Vienna Circle of *Wiener Kreis* was a band of cutthroats that went after the fat burghers of Continental metaphysics who had become intolerably inbred and pompously verbose. The *kris* is a Malaysian knife, and the *Wiener Kreis* employed a kind of Occam's Razor called the Verifiability Principle. It performed a tracheotomoy that made it possible for philosophy to breathe again.

It is intriguing to note that the reaction against the quantitative paradigm is itself a reaction against a reaction—the pendulum has swung again. However, the reaction against the quantitative paradigm may *not be a reaction involving inherent features of the paradigm.* As Phillips (1983, p. 8) notes, "There is nothing in the doctrines of positivism that necessitates a love of statistics or a distaste for case studies."

"Philosophers have attached a considerable number of meanings to the term positivism" (Donmoyer, 1985, p. 14). Thus, Lincoln and Guba (1985, p. 24) observe that

> It is very clear from this sample of statements about positivism that there is no clear agreement about what either the philosophy or the method encompasses . . . One might venture to say that the particular form of definition offered by any commentator depends heavily upon the counterpoints he or she wishes to make.

However, a few of the important features of positivistic thought can be identified. First, positivists disclaim any interest in metaphysical realities or explanations. Of course, this is sensible given the origins of the school of thought. Second, positivists presume the existence of a reality that has existence independent of man. Thus, positivists are philosophically realists.

Inherent Features of the Qualitative Paradigm

Just as there are many schools of positivism, there are myriad views of the qualitative paradigm. Thus, with respect to the several approaches to anthropolical method, Overholt and Stallings (1976, p. 12) note that "The anthropoligist who goes into the field armed with one of these [several anthropological method] theory bases is likely to employ field methods different from those employed by an adherent of a different theory.'' Most qualitative researchers believe that subjective interpretation of experiences is a part of the essence of the paradigm, but some qualitative researchers do not agree:

> Not all qualitative researchers believe we should interpret; some strive to separate interpretations from descriptions (e.g., Smith & Geoffrey, 1968), and others attempt to describe without interpreting events, leaving this to the reader (e.g., Barker, 1968). (McCutcheon, 1981, p. 5)

Qualitative researchers have been rather upset with some implementations of the paradigm. For example, the Federal support of large-scale multi-site qualitative program evaluation projects has provoked serious comment. These projects have typically employed semi-structured field studies for which selected issues and procedures were specified a priori; the a priori specifications were deemed necessary in order to assure some comparability of results across various sites. But as Herriott and Firestone (1983, pp. 16–17) observe:

> The heavy reliance on semi-structured procedures is clearly a major departure from the traditional, single-site case study approach. It seems to represent an accomodation in the direction of quantitative methods, one made to facilitate cross-site comparison.

Fetterman (1982, p. 18) has protested that in studies of this sort ''the values, the most important elements of the anthropological culture system, have been left behind: phenomenology, holism, nonjudgmental orientation, and contextualization.''

Paradigm conflicts naturally provoke thoughtful articulation of many views of the ''correct'' way to operate. Each view incites its own loyalists. But some characteristics of the paradigms under discussion must be presented so that confusion can be minimized. A number of researchers have offered their perspectives on the distinguishing features of the qualitative and the quantitative paradigms (Lincoln & Guba, 1985, pp. 24–44; Rist, 1977; L. Smith, 1979; Wolcott, 1975). Quite a few distinguishing features might be cited. However, three fundamental and inherent characteristics distinguish the two paradigms being considered here.

Inductive versus Hypothetico-Deductive

One important distinguishing feature of the two paradigms involves the role of hypotheses. All empirical science tests hypotheses, but the hypotheses may be derived differently and researchers may test their hypotheses in different ways. Overholt and Stallings' (1976, p. 12) comments generalize to cover both the paradigms:

> The chief distinctive feature of the methodology that leads to empirically grounded anthropological theory is its use of what can be termed ethnographic hypotheses . . . As a rule, anthropologists begin their research with a general theory while experimental researchers begin their investigations with a specific hypothesis.

Qualitative researchers reject the concept of scientific objectivity, especially as regards inquiry in social science. As Piel (1978, p. 9) argues, "In the social sciences the act of observation perturbs the observer. The social scientist is himself caught up in the web of circumstances under study; he cannot escape his role as an actor in society." Similarly, Rist (1975, pp. 92–93) argues that

> The presence of preconceived ideas held by the investigator may distort the findings and interpretations to such a degree that they no longer reflect the original observed behavior. Additionally . . . it has been well documented that individuals often see in a social situation what they wish to see or what them deem important and salient to themselves.

The empirical observations of the qualitative researcher are protected against bias by the requirement that the subjects in the inquiry themselves determine what events are worthy of interpretation and what meanings must be ascribed to these events. Thus, Donmoyer (1986, p. 26) notes that anthropologists must "resolve questions of meaning by adopting the interpretations of their subjects." Filstead (1970, p. 6) suggests that "Qualitative methodology allows the researcher to 'get close to the data,' thereby developing the analytical, conceptual, and categorical components of explanation from the data itself."

The views of LeCompte and Goetz (1982, p. 32) regarding ethnography apply to qualitative approaches more generally: "By admitting into the research frame the subjective experiences of both participants and investigator, ethnography may provide a depth of understanding lacking in other approaches to investigation." Thus, Overholt and Stallings (1976, p. 14) argue that:

> The anthropologist manipulates hypotheses in order to arrive at statements that account for as many of the observed facts as possible with the greatest degree of economy, simplicity, and elegance possible. It is for this reason that the ethnographic hypothesis remains empirically grounded in a way that the experimental hypothesis does not.

LeCompte and Goetz argue for the superiority of "empirically grounded" hypotheses and interpretations. They (1982, p. 43) suggest that working closely with subjects

> and collecting data for long periods provides opportunities for continual data analysis and comparison to refine constructs and to ensure the match between scientific categories and participant reality. Second, informant interviewing, a major ethnographic data source, necessarily is phrased more closely to the empirical categories of participants and is formed less abstractly than instruments used in other designs. Third, participant observation, the ethnographer's second key source of data, is conducted in natural settings that reflect the reality of the life experiences of participants more accurately than do contrived settings.

Quantitative researchers, on the other hand, also acknowledge their lack of objectivity. The a priori declaration of a hypothesis is itself, in a very real sense, a declaration of expectation and bias. Thus, checks on distortion are required in this paradigm too. The check in the quantitative paradigm is replication. As McGuigan (1983, p. 231, emphasis in original) explains:

> We have emphasized the *self-correcting feature of science*—if a scientist errs, for whatever reason, the error will be discovered, at least if it has any importance. The basic criterion in science for evaluating the validity of our conclusions is that research is repeated.

The check is effective enough to even detect bias in the form of fabrication of results. Piel (1978) elaborates the example.

Holistic versus Reductionistic

Quantitative researchers measure their constructs ''operationally'' by selecting precise instruments that they hope will provide reliable and valid measurement in a given application. Qualitative researchers believe that this quantitative process of delimitation introduces distortion as a function of oversimplification. Thus, Patton (1975, p. 29) observes:

> It is the constraints posed by controlling the specific treatment under study that necessitates simplifying and breaking down the totality of reality into small component parts. A great deal of the scientific enterprise revolves around this process of simplifying the complexity of reality.

LeCompte and Goetz (1982, p. 35) are disturbed by what they believe are the consequences of reductionism:

> Accomodating the strictures of experimental control requires manipulation of phenomena, which distorts their natural occurence. Attempts at rigorous measurement may impede construction of powerful analytic categories if the phenomena observed are prematurely or inappropriately reduced or standardized.

Qualitative researchers argue that the focus of social science is human, and that this poses serious difficulties for the possibility of acceptable reductionism. As Soltis (1984, pp. 6–7) notes,

> This segment of educational research [qualitative inquirers] takes its work to be inquiry into human intersubjective meaning so that we can understand how education initiates us into our culture. They are opposed to the logical empiricists, not with regard for the need for objectivity or empirical evidence, but because they believe that the empiricist has too narrow a view of the concepts of objectivity and evidence and therefore fails to investigate what is distinctly human in our publicly shared social world.

Rist (1975, p. 89) provides a succinct summary of this qualitative view:

> Only select aspects of the influences of the school on the child can be ascertained by relying on abstract measures of aptitude, attitude, grades, or IQ. Granted, these indices may provide guidelines as to the current performance of the child, but they do not elucidate the complexities of the classroom by which such "products" as grades or test scores are generated.

Byrne (1983, p. 23) provides an incisive analogy of the qualitative paradigm view of reductionism. The analogy involves inquiry into the dynamics of good versus poor chess players:

> If our researcher should then proceed—by analogy with many an educational researcher—by determining the frequencies with which pawns, knights, bishops, rooks, and the other pieces on a chess board are moved by representatives of the two [good versus bad] groups in the course of their games, then his understanding of the players and of the game will be slight indeed, no matter how objective may be his research. For although differences between the groups will be found to exist, little will be gleaned of players' strategies and tactics, which are what distinguish the more able from the less able players.

McCutcheon (1981, p. 9) notes that "We can only see, only count, only code those items admitted to perception by the instrument." Rist (1982, p. ix) argues that:

> We as human beings are more than simply the sum total of psychological measures, survey instrument responses, and bits of data on a laboratory checklist. That our experiences, fears, anxieties, emotions, beliefs, reactions, hopes, behaviors, and irrationalities are not well captured or explained by the rush to quantification is one reason that qualitative research is experiencing the renaissance it is.

Lincoln and Guba (1985, p. 39) concur:

> It would be virtually impossible to devise a priori a nonhuman instrument with sufficient adaptability to encompass and adjust to the variety of realities that will be encountered.

In summary, Rist (1977, p. 49) argues that "It is, from this [qualitative] perspective, precisely because reality cannot be broken down into component parts without the severe risk of distortion that a holistic analysis is necessary."

Idealist versus Realist Concepts of Reality

Qualitative researchers argue that the unique nature of human reality was not honored by the attempt to transport the methods of the natural sciences into social science inquiry. It is therefore intriguing to note that much of "the philosophical and epistemological soul-searching that currently pervades the social sciences also has been occurring in the physical sciences" (Tuthill & Ashton, 1983, p. 7).

The quantitative paradigm is based on a realist philosophy regarding the nature of reality. As J. Smith (1983, pp. 7, 9) explains:

When Durkheim said that we should treat social facts as things, he was saying in effect that the objects of study in the social sciences should be treated in the same way physical scientists treat physical things. This means that if physical scientists can stand apart from their subject and think of it as having an independent, object-like existence with no intrinsic meaning, the same is true for social scientists. . . . In this perspective reality exists not only independent of but prior to any interest or activity on the investigator's part.

The qualitative paradigm under discussion here, on the other hand, is idealist in its world view. As an important caveat, it must be noted that not all qualitative researchers share this philosophical predisposition. As Bogdan and Biklen (1982, p. 32) note,

While qualitative researchers tend to be phenomenological in their orientation, most are not radical idealists. They emphasize the subjective, but they do not necessarily deny a reality "out there" that stands over and against human beings, capable of resisting action toward it.

But idealist philosophy is more common in qualitative research than Bogdan and Biklen would have one believe.

The qualitative paradigm is idealist to the extent that it presumes that reality can only be known phenomenologically. That is,

Qualitative methodologies assume there is value to an analysis of both the inner and outer perspectives of human behavior . . . A complete and ultimately truthful analysis can only be achieved by actively participating in the life of the observed and gaining insights by means of introspection. (Rist, 1977, p. 45)

As J. Smith (1983, p. 12) explains the position, "One knows what another is experiencing by engaging in a recreation of those experiences in oneself. At its core, the essence of understanding is to put oneself in the place of the other."

Lincoln and Guba (1985, p. 37) argue that, "The inquirer and the 'object' of inquiry interact to influence one another; knower and known are inseparable." As J. Smith (1983, p. 8) summarizes this perspective,

The subject and the object, perceived by realists as two elements, become one to idealists, who perceive no reality independent of the shaping or creating efforts of the mind. To idealists the relationship of investigation to subject can be more accurately described as subject-subject rather than subject-object; what is investigated is not independent of the process of investigation.

Lincoln and Guba (1985, p. 87, emphasis in original) are frank in declaring that they are idealists:

We shall settle for a less extreme alternative: position 3, constructed reality . . . [The ontological position of constructed reality and the more extreme position of created reality are similar] in their basic assumptions about the *nature* of reality—that is, *it doesn't exist until either* (1) it is *constructed* by an actor or (2) it is *created* by a participant.

The reaction against positivism can be seen in their declaration that metaphysical reality is *the* standard of truth in their paradigm perspective.

> Truth 1, with which we are most concerned here, may be called *metaphysical* truth. . . . [Truth 1 or metaphysical truths] represent the ultimate benchmarks against which *everything else* is tested, for if there were something more fundamental against which a test might be made, then that more fundamental entity would become *the* basic belief whose truth (T 1) must be taken for granted (Lincoln & Guba, 1985, pp. 14–15, emphasis in original).

These positions have major implications for the conduct of scientific inquiry. For example, the progress of natural science depends upon a postulate of permanism. Once lawful relationships are discovered, they are presumed to remain lawful. Thus, once gravity is discovered, one does not feel that it is necessary to confirm the continuing existence of this force on a daily basis. The postulate allows scientists to move beyond old discoveries, and is also important in inquiry in social science. But the qualitative paradigm view of reality means that every social phenomenon is embued with its own human meaning, and that this meaning is also constantly changing. Thus, Lincoln and Guba (1985, p. 38) argue that "All entities are in a state of mutual simultaneous shaping so that it is impossible to distinguish causes from effects." In Stake's (1978, p. 6) view, "To know particulars fleetingly of course is to know next to nothing. What becomes useful understanding is a full and thorough knowledge of the particular."

THE PURPOSES OF SCIENCE

Toulmin (1961, p. 20) has cautioned against evaluating a paradigm against the criterion of a single purpose. He analogizes such an evaluation to a hypothetical effort to discover a single purpose in a game:

> Competitive games are of course competitive, and this fact determines the general *sorts* of purposes they will have. Yet in playing any particular game a man will be trying to do a large number of different things—to ace his opponent, tire him out, get him out of position, and so on—pursuing a range of different aims, any of which may contribute to his overall success . . . And we shall understand the game in question only when we understand, in outline at any rate, this whole plural range of aims and purposes which a participant in it has to pursue.

Nevertheless, some conclusions about purpose must be drawn if the tenets of the two paradigms are to be fully compared.

Paradigm Differences Regarding the Import of Theory

Social scientists differ over the purposes of their science. These differences of opinion have clouded the evaluation of the inherently contradictory quantitative and qualitative paradigms. As Tuthill and Ashton (1983, p. 6) have observed, "Much of the uncertainty surrounding the use of science in education can be traced to the question of the purpose of educational science." Schubert (1980, p. 18) delineates two basic positions that social scientists have taken regarding the question of scientific purpose:

> The theoretical position holds that the end of inquiry is the creation of knowledge for its own sake. Further, a faith is held in the potential utility of such knowledge, though there may be a considerable time lag before results of basic research become applied. The practical position criticizes this stance on grounds that it abstracts concepts from the stream of existence and treats them as if they are realities.

Quite a number of education scholars have taken the position that educational research is primarily a practical endeavor:

> My test of the worth of a piece of education research, therefore, is whether it promotes or hinders that enterprise. (Piel, 1978, p. 8)
>
> But the aim of the practical arts is to get things done . . . In fields such as education and social work, where few laws have been validated and where inquiry can be directed toward gathering information that has use other than for the cultivation of laws, a persistent attention to laws is pedantic. (Stake, 1978, p. 7)
>
> In the practical sciences we are looking for solutions to problems, not just explanations of the failures that led to the problems . . . It does not take a theory. (Scriven, 1980, p. 18)

However, some researchers have argued that educational research could have both theoretical and practical orientations, or perhaps that theory might be viewed as the servant of practical purposes. Thus, Shulman (1981b, p. 40) argues that "It is the marriage of theoretical knowledge with practical action which characterizes education (along with medicine, law and other 'professional fields') and requires a philosophical perspective of its own."

Kerlinger (1977, pp. 5–6), on the other hand, has been adamant that theory is the sole purpose of science:

> Science, then, really has no other purpose than theory, or understanding and explanation . . . Scientific research never has the purpose of solving human or social problems, making decisions, and taking actions. The researcher . . . should never be required to think about or spell out the educational implications of what he is doing or has done.

Of course, the qualitative paradigm completely rejects theory as a legitimate purpose of science. As J. Smith (1983, p. 12) notes,

> The overall idea [underlying quantitative science] is that the accumulation of evidence will allow us to "sort out" the educational world in a systematic fashion . . . Not surprisingly, the interpretive-idealist approach to research rejects the possibility that laws will ever be found, at least laws analogous to those set forth in the physical sciences.

Lincoln and Guba (1985, p. 38) contrast, respectively, the quantitative and the qualitative paradigm in this manner:

> *Positivist version*: The aim of inquiry is to develop a nomethetic [lawlike generalizations] body of knowledge in the form of generalizations that are truth statements free from both time

> and context (they will hold anywhere and at any time). *Naturalist version*: The aim of inquiry is to develop an idiographic [limited to the particulars of the case] body of knowledge in the form of "working hypotheses" that describe the individual case.

Similarly, Eisner (1981, p. 9) notes that

> Artistic approaches to research are less concerned with the discovery of truth than with the creation of meaning. What art seeks is not the discovery of the laws of nature about which true statements or explanations can be given, but rather the creation of images that people will find meaningful and from which their fallible and tentative views of the world can be altered, rejected, or made more secure.

The quantitative paradigm, however, posits the existence of an external reality. It is believed that true general statements about aspects of that reality can be identified, although the reality is complex and so identification of general explanations is no easy feat. Some quantitative researchers heavily emphasize the importance of theoretically grounded research because they believe that this sort of research leads to more economical accumulation of knowledge about external reality. For example, when Jenner discovered many years ago that milkmaids did not get smallpox if they had been exposed to cowpox, he had the basis for suggesting a possible cure for smallpox. But absent any understanding of the mechanics of the cure, if he had then attempted to identify a cure for polio, his original discovery would have been of no assistance at all. If this discovery had enlightened him regarding the processes of immunology and the nature of viruses, however, his new hypothetical quest would have been more likely to be successful. As Gergen (1969, p. 13) notes, theoretically grounded research "not only satisfies our curiosity, but also has the advantage of maximum heuristic value. It leads to new investigations and suggests interesting links to other areas of concern."

If an external reality about which one can generalize exists, then orientation toward theory becomes important in comparing the two paradigms. A theoretically oriented paradigm may have the advantage if it leads to more empirical findings *or* to better concepts of reality. As MacMillan and Garrison (1984, p. 16) summarize some of the literature on this matter:

> A major advance of Laudan's [1978] scheme of research traditions is the emphasis given to *conceptual* as well as *empirical* problems; evaluation of a tradition of research must deal not only with the increase in empirical content (emphasized particularly by Popper, 1959, and Lakatos, 1970) but also with the conceptual problems that come up in any treatment.

Prediction as the Test of Theory

The qualitative paradigm does not admit prediction as the test of its findings. This is because, among other reasons, reality is seen as ever changing with different meaning intrinsic in the ever changing cast of the human characters that construct reality. As Lincoln and Guba (1985, p. 37) explain:

> There are multiple constructed realities that can be studied only holistically; inquiry into these multiple realities will inevitably diverge (each inquiry raises more questions than it answers) so that prediction and control are unlikely outcomes although some level of understanding (verstehen [shared meaning of researcher with persons in the research context]) can be achieved.

But traditional quantitative views have seen prediction as the acid test of the truth of theoretical tenets. If one truly understands, then one must be able to predict. For example, Watson (1948, p. 457), one of the behavorist fathers of contemporary psychology as a discipline, writes that "Psychology as the behaviorist views it is a purely objective experimental branch of natural science. Its theoretical goal is the prediction and control of behavior."

Qualitative researchers have noted that:

> In deduction, given the validity of the premises, the conclusion must be true and it is the only conclusion possible. But in induction, there are always many conclusions that can reasonably be related to certain premises. Deductions are closed but inductions are open (Lincoln & Guba, 1985, p. 26).

However, the quantitative paradigm has moved toward accepting the view that prediction is not the sole (or perhaps even the best) test of theory. Theoretical tenets should give reasonable probabilistic statements about reality (Hempel, 1986, p. 183), but theory cannot reasonably be judged against the criterion of perfect prediction.

As Neale and Liebert (1986, p. 289) suggest, "One implication of this new view is that the ability to explain does not always (or even usually) imply the ability to predict." Eisner (1981, p. 8) concurs, noting that "Most social science fields neither control nor successfully predict, they explicate." Scriven (1980, p. 18, emphasis in original) provides a graphic illustration of one test of theory other than prediction:

> Coroners do not promise that they could predict whether someone 50 pounds overweight would die of a heart-attack if they ran up 50 stairs. But they can nevertheless be sure of that exertion as the cause of death if death occurs, after an autopsy. The pattern is open-ended, but the fit can be made *exact* when the events fall into place. Explanations are possible where predictions are not.

CRITIQUE OF THE QUALITATIVE PARADIGM

The qualitative paradigm has been subjected to various criticisms of varying intensity. For example, Foster (1972, p. 481) has suggested that the anthropological study of education has gone nowhere for 20 years and may be "singularly *unfitted* to conduct educational research." Three criticisms of the paradigm can be noted, though they differ in their significance.

Inadequate Checks Against Bias

A fundamental tenet of the quantitative paradigm is that science must be self-correcting. As J. Smith, (1983, p. 10) notes "A basic criterion for separating what is considered objective [i.e., true] from what is not is whether the findings can be duplicated by anyone using the same instruments and procedures (presuming a similar level of skill)." Thus, Miles and Huberman (1984, p. 22) argue that "We need to be confident that the conclusions are not unreasonable, that another researcher facing the data would reach a conclusion that falls in the same general 'truth space.'"

Bias can be introduced in qualitative research both in observation and in the analysis and reporting of results. Consider Mulhauser's (1974, p. 7) reflections as a qualitative researcher:

> After I had been observing the administration of a school system all day every day for two years, I had a strong urge to show that I had it under intellectual control . . . I had a stake in showing that I could interpret most of the behavior I saw by pointing out its links and relations to the rest of the system which I thought I saw more comprehensively than any particular actor within it, thanks to the extraordinary patience of everyone in putting up with me and my notebook.

With respect to bias in analysis and reporting, Herriott and Firestone (1983, p. 18) observes that "The potential of any study for useful, valid description and generalization depends on the analysts' ability to reduce data to a manageable form without distortion or loss of meaningful detail." However, there is ample room for bias in qualitative research, because "Many qualitative researchers still consider analysis an art and stress intuitive approaches to it" (Miles & Huberman, 1984, p. 22). Indeed, some qualitative researchers would argue that the subjective phenomenological interpretation of experiences is within the essence of the method. Miles and Huberman (1984, p. 20) note that "There are few agreed-on canons for analysis of qualitative data, and therefore the truth claims underlying such work are uncertain." Furthermore, they acknowledge that:

> There is a license [in qualitative work] to amplify or interpret the results of observations at a higher level of inference than might be warranted under classical canons of inductive, Bayesian, or statistical inference (Miles & Huberman, 1984, p. 21).

The grounding of observation in the context of the field and the grounding of interpretation in the meanings of the subjects have some appeal. But the grounding may not be much better than the qualitative researcher's judgment that observation and interpretation were correctly grounded. This flaw is inherent in the qualitative paradigm.

Unfortunately, a post-paradigmatic view requires quantitative researchers to recognize that their single studies *taken singly* are equally subject to the risks of bias. As Eisner (1981, p. 8) notes:

> Making things vivid through selective reporting and special emphasis occurs inevitably in any form of reporting, including scientific reporting. Artistically oriented research acknowledges what already exists and instead of presenting a facade of objectivity, exploits the potential of selectivity and emphasis to say what needs saying as the investigator sees it.

However, unlike the qualitative paradigm, the quantitative paradigm seeks general theory through the integration of multiple inquiries. In the quantitative paradigm, since a single study per se is of little interest, the check of replication is available to the field of quantitative inquiry, though bias may operate in any given single study.

The Dilemma of Thick Description

Practitioners of the qualitative paradigm confront a difficult dilemma involving reports of their scholarly inquiries. An essential feature of qualitative research involves the "thick description" of the context that the research investigated. These descriptions are intended to provide sharing of the intersubjective meanings and experiences noted in the field. However, truly thick description may "yield prolix, undigested 'findings' that only the most obsessive scholar can wade through" (Huberman & Miles, 1986, p. 25).

Furthermore, editors may resist the allocation of precious pages in service of thick description. Thus Lecompte and Goetz (1982, p. 40) note that

> Failures to specify methods of data collection and analysis may be related to the aforementioned brevity that journals often require in manuscripts. Pelto and Pelto (1978) note the regularity with which journal authors fail to report sufficiently their research designs and methodology.

Thus, Mulhauser (1974, p. 20) reports that, "It has been my own high hopes for non-reductionist methods of study of complex institutions that cause my acute disappointment when I see how difficult it is to communicate the results."

B. Thompson (1981b) discusses an example of a qualitative study that was reported in several outlets in varying detail, but that in some outlets was not reported in meaningful detail. It should be noted, however, that this difficulty partially involves a poor correspondence between an inherent feature of the qualitative paradigm and features of our mechanisms for sharing insights from scholarly inquiries with each other. The problem could be mitigated by changes in contemporary editorial practices.

Unitary Criterion for the Test of Meaning

Contemporary social science can be seen as an attempt to escape the previous obsessive interest in the metaphysical. Yet the qualitative paradigm too is a reaction—a reaction against the strictures of positivism. The problem is that the qualitative paradigm tries to assign the responsibility for observation and interpretation decisions to the subjects being studied. A serious problem with this effort is that the use of subjects' beliefs as the *sole* criterion of meaning represents an attempted "escape from freedom" that may not be appropriate.

As Miles and Huberman (1984, p. 19) note, "Even if people [subjects] do not themselves apprehend the same analytical constructs as those derived by researchers, this does not make such constructs invalid or contrived." Donmoyer (1985, p. 17) argues that

> Certain social scientists, of course—emic-oriented anthropologists in particular—simply convert questions of meaning into questions of truth by preselecting as their language the language that subjects themselves use to characterize phenomena. These researchers do not ask what is the valid meaning to attribute to phenomena . . . The problem with this approach is that there is no reason to believe that an insider's view of particular phenomena is necessarily more valid than an outsider's view of the same phenomena.

A post-paradigmatic view suggests that all researchers can benefit from considering the meanings and the perceptions of the human participants in studies through the eyes of the participants. The view acknowledges the reflexivity and intentionality of the participants. But this does not warrant the use of these perspectives as the sole criterion for meaning. Scientists must not allow the delineation of scientific paradigms to continue as a cyclical process of swinging between extreme positions such as positivism and idealism.

THE "NEW" PHILOSOPHY OF SCIENCE

Historically any number of philosophical views on the nature of science have been available to researcher. As Soltis (1984, p. 6) notes:

> From low-level inductivist accounts from Bacon (1960) of correlational studies, to experimental strategies based on Mill's (1961) canons, to a deductive theory of hypothesis generation a la Braithwaite (1953), to Nagel's (1961) view of a two-tiered empirical-theoretical structure of science, to Popper's (1965) fallibist program of conjecture and refutation, to Lakatos' (1970) progressive and retrogressive research programs, to Kuhn's (1962) normal and revolutionary scientist, we have been given different philosophical views of what constitutes the proper form of empirical science.

Recently, new views of the scientific paradigm have emerged from the conflicts between the quantitative and the qualitative paradigms. The "new" philosophy of science represents considerable effort to realize post-paradigmatic insight. Much of this thought was stimulated by consideration of a fundamental conflict between the quantitative and the qualitative paradigms, that is, standards for testing truth.

Tests of Truth

Standards for testing truth are at the core of any meaningful scientific paradigm. Any number of views regarding appropriate standards have been presented. Some seem unduly nehilistic:

> What we should do, I suggest, is to give up the idea of ultimate sources of knowledge, and admit that all knowledge is human; that it is mixed with our errors, our prejudices, our dreams, and our hopes; that all we can do is to grope for truth even though it be beyond our reach. (Popper, 1965, pp. 29–30)

The traditional quantitative paradigm had its roots in positivistic thought. The paradigm has always presumed the existence of a reality external to the researcher. The paradigm has traditionally employed a *correspondence* theory of truth in order to test facts. As J. Smith (1983, p. 9) notes:

> The basic feature of realist epistemology is that it espouses a correspondence theory of truth. According to this theory, truth has its source in reality; a statement will be judged true if it corresponds to an independently existing reality and false if it does not.

However, this test is not available to the idealist qualitative paradigm, since an independent external reality is not presumed to be available. In its stead, the qualitative paradigm employs a *consensus* theory of truth. As J. Smith (1983, p. 10) explains:

> From the interpretive perspective, objectivity is therefore nothing more than social agreement: What is objectively so [i.e., true] is what we agree is objectively so. This agreement is based on justification or persuasion, which is of course a question of values and interests; agreement is not a product of an external reality [since there is no external reality].

Smith and Heshusius (1986, p. 9) note that, "Since reality is mind-dependent (for the idealist/qualitative researcher), a description can only be matched to other descriptions and not to an unconceptualized reality."

McCutcheon (1981, p. 9) acknowledges that qualitative or "interpretive work is intersubjective; potentially, the audience can share the understanding and the interpretation the researcher has constructed." Eisner (1981, p. 6) is perfectly comfortable with this standard:

> Validity in the arts [and in artistic approaches to qualitative research] is the product of the persuasiveness of a personal vision; its utility is determined by the extent to which it informs . . . What one seeks is illumination and penetration. The proof of the pudding is the way in which it shapes our conception of the world or some aspect of it.

However, the view does fly straight in the face of the traditional quantitative paradigm:

> Disciplined inquiry has a quality that distinguishes it from other sources of opinion and belief. The disciplined inquiry is conducted and reported in such a way that the argument can be painstakingly examined. The report does not depend for its appeal on the eolquence of the writer or on any surface plausibility. (Cronbach & Suppes, 1969, p. 15)

To many the consensus theory of truth, at least as it is applied to test facts, seems hollow and relativistic. Miles and Huberman (1984, p. 27) paint a rather horrifying view of results being incommensurable because the qualitative and the quantitative paradigms are incompatible:

> Researchers doublechecking the site come up with discrepant findings. Site informants, asked to report on the findings, plausibly contest some or all of them. The [idealist, qualitative researcher] chuckles, reinforced by the idea that there is no single reality out there to "get right." The [realist, quantitative) psychometrician concludes that nonstatistical research is an albatross.

Smith and Heshusius (1986, p. 10) seem to dispair:

> If there is no God's Eye view, and one description based on values and interests can only be matched to other descriptions based on other values and interests, are we trapped in a never-ending circle of descriptions? Does qualitative inquiry leave us with the prospect that we cannot break out of the circle and that there are no criteria and procedures to be specified to prevent "anything goes"?

Cole (1980, pp. 129–130) laments, "Even if Kuhn's view turns out to be correct, it is possible that it might be necessary for scientists to believe in the more traditional view in order to proceed with the work of science." Manicas and Secord (1983, p. 401) ask, "Does the [Kuhnian] paradigmatic view lead to a consensus theory of truth in which, in fact, there are no independent checks on the nature of consensus?"

Tenets of the New Philosophy of Science

The new philosophy of science represents a paradigm shift from the traditional quantitative paradigm. The new philosophy is distinctly non-positivistic, but still honors many aspects of contemporary research practice. Furthermore, the new philosophy accomodates many of the practices and precepts of the qualitative paradigm. Three tenets in particular distinguish this new view of science.

First, *the new philosophy of science acknowledges that all aspects of scientific inquiry are value laden.* Even the selection of research questions is itself a matter of value. As Strike (1979, p. 10, emphasis in original) observes, "Situations do not become [research] problems unless we approach them with values which specify what properties these situations *ought* to have." Perceptions are inherently value laden:

> Hermeneutics (a term derived from Hermes, the messenger god of Greek mythology) is the art of explaining or interpreting; the hermeneutic view states that all perception is interpretive. The hermeneutic approach to knowledge states that we see what we expect to see or intend to see; perception is the interpretation (or "reading") of sensation and is therefore always fallible. (Neale & Libert, 1986, p. 288)

Similarly, Strike (1979, p. 10) notes that "Unhappily, no theory of any sophistication and power is ever refuted by a single counter instance. Theories can typically be protected from negative data by the manipulation of assumptions of lesser scope."

Manicas and Secord (1983, p. 401) summarize some of the insights gained from the conflict between the quantitative and the qualitative paradigms:

> These [Kuhnian] philosophers made clear that observations were not "given" but were profoundly shaped by the observer's preconceptions and theoretical notions. They demonstrated convincingly that scientific meanings could not be found in observations alone, as the logical empiricists had maintained. And the idea that there could be unambiguous logical connections between theory and observation was overthrown. Finally, that scientists were human observers was demonstrated to make science a social activity, which subjected it to normative or paradigmatic influences operating apart from the internal criteria of science.

However, these new perspectives do not represent a submission to relativism. "All our perceptions, categories, and frames of meaning are mediated and are culturally and historically loaded. But this does not eliminate the possibility of objectivity, construed here as warranted assertibility" (Manicas & Secord, 1983, p. 410). As Soltis (1984, p. 8) notes, "Although I argue that the study of pedagogy must include value judgments and cannot be value free, it is not therefore necessarily cut loose from rational modes of public appraisal."

Second, *the new philosophy of science acknowledges that interpretations of scientific findings must be tested against several criteria in addition to testing through the correspondence theory of truth.* As MacMillan and Garrison (1984, p. 19) suggest,

> Correlations [and sums of squares partitions] do not provide an explanation of the observations they summarize, but only descriptions of phenomena that need causal explanation. What is lacking is the connective causal story, a narrative account with a beginning, middle, and end, a cast of recognizable characters, and a coherent plot.

With respect to casting for these characters, "Most post-positivistic philosophers of science are united behind the view that empirical evidence alone is inadequate for assessing the potency of interpretations, for contemporary philosophers recognize that what counts as empirical evidence depends on the interpretive framework being employed" (Donmoyer, 1985, p. 16).

The new philosophy of science emphasizes replication as an important component of truth testing. As Neale and Liebert (1986, p. 290) explain,

> No one study, however shrewdly designed and carefully executed, can provide convincing support for a causal hypothesis or theoretical statement in the social sciences . . . Too many possible (if not plausible) confounds, limitations on generality, and alternative interpretations can be offered for any one observation. Moreover, each of the basic methods of research (experimental, correlational, and case study) and techniques of comparison (within- or between-subjects) has instrinsic limitations. How, then, does social science theory advance through research? The answer is, by collecting a diverse body of evidence about any major theoretical proposition.

Third, *the new philosophy of science presumes the existence of an external reality and assumes the preeminence of theory as a component of reality.* As Manicas and Secord (1983, p. 401, emphasis in original) argue,

> The practices of science generate their own *rational* criteria in terms of which theory is accepted or rejected. The crucial point is that it is possible for these criteria to be rational precisely because on realist terms, there is a world that exists independently of cognizing experience.

In Huberman and Miles' (1986, pp. 25–26) terms:

> [''Transcendental realism''] is a ''middle-ground'' epistomology that refutes correspondence theory, empirical probabilism, and predictive validity, while still making claims to verifiable explanation. This position incorporates some of the core components of causal idealism as well—socially generated meanings, intentionality and reflexivity, historicism.

Manicas and Secord (1983, pp. 402–403, emphasis in original) emphasize the importance of theory in this new view:

> The patterns of experience are where we begin. Led by a hypothesis that there is some causally efficacious mechanism at work, we construct theory about it. The theory tells us what we can expect if, with ingenuity, we can isolate the theorized mechanism. A good experiment confirms a theory precisely because if it establishes the right conditions and eliminates interfering causal mechanisms, the experiment yields what would *not* have been observed without the experiment.

As Neale and Liebert (1986, p. 289, emphasis in original) note,

> The business of science, all the philosophers of [''new''] science claim, is to invent theories rather than to discover facts. Theories, therefore, must rest on rational as well as empirical criteria. Theories are in fact judged by their goodness-of-fit with the understood or perceived world (which is not the same as *the* world).

THE PLACE OF OLD PRECEPTS IN THE NEW VIEW

The new philosophy of science rejects both the idealist assumptions of the qualitative paradigm and the positivistic assumptions of the quantitative paradigm. However, the new philosophy of science accomodates some of the assumptions and some of the methods of both paradigms.

Kerlinger (1977, p. 9) has observed that "Methodology is, after all, different ways of doing things for different purposes. Change methodology and you change, to some extent at least, the problems we attack." Shulman (1981a, p. 11) notes that

> One of the enduring problems in research methodology has been the tendency to treat selection of method as primarily a technical question not associated with the underlying theoretical or substantive rationale of the research to be conducted.

Toulmin (1972, p. 64) notes that methods have their limits:

> Where our task is to judge alternative hypotheses within the scope of a [conceptually] single scientific theory, the formal procedures of logic and probability-theory—significance tests, techniques of curve fitting, and so on—may serve us well; but the moment we have to compare hypotheses framed in terms of different theories, we go outside the scope of these procedures.

Certainly quantitative methods have left many questions unanswered. As Glass (1979, p. 13, emphasis in original) notes

> In none of the dozen or so research literatures that we have integrated in the past five years have we ever encountered a cross-validated multiple correlation between study findings and study characteristics that was larger than approximately .60. That is, I haven't seen a body of literature in which we can account for much more than a *third* of the variability in the *results of studies*.

Reickenbach (1938, p. 7) distinguishes between the "context of discovery" and the "context of justification." He notes that the scientific process of formalizing knowledge has different characteristics than the process of formulating insight or theory. In many respects the traditional quantitative paradigm has not been theoretically oriented, and thus has made more limited contributions to discovery. As Manicas and Secord (1983, p. 400) note, for those practicing science from the standard view,

> research is more or less atheoretical, with many researchers avoiding theory as far as possible and seeking to test only hypotheses related to variables that can be closely tied to observations. Few investigators attempt to develop full-blown theories.

Lincoln and Guba (1985, p. 25) argue that "Verification has taken precedence over discovery within positivism [read as quantitative research] because proponents of that formulation could not devise a means for coming to grips with it [discovery] systematically."

Qualitative methods make a particularly important contribution to science in the "context of discovery," though this view can be taken too strictly. As LeCompte and Goetz (1982, p. 34) note,

> A stereotypic distinction labels experimentation as hypothesis verifying and ethnography as hypothesis generating. This simplification has been challenged legitimately by some scholars. Our position is that such dimensions as generation-verification and induction-deduction are continuous rather than discrete processes and that researchers shift along these continua as they proceed through any particular research project and follow some line of investigation.

Nevertheless, qualitative views can make a major contribution to discovery:

> When explanation, propositional knowledge, and law are the aims of an inquiry, the case study will often be at a disadvantage. When the aims are understanding, extension of experience, and increase in convinction in that which is known, the disadvantage disappears (Stake, 1978, p. 6).

Though Cooley (1978, p. 9) may overstate the case, "It is important to remember that most of what is known about people and the universe has not been based on experimentation, but on observation." For example, Ginsburg and Opper (1969, p. ix) suggest that "Since the early 1950's, it has become increasingly clear to child psychologists, educators, and others in diverse areas that Jean Piaget is the foremost contributor to the field of intellectual development." Yet, as Wadsworth (1971, p. 7) notes,

> The main sources for three of Piaget's books were observations of his own three children, born between 1925 and 1931 . . . From these exceedingly complete and careful descriptions of behavior over a period of years, major conclusions have been drawn regarding intellectual development from birth to age 2.

These considerations suggest the post-paradigm position that quantitative researchers must become more thoughtful and reflective in their work. Cronbach (1975, p. 124) has observed that

> Originally, the psychologist saw his role as the scientific observation of human behavior. When hypothesis testing became paramount, observation was neglected, and even actively discouraged by editorial policies of journals. Some authors now report nothing save *F* ratios.

J. Thompson, Hawkes, and Avery (1983, p. 13) argue that the

> scientist who is overly disciplined to current theories and to current experimental evidence is not the one who will achieve creative insight . . . Scientific insight usually comes from someone on the periphery of a discipline rather than someone squarely in that discipline.

The findings of M. Thompson and Brewster (1978) support this position; they report that faculty in more developed disciplines are more dogmatic, authoritarian, and less democratic than faculty in less developed disciplines.

CONCLUDING REMARKS

Social scientists are currently participating in a paradigm conflict and shift of historical proportions. Most contemporary social scientists were not alive during the previous major shift at the turn of the century. These are difficult times, but also times of great opportunity. Lincoln and Guba (1985, p. 15) suggest that "Paradigms represent a distillation of what we *think* about the world (but cannot prove). Our actions in the world, including actions that we take as inquirers, cannot occur without reference to those paradigms."

However, post-paradigmatic thought may be possible during such extraordinary periods of science. Scientists must be thoughtful and thorough in their deliberations over contemporary choices. Definitive positions that are explicitly justified facilitate deliberations regarding these choices. And researchers must be prepared to be wrong and to make necessary corrections. Strike's (1979, p. 11) comments about ontological paradigm testing, that is, theory testing, may apply to elaboration of epistemological paradigms as well:

> It is unlikely that any theory can be mapped onto experience unless a process of testing auxillary hypotheses and replacing them in light of the sort of failure achieved takes place. Good research, thus, requires tolerance for failure.

Scientists must also approach resolution of the paradigm conflict with tolerance. Thus, Cooley (1978, p. 13) has noted "the importance of the interaction between qualitative and quantitative 'types' in working toward an improved understanding of educational processes. We have to talk to each other and read each other's work, not shout at each other." In Strike's (1984, p. 7) view,

> Each of us should have an interest in seeing that everything gets done and done well. I will also argue that we need to try to understand what others are doing and be willing to be reasonable and fair when we judge their claims rather than use our own methodological biases to prejudge their worth. We need to become a real community of researchers.

The new philosophy of science may provide the epistemological paradigm that accomodates just such a community.

REFERENCES

Assimov, I. (1972). *The gods themselves*. New York: Doubleday.

Blalock, H. M. (1960). *Social statistics*. New York: McGraw-Hill.

Bogdan, R. C., & Biklen, S. K. (1982). *Qualitative research for education: An introduction to theory and methods*. Boston: Allyn and Bacon.

Byrne, C. J. (1983, October). *Teacher knowledge and teacher effectiveness: A literature review, theoretical analysis and discussion of research strategy*. Paper presented at the annual meeting of the Northeastern Educational Research Association, Ellenville, NY.

Campbell, D. T., & Erlebacher, A. (1975). How regression artifacts in quasi-experimental evaluations can mistakenly make compensatory education look harmful. In M. Guttentag & E. L. Struening (Eds.), *Handbook of evaluation research* (Vol. 1, pp. 597–617). Beverly Hills, CA: Sage.

Campbell, D. T., & Stanley, J. C. (1963). *Experimental and quasi-experimental designs for research.* Chicago: Rand McNally.

Carlberg, C. G., & Kavale, K. (1980). The efficacy of special versus regular class placement for exceptional children: A metaanalysis. *Journal of Special Education, 14,* 295–309.

Carver, R. P. (1978). The case against statistical significance testing. *Harvard Educational Review, 48,* 378–399.

Cohen, J. (1968). Multiple regression as a general data-analytic system. *Psychological Bulletin, 70,* 426–443.

Cole, S. (1980). *The sociological method: An introduction to the science of sociology.* Chicago: Rand McNally.

Cooley, W. W. (1978). Explanatory observational studies. *Educational Researcher, 7*(9), 9–15.

Cornfield, J., & Tukey, J. W. (1956). Average values of mean squares in factorials. *Annals of Mathematical Statistics, 27,* 907–959.

Cronback, L. J. (1975). Beyond the two disciplines of scientific psychology. *American Psychologist, 30,* 116–127.

Cronbach, L. J., Ambron, S. R., Dornbusch, S. M., Hess, R. D., Hornik, R. C., Phillips, D. C., Walker, D. F., & Weiner, S. S. (1980). *Toward reform of program evaluation.* San Francisco: Jossey-Bass.

Cronbach, L. J., & Suppes, P. (Eds.). (1969). *Research for tomorrow's schools: Disciplined inquiry for education.* New York: MacMillan.

Culbertson, J. (1983). Theory in educational administration: Echoes from critical thinkers. *Educational Researcher, 12*(10), 15–22.

Donmoyer, R. (1985). The rescue from relativism: Two failed attempts and an alternative strategy. *Educational Researcher, 14*(10), 13–20.

Donmoyer, R. (1986). The problem of language in empirical research: A rejoinder to Miles and Huberman. *Educational Researcher, 15*(3), 26–27.

Edgington, E. S. (1974). A new tabulation of statistical procedures in APA journals. *American Psychologist, 29,* 25–26.

Eisner, E. W. (1981). On the difference between scientific and artistic approaches to qualitative research. *Educational Researcher, 10*(4), 5–9.

Eisner, E. W. (1983). Anastasia might still be alive, but the monarchy is dead. *Educational Researcher, 12*(5), 13–14, 23–24.

Elashoff, J. D. (1969). Analysis of covariance: A delicate instrument. *American Educational Research Journal, 6,* 383–401.

Fetterman, D. M. (1982). Ethnography in educational research: The dynamics of diffusion. *Educational Researcher, 11*(3), 17–22, 29.

Filstead, W. J. (1970). *Qualitative methodology.* Chicago: Markum.

Foster, P. (1972). [Review of *Anthropological perspectives on education*]. *American Journal of Sociology, 78,* 489–492.

Gage, N. L. (1963). Paradigms for research on teaching. In N. L. Gage (Ed.), *Handbook of research on teaching.* Chicago: Rand McNally.

Gardner, G. T. (1978). Effects of Federal human subjects regulations on data obtained in environmental stressor research. *Journal of Personality and Social Psychology, 36,* 628–634.

Gergen, K. J. (1969). *The psychology of behavior exchange.* Reading, MA: Addison-Wesley.

Ginsburg, H., & Opper, S. (1969). *Piaget's theory of intellectual development: An introduction.* Englewood Cliffs, NJ: Prentice-Hall.

Glass, G. V. (1979). Policy for the unpredictable (uncertainty research and policy). *Educational Researcher, 8*(9), 12–14.

Glass, G. V., McGaw, B., & Smith, M. L. (1981). *Meta-analysis in social research.* Beverly Hills, CA: Sage.

Goodwin, L. D., & Goodwin, W. L. (1985). Statistical techniques in *AERJ* articles, 1979–1983: The preparation of graduate students to read the educational research literature. *Educational Researcher, 14*(2), 5–11.

Gorsuch, R. L. (1983). *Factor analysis* (2nd ed.). Hillsdale, NJ: Erlbaum.

Guilford, J. P. (1965). *Fundamental statistics in psychology and education* (4th ed.). New York: McGraw-Hill.

Hays, W. (1963). *Statistics.* New York: Holt, Rinehart and Winston.

Hempel, C. G. (1968). The logic of functional analysis. In M. Brodbeck (Ed.), *Readings in the philosophy of social science.* New York: MacMillan.

Herriott, R. E., & Firestone, W. A. (1983). Multisite qualitative policy research: Optimizing description and generalizability. *Educational Researcher, 12*(2), 14–19.

Hiltner, S. (1973). Tuskegee syphillis study under review. *Christian Century, 90,* 1174–1176.

Homans, G. C. (1967). *The nature of social science.* New York: Harcourt, Rinehart and Winston.

Huberman, A. M., & Miles, M. B. (1986). Concepts and methods in qualitative research: A reply to Donmoyer. *Educational Researcher, 15*(3), 25–26.

Hudson, W. D. (1969). *The is/ought question.* London: MacMillan.

Hume, D. (1957). *An inquiry concerning human understanding.* New York: The Liberal Arts Press.

Kaiser, H. F. (1976). [Review of *Factor analysis as a statistical method*]. *Educational and Psychological Measurement 36,* 586–589.

Kerlinger, F. N. (1973). *Foundations of behavioral research* (2nd ed.). New York: Holt, Rinehart and Winston.

Kerlinger, F. N. (1977). The influence of research on education practice. *Educational Researcher, 6* (8), 5–12.

Knapp, T. R. (1978). Canonical correlation analysis: A general parametric significance-testing system. *Psychological Bulletin, 85,* 410–416.

Koch, S. (1959). *Psychology: A study of a science* (Vol. 3). New York: McGraw-Hill.

Kuhn, T. S. (1970). *The structure of scientific revolutions* (2nd ed.). Chicago: University of Chicago Press, (1st ed., 1969).

LeCompte, M. D., & Goetz, J. P. (1982). Problems of reliability and validity in ethnographic research. *Review of Educational Research, 52,* 31–60.

Laudan, L. (1978). *Progress and its problems.* Berkeley: University of California Press.

Lincoln, Y. S., & Guba, E. G. (1985). *Naturalistic inquiry.* Beverly Hills, CA: Sage.

Lord, F. M. (1960). Large sample covariance analysis when the control variable is fallible. *Journal of the American Statistical Association, 55,* 309–321.

MacMillan, C. J. B., & Garrison, J. W. (1984). Using the "new philosophy of science" in criticizing current research traditions in education. *Educational Researcher, 13*(10), 15–21.

McCutcheon, G. (1981). On the interpretation of classroom observations. *Educational Researcher, 10*(5), 5–10.

McGuigan, F. J. (1983). *Experimental psychology: Methods of research* (4th ed.). Englewood Cliffs, NJ: Prentice-Hall.

Marascuilo, L. A., & Levin, J. R. (1970). Appropriate post hoc comparisons for interaction and nested hypotheses in analysis of variance designs: The elimination of Type IV errors. *American Educational Research Journal, 7,* 397–421.

Manicas, P. T., & Secord, P. F. (1983). Implications for psychology of the new philosophy of science. *American Psychologist, 38,* 399–413.

Miles, M. B., & Huberman, A. M. (1984). Drawing valid meaning from qualitative data: Toward a shared craft. *Educational Researcher, 13*(5), 20–30.

Miles, M. B., & Huberman, A. M. (1984). *Qualitative data analysis: A sourcebook of new methods.* Beverly Hills, CA: Sage.

Morrison, D. E., & Henkel, R. E. (1970). *The significance test controversy—A reader.* Chicago: Adeline.

Mulhauser, F. (1974, April). *Ethnography and educational policymaking.* Paper presented at the annual meeting of the American Educational Research Association, New Orleans.

Neale, J. M., & Liebert, R. M. (1986). *Science and behavior: An introduction to methods of research* (3rd ed.). Englewood Cliffs, NJ: Prentice-Hall.

Nunnally, J. C. (1975). Psychometric theory—25 years ago and now. *Educational Researcher, 4* (10), 7–14, 19–20.

Overholt, G. E., & Stallings, W. M. (1976). Ethnographic and experimental hypotheses in educational research. *Educational Researcher, 5*(8), 12–14.

Patton, M. Q. (1975). *Alternative evaluation research paradigm.* Grand Forks: University of North Dakota Press.

Phillips, D. C. (1980). What do the researcher and the practitioner have to offer each other? *Educational Researcher, 9*(11), 17–20, 24.

Phillips, D. C. (1983). After the wake: Postpositivistic educational thought. *Educational Researcher, 12*(5), 4–12.

Piel, G. (1978). Research for action. *Educational Researcher, 7*(2), 8–12.

Popper, K. (1965). *Conjectures and refutations* (2nd ed.). New York: Harper Torchbooks.

Reickenbach, H. (1938). *Experience and prediction.* Chicago: University of Chicago Press.

Rist, R. C. (1975). Ethnographic techniques and the study of an urban school. *Urban Education, 10,* 86–108.

Rist, R. C. (1977). On the relations among educational research paradigms: From disdain to detente. *Anthropology and Education Quarterly, 7*(2), 42–50.

Rist, R. C. (1980). Blitzkrieg ethnography: On the transformation of a method into a movement. *Educational Researcher, 9*(2), 8–10.

Rist, R. C. (1982). Foreword. In R. C. Bogdan & S. K. Biklen, *Qualitative research for education: An introduction to theory and methods.* Boston: Allyn and Bacon.

Schubert, W. H. (1980). Recalibrating educational research: Toward a focus on practice. *Educational Researcher, 9*(1), 17–24, 31.

Scriven, M. (1969). Logical positivism and the behavioral sciences. In Achinstein, P. & F. Barker. *The legacy of logical positivism* (pp. 195–209). Baltimore: Johns Hopkins Press.

Scriven, M. (1980). Self-referent research. *Educational Researcher, 9*(6), 11–18, 30.

Shapiro, J. Z. (1984). On the application of econometric methodology to educational research: A meta-theoretical analysis. *Educational Researcher, 13*(2), 12–19.

Shaver, J. P. (1979). The productivity of educational research and the applied-basic research distinction. *Educational Researcher, 8*(1), 3–9.

Shaver, J. P ., & Norton, R. S. (1980). Randomness and replication in ten years of the *American Educational Research Journal. Educational Researcher, 9*(1), 9–15.

Shulman, L. S. (1981a). Disciplines of inquiry in education: An overview. *Educational Researcher, 10*(6), 5–12, 23.

Shulman, L. S. (1981b). A view from educational psychology. *Educational Theory, 31*(1), 37–42.

Smith, J. K. (1983). Quantitative versus qualitative research: An attempt to clarify the issue. *Educational Researcher, 12*(3), 6–13.

Smith, J. K., & Heshusius, L. (1986). Closing down the conversation: The end of the quantitative-qualitative debate among educational inquirers. *Educational Researcher, 15*(1), 4–12.

Smith, L. M. (1979). An evolving logic of participant observation, educational ethnography, and other case studies. *Review of Research in Education, 6,* 316–377.

Soltis, J. F. (1984). On the nature of educational research. *Educational Researcher, 13*(10), 5–10.

Stake, R. E. (1978). The case study method in social inquiry. *Educational Researcher, 7* (2), 5–8.

Strike, K. A. (1979). An epistomology of practical research. *Educational Researcher, 8*(1), 10–16.

Tatsuoka, M. M. (1973). *An examination of the statistical properties of a multivariate measure of strength of relationship*. Urbana: University of Illinois. (ERIC Document Reproduction Service No. ED 099 406)

Thompson, B. (1981a, November). *The problem of OVAism*. Paper presented at the annual meeting of the Mid-South Educational Research Association, Lexington, KY. [Document No. 03980, National Auxillary Publication Service, P. O. Box 3513, Grand Central Station, New York, NY 11017]

Thompson, B. (1981b). [Review of *Utilization of evaluative information*]. *Educational Evaluation and Policy Analysis, 3,* 106–107.

Thompson, B. (1984). *Canonical correlation analysis: Uses and interpretation*. Beverly Hills, CA: Sage.

Thompson, B. (1985a). Alternate methods for analyzing data from experiments. *Journal of Experimental Education, 54,* 50–55.

Thompson, B. (1985b, April). *Heuristics for teaching multivariate general linear model concepts*. Paper presented at the annual meeting of the American Educational Research Association, Chicago. (ERIC Document Reproduction Service No. ED 262 073)

Thompson, B. (1986). A Monte Carlo study of the use of ANOVA with ATI designs. *Educational and Psychological Measurement, 46,* 917–928.

Thompson, B. (1988, April). *Canonical correlation analysis: An explanation with comments on correct practice*. Paper presented at the annual meeting of the American Educational Research Association, New Orleans. (ERIC Document Reproduction Service No. ED 295 957)

Thompson, B., & Borrello, G. M. (1985). The importance of structure coefficients in regression research. *Educational and Psychological Measurement, 45,* 203–209.

Thompson, J. D., Hawkes, R. W., & Avery, R. W. (1969). Truth strategies and university organization. *Educational Administration Quarterly, 5*(2), 4–25.

Thompson, M. E., & Brewster, D. A. (1978). Faculty behavior in low-paradigm versus high-paradigm disciplines: A case study. *Research in Higher Education, 8,* 169–175.

Thompson, W. N. (1971). *Modern argumentation and debate: Principles and practices*. New York: Harper and Row.

Toulmin, S. (1961). *Foresight and understanding*. New York: Harper and Row.

Toulmin, S. (1972). *Human understanding*. Princeton: Princeton University Press.

Tuthill, D., & Ashton, P. (1983). Improving educational research through the development of educational paradigms. *Educational Researcher, 12*(10), 6–14.

Wadsworth, B. J. (1971). *Piaget's theory of cognitive development*. New York: David McKay.

Watson, J. (1948). Psychology as the behaviorist views it. In W. Dennis (Ed.), *Readings in the history of psychology* (pp. 457–471). New York: Appleton-Century-Crofts.

Weimer, W. B. (1979). *Notes on the methodology of scientific research*. Hillsdale, NJ: Erlbaum.

Welch, W. W., & Walberg, H. J. (1974). A course evaluation. In H. J. Walberg (Ed.), *Evaluating educational performance: A sourcebook of methods, instruments, and examples* (pp. 113–124). Berkeley: McCutchan.

Willson, V. L. (1980). Research techniques in *AERJ* articles: 1969 to 1978. *Educational Researcher, 9*(6), 5–10.

Wolcott, H. F. (1975). Criteria for an ethnographic approach to research in schools. *Human Organization, 34,* 111–128.

PROBLEMS WITH STEPWISE METHODS—BETTER ALTERNATIVES

Carl J Huberty

The conduct of analytical procedures in "steps" is quite common. Calculations in the steps vary from the simple-in-routine procedures (such as formula plug-in steps) to the complex in what have been called "stepwise" and "stepdown" and "stepup" procedures. The latter procedures have enjoyed widespread use by social and behavioral science researchers in the analyses of data obtained on multiple response variables. The widespread use is undoubtedly due to the availability of computer software to accomplish the complex calculations. All three popular computer software packages—BMDP, SAS, SPSS—include a computer program to conduct what is called a "stepwise multiple regression analysis" and a program for a "stepwise discriminant analysis." Although regression analysis and discriminant analysis problems are, without a doubt, the most popular contexts for the use of step-type computational algorithms, these approaches have also been suggested in multivariate analysis of variance (Stevens, 1973) and in canonical correlation analysis (Thompson, 1984, pp. 47–51; Thorndike & Weiss, 1983). The focus of the current paper is on the use of stepwise methods and alternatives thereof in regression and discriminant analyses.

The notion of stepwise analysis is believed to have been first advanced by Efroymson (1960), and is fully described by Draper and Smith (1981, chap. 6)

Advances in Social Science Methodology, Volume 1, pages 43–70.

ISBN: 0-89232-736-7

and Jennrich (1977a, 1977b). [See also, Klecka, 1980, chap. 5; Norusis, 1985, chaps. 2 and 3; and Younger, 1985, chap. 15.] Essentially, a stepwise analysis develops a sequence of linear models (actually, model *equations*), at each step adding or deleting a response variable. Various criteria may be employed for variable addition/deletion. The criteria used depend on the type of analysis (regression versus discriminant), on the purpose of the analysis (e.g., model building, prediction), and on personal preference or expert advisement. Available to researchers are forward stepwise and backward stepwise procedures. In the former, a single-variable model is the starting point, assuming the criterion for considering a single variable is met at the outset. In the second step another variable is added, with the possibility that the first-entered variable is removed. This continues with a "step" being accomplished whenever a new variable is added, or when a variable already entered is removed. The process continues until all variables are considered for addition or until a criterion is met for stopping. [In rare cases, a "looping" may result when one variable is removed and added repeatedly. To limit looping, the user may specify a maximum number of steps to be executed.]

The backward stepwise procedure begins with all variables on hand in the model. One variable is deleted according to some criterion chosen by the user. Again, a step is accomplished when a variable is eliminated or when one that was earlier eliminated is added. In practice, the backward stepwise procedure is not nearly as popular as the forward stepwise procedure.

What is, perhaps, most popular is simply a so-called forward selection procedure, which is a simplified version of the forward stepwise procedure, omitting the test of whether a variable once entered should be removed. Another procedure, albeit not commonly used by social and behavioral science researchers, is the backward elimination procedure (see Mantel, 1970). Although many researchers claim to have used a stepwise procedure, what they in fact used was simply a forward selection procedure.

This chapter begins by discussing uses of stepwise regression and discriminant analyses, and the interpretation of F-values in stepwise analyses. The bulk of the chapter deals with proposed alternatives to stepwise analyses for purposes of variable selection and ordering. The chapter concludes with three caveats pertaining to inferences based on, and a data analysis approach to, variable selection and ordering, and a brief discussion section.

USES OF STEPWISE ANALYSES

Uses of multiple regression analysis and discriminant analysis are, to repeat, fairly common in the behavioral and social sciences. But misuses of such analyses are also fairly common. The uses (and misuses) of interest in the current paper pertain to stepwise analyses. [See Box (1966), Huberty (1984), and Tabachnick and Fidell (1989, chap. 5) for additional discussions of analysis issues.] Stepwise analyses have basically been used for three purposes: (1) selection or deletion of variables, (2) assessing relative variable importance; or (3) both variable selection and variable ordering. Note that these are uses often made of stepwise analyses, not uses that necessarily *should* be made. Problems with these uses will be discussed in this section, with alternatives—posited as being preferable—being presented later.

Variable Selection

One goal of analyses suggested by stepwise advocates is to select a "good" subset of response variables from an initial set of variables. That is, the analyses are used to discard "poor" variables. The idea of variable selection is perhaps a worthy one. The notion of parsimony in explanation or in description or in model building is "scientific." If one is dealing with prediction—either of a continuous variable as in multiple regression analysis, or of group membership as in predictive discriminant analysis—then it is desirable to determine if the number of predictors can be reduced without an appreciable loss (or to obtain a gain) in predictive accuracy. Variable reduction may also be informative and helpful in describing/explaining predictor-criterion relationships. Further, a reduction may be helpful in lowering the costs of data collection if interest is on predictive accuracy in the future or in replicative studies. From a parameter estimation viewpoint, too, variable reduction is desirable, particularly if the ratio of number of units to number of variables is not too large.

In variable selection, one wishes to arrive at a "good" subset of variables, if not a "best" subset of variables, of a given size. A thesis advanced here is that stepwise analyses should *not* generally be used for variable selection purposes. A basic defect of stepwise procedures is attributable to "their consideration of variables one-at-a-time . . . , direct tests for the additional information supplied jointly by several variables are not made" (McKay & Campbell, 1982a, p. 13).

A user of stepwise analyses may be led to believe that the first q variables entered into the analysis would constitute a good subset (of size q) of the initial set of p variables, or even the *best* subset of size q. This very clearly is the conclusion drawn by many, many researchers who employ stepwise analyses. It is not easy to determine what is "good" and what is "best." Hocking (1983, p. 226) posits that in a regression analysis context, "there is not likely to be a well-defined 'best' equation"; the same statement would apply in discriminant analysis. The typical index used to assess the goodness of a variable subset in regression analysis is the squared multiple correlation coefficient (R^2), and in discriminant analysis is the Wilks lambda. Three other indices in regression analysis are an adjusted R^2, the residual mean square, and the C_p statistic (see Draper & Smith, 1981, pp. 298–302; Hocking, 1976). Two other indices in discriminant analysis are Rao's V, and pairwise inter-group distances.

It is generally understood by methodologists that the first q variables entered into either a regression analysis or a discriminant analysis do not necessarily constitute the "best" subset of size q, that is, best in the sense of any of the indices mentioned above. In regression analysis there may be one or more subsets of size q that would, for the data on hand, yield a larger R^2 value. In discriminant analysis there may be one or more subsets of size q that would yield a smaller lambda value. Furthermore, and perhaps more importantly, if a given subset of size q yielded the largest R^2 (or, smallest lambda) of all subsets of that size, there may very well be other subsets of size q that yield nearly the same R^2 value (or, lambda value). And one or more of these subsets may be more interesting or relevant in a substantive sense.

Variable Ordering

In reading reports of research that involve the use of stepwise analyses, it is not uncommon to find the following type of statement: "The most important variable turned out to be, say, Variable 1 (since it was entered first), and the next most important was Variable 2 (since it was entered second)." Some writers go on to conclude, either explicitly or implicity, that some variables (those that entered late in the stepping process, or not at all because a criterion was not met for entering) are not "important." The notion of relative variable importance in a multivariate context in general is not at all a clear notion; little consensus of meaning of variable importance or of relative variable contribution exists among social and behavioral science methodologists.

The idea of variable ordering (in terms of relative "importance") is, perhaps, worth considering while interpreting the results of a regression/discriminant analysis, though less attention has been paid to this notion in the context of other multivariate domains such as factor analysis, canonical correlation/regression, cluster analysis, and multidimensional scaling. The subject-matter researcher typically desires to make an assessment of relative variable contribution/importance. Sometimes the researcher wants to assess relative contributions of variable clusters as opposed to individual variables. Variable contribution information may be relevant for theory verification, theory building, or simply for descriptive purposes. Same-variable, across-study or across-context comparisons of variable importance are also sometimes of interest.

A second thesis advanced here is that order of variable entry in a stepwise analysis should *not* be used to assess relative variable contribution/importance. The first variable entered with a stepwise regression analysis is determined by the correlation between each predictor variable and the criterion variable. The first variable entered with a stepwise discriminant analysis is determined by the correlation between each outcome variable and the grouping variable or, equivalently, by multiple univariate group-comparison statistics (e.g., multiple one-way ANOVA F values). As such, the inter-relationships of the response variables are completely ignored when the most "important" variable is determined. However, a fundamental reason for conducting a multivariate analysis is to study a collection of response variables as a "system," as opposed to studying multiple bivariate or univariate subsystems (see Huberty & Morris, 1989). Suppose, again, there are p response variables—predictors in regression analysis, outcome variables in (descriptive) discriminant analysis. The third, say, variable to be entered (and often considered to be the third most important) is dependent on the two variables already entered. If one or two of the variables already entered would be changed, then the third variable entered may also be different. This dependence or conditionality truly makes variable importance as determined by stepwise analyses *very* questionable.

It should, perhaps, go without saying that attempting to assess *absolute* variable contribution is fruitless. A few proposals for such assessment have been made for the regression context, but the comment by Darlington (1968, p. 169) seems appropriate: ". . . the notion of 'independent contribution to variance' has no meaning when predictor variables are intercorrelated." [See, also, Goldberger, 1964, p. 201.] Proposals for absolute variable contribution in discriminant analysis have not been advanced for use with intercorrelated response variables. For orthogonal two-way design layouts, an eta-squared-type index may be useful; variable ordering in nonorthogonal designs is problematic.

Selecting and Ordering Variables

A researcher may be tempted to solve both the variable selection and variable ordering problems with a single stepwise analysis. That is, the first q variables entered might be considered as constituting a "good" variable subset, with the first variable entered considered the most important and the qth variable entered the qth most important. It might be argued that these two problems should be considered separately; first, determine that system of variables to be considered for final interpretation, and then for the resultant system, order the variables. An ordering should not be dependent upon variables that are not retained for final interpretation.

It might also be argued that variable selection and variable ordering should be considered as essentially the same problem. That is, the q most important variables should constitute a good subset to retain for interpretation. The presenter of such an argument must have a clear, acceptable meaning of "importance"; even so, the obtained variable subset may not be as "good" as any number of other subsets of the same size, depending on the meaning of goodness. There are some differences of opinion regarding the meaning of subset goodness to use, but these differences are pretty much centered around the three indices for each type of analysis mentioned in a previous subsection, Variable Selection. The meaning of importance, however, is another story. From a descriptive (i.e., sample-specific) perspective, several indices have been proposed for both regression analysis

(Darlington, 1968) and for discriminant analysis (Huberty, 1984). From an inferential perspective, little, if any, guidance has been given. The descriptive-inferential issue is expressed in the caveat section.

F-VALUES IN STEPWISE ANALYSES

F-values are typically reported for each step in both stepwise regression and stepwise discriminant analyses. Definitions of the "F-to-remove" and "F-to-enter" statistics are given by Jennrich (1977a, 1977b). It is quite clear what hypotheses are intended to be tested via these statistics. However, the distributions of these statistics are not so clearly understood. The tail probabilities often associated with the (so-called) F statistics, and found in output of the package programs, should *not* be taken too seriously. And one should certainly not refer such probabilities to conventional significance levels to determine the "significance" of an entered or removed response variable. There are two problems with these reported tail probabilities. One problem refers to the fact that with a p-variable data set, a large number of statistical tests could be considered. With multiple tests there is a "probability pyramiding" phenomenon (see Wilkinson, 1979).

The second problem is more basic and is with the "F statistics" themselves. The distributions of nearly all of these statistics for a given analysis are quite complicated, indeed. Although the statement by Krishnaiah (1982, p. 811) is made in the context of forward stepwise regression analyses, it is equally appropriate in a forward stepwise discriminant analysis: ". . . at most one of the F statistics is distributed as central F distribution . . . since at most one of the models considered at that (step) is the true model." [See, also, Pope and Webster (1972).] Therefore, one should be very cautious about concluding, on the basis of reported tail probabilities, that, at a given step, one variable significantly adds to predictive accuracy (or, separation) while one or more others do not. If one is compelled to use stepwise analyses with the reported tail probabilities, it has been recommended that nonconventional probability levels be employed (Bendel & Afifi, 1977; Costanza & Afifi, 1979).

ALTERNATIVES TO STEPWISE ANALYSES

As is perhaps obvious from the discussion in the earlier sections of this paper, the current writer does not generally espouse the use of stepwise analyses. There is, however, a situation for which a stepwise analysis might be considered. Some of the alternative analyses suggested below are relatively expensive to carry out when the number of response variables is large, say, greater than $p = 30$. Therefore, a stepwise analysis *might* be used for the purpose of getting the system of response variables down to a manageable size. Such an analysis should be considered as a preliminary analysis. It may be argued, however, that there are other means of discarding variables in a "preliminary" way: (1) discard variables that are highly correlated with others; (2) discard variables that are contributing nothing but "noise" to the system, as reflected by extremely low predictive validity index values; (3) discard variables that have yielded relatively little contribution in previous studies; and (4) discard variables by judiciously choosing variables while designing the investigation. A "judgment analysis" by the substantive researcher along with, perhaps, a methodologist might be conducted to determine an initial collection of response variables that are relevant to the proposed study. If the idea of discarding variables prior to final analyses is distasteful, it might be wise to consider multiple analyses on clusters of variables. Clusters may be arrived through intellectual intuition, through some type of "dimension analysis" such as factor analysis, or through "scoring" some variables using meaningful scales (e.g., subtotal scores).

The alternatives to stepwise analyses proposed in the following subsections are based on some assumptions: (1) the collection of variables to be studied constitutes a meaningful system from a substantive standpoint; (2) the size of the initial variable system is manageable, that is, the number of response variables is about 30 or less; (3) there is a theoretical or substantive or practical reason for wanting to delete some variables; and (4) the researcher has access to a computer and some computer package software. Because of different analysis objectives, the variable selection and ordering alternatives will be discussed separately for regression analysis and discriminant analysis. Variable selection is discussed first since determination of the variable system to be interpreted should be made prior to the assessment of variable contribution. Caveats pertaining to the interpretation of any variable selection or ordering analysis will be offered after the specific alternatives are discussed. It is assumed that required data conditions, including lack of outliers, are satisfied.

Regression Analysis

Variable Selection

Two problems related to variable selection confront the researcher: (1) finding good variable subsets of a given size; and (2) determining the size of the subset to consider for final interpretation/use. The solutions to these problems should be considered in light of the intended use of the decided-upon final regression equation. Six potential uses of an equation are presented by Hocking (1976, pp. 14–15): (a) pure description; (b) prediction and estimation; (c) extrapolation; (d) estimation of parameters; (e) control; and (f) model building. It is conjectured that one of the most common intended uses of regression equations in the social and behavioral sciences is for prediction and estimation (of predicted outcome values). [Another possibility is description, a use alluded to later.] It is under this supposition that the two problems will be discussed, in turn.

The approach herein recommended to solve the first variable selection problem is to consider regression equations for all possible variable subsets. To accomplish this, it might appear that one would need to assess 2^p-1 equations, where p is the number of predictors. This is precisely what is claimed to be done via the SAS RSQUARE procedure. Computational algorithms have been developed, however, which necessitate the assessment of only a small fraction of the total number of potential equations (see Hocking, 1976, p. 10). The BMDP All Possible Subsets Regression program (P9R) does precisely this. Another computer program that employs a very similar regression selection algorithm is one due to Purdue University statistician George P. McCabe. These algorithms are extremely computationally efficient, and thus a sizeable number of predictors can be accomodated—for example, BMDP9R can analyze problems with up to 27 predictors, at a cost claimed to be comparable for a stepwise analysis.

A "natural" criterion to use to determine the best subset size in the context of prediction and estimation is to minimize the residual sum-of-squares value. That is, the best subset of size q, say, is the subset that yields the smallest residual sum of squares when compared to other subsets of size q. Equivalent to this criterion is to determine the subset that yields the largest squared multiple correlation coefficient. The latter criterion may be specified (by "RSQ") when using the BMDP9R program. The BMDP9R program also allows for specification of two other subset selection criteria: an adjusted R^2, and the C_p statistic (often attributed to C. L. Mallows). These criteria may yield "best" subsets that are slightly different from those obtained when using RSQ. Empirical comparisons of these criteria, and others (see Hocking, 1976, pp. 15–16), have not lead to a single preferred criterion.

Whether the intended use of the decided-upon regression equation is prediction and estimation or is description, the preference of the current writer is an adjusted R^2 value (see Morris, 1981). The adjusted R^2 used by BMDP (and, for other purposes, by SPSSX) is that originally proposed by M. Ezekiel:

$$\text{adj } R^2 = R^2 - p(1-R^2)/(N-p-1).$$

This value would be quite appropriate in the context of description; in the prediction context a more appropriate adjustment would be the Olkin-Pratt or the Nicholson-Lord or the Stein-Darlington adjustment (see Huberty & Mourad, 1980). From a practical standpoint, the choice among these four criteria has minor implications, since numerical differences among the adjustments tend to be small.

In this "best subset" regression analysis, computer algorithms yield not only *the* best subset of a given size, but also the second best, the third best, and so forth, to the Mth best. For example, a user of BMDP9R with the RSQ option may specify an M value of 10 or less so as to obtain at most 10 best subsets of each size; 10 best single-variable equations, 10 best two-variable equations, and so forth, to 10 best (p-1)-variable equations (provided, of course, p is at least 10). This information can be extremely valuable and, perhaps, more useful than merely knowing the one "best" equation for a given variable subset size. The user can observe where variables or collections of variables are interchangeable, or observe patterns in which a particular variable shows up consistently in various subsets. Furthermore, from a substantive theory standpoint, the second or third best subset of a given size may "make more sense," or may contain variables on which measures are easier to collect or are more reliable.

The second variable selection problem—that of determining the size of the final subset to use—is a more difficult one to solve. Indeed, as Hocking (1977, p. 40) puts it, "it is quite likely that a single criterion does not exist that is uniformly applicable" in determining the final subset size, say, q. This is a situation in data analysis that calls for studying the results and applying common sense. The index suggested above, an adjusted R^2, may be helpful in providing some information leading to determining a value of q. What might be done is to plot the adjusted R^2 value for the "best" subset of each size (determined by the researcher using information from computer output plus sound judgment) against subset size. This approach involves examining "scree" and utilizing two "physical tests," the "elbow test" and the "eyeball test." As q increases, the adjusted R^2 values generally (but not necessarily) increase. The increase is expected to be sharp at first, and then taper off. The value of q for which the plot turns abruptly upward may be chosen. A problem with this approach is that the value of q may not be clearly defined due to a gradually increasing plot. Another visual approach to isolating adequate predictor subsets is presented by McKay (1979). This approach involves the plotting of P-values for a few best subsets of each size against the value of p. Neter, Wasserman, and Kutner (1985, pp. 424–427) suggest plots of the unadjusted R^2, error mean square, and C_p against the value of q.

Still another approach to the second problem is to consider, for the various subset sizes, the residual mean square, an estimate of the variance of the prediction errors, which is proportional to

$$(1 - R_q^2)/(N - q - 1),\ q = 1, 2, \ldots, p - 1,$$

where R_q^2 is the squared multiple correlation for q predictors. This is, in essence, what Achen (1982, p. 62) suggests as an index of fit. Wonnacott and Wonnacott (1981, pp. 186–187), however, suggest squaring the denominator df-value so that we do not "go on finding discernible regressors too long." With either ratio, when subset size increases, the denominator decreases. At the same time, R_q^2 increases, so the numerator decreases; only if the increase in R_q^2 is sufficient will the ratio decrease, with the increase in subset size being justified. A sample plot of ratio versus subset size will reveal the low point and, therefore, a candidate subset size.

A researcher might feel compelled to compare the predictive accuracy of a number of variable subsets each to the predictive accuracy of the complete set of predictors via some statistical testing procedure. If so, he/she could employ a simultaneous test procedure (STP) as suggested by some methodologists (e.g., Aitkin, 1974). The idea of conducting such fairly complicated tests, however, is not expected to be very well received by the practicing social and behavioral science researcher.

It may be informative to carry out regression analyses for two or three different values of q. Output from these analyses could be examined for outliers, for predictive accuracy for subgroups of units, and for patterns of residuals, following the adage, "look at your data."

Variable Ordering

A meaning of variable importance that seems reasonable to the current writer is one that takes into consideration the intercorrelations of the p variables and the contribution each variable makes to the fit of the variable measures to an (assumed appropriate) rectilinear model. The index of fit considered here is the squared multiple correlation coefficient (see Kvalseth, 1985). A relative ordering of the variables, then, may be simply obtained by considering the p differences,

$$R_p^2 - R_{(i)}^2, \; i = 1, 2, \ldots, p - 1,$$

where R_p^2 is the squared coefficient involving all p response variables, and $R_{(i)}^2$ is the squared coefficient involving all variables but the ith one. To be consistent with the position taken in the immediately preceding section, one might prefer to consider differences of adjusted R^2 values. The rank order of these differences would, however, be identical to those considered here. The variable that yields the largest difference would be considered the most "important" variable, since the deletion of this variable would give a model whose fit is poorer than any other (p-1)-model. The second largest difference would indicate the second most important variable. And so on.

Such a variable ordering may be accomplished by using some results from a stepwise analysis with any of the three program packages. Having decided upon the collection of predictor variables to investigate (with or without a variable selection analysis), all predictors need to be forced into the analysis. This can be accomplished with the BMDP2R program using the statement, "FORCE=1" in the REGR paragraph. Alternately, entry and removal statistics—either probability values or so-called F values—can be specified so that all variables are entered into and remain in the model. For example, with the SPSS-X regression program, FIN and FOUT values of .00001 should do. Then the F-to-remove values *at the last step* may be used for variable ordering. The largest F-to-remove value would be associated with the largest $R_p^2 - R_{(i)}^2$ difference, and so on. Note that the F-to-remove values are simply used as index values for variable ordering purposes—the reported probability values for these F-to-remove values are ignored.

It may be noted that the F-to-remove values are the same statistic values used in testing the significance of the individual regression weights. Harris (1985, p. 515) shows that $R_p^2 - R_{(i)}^2 = (b_i^*)^2 (1 - R_{i.oth}^2)$ where b_i^* is the standardized regression weight for predictor i, and $R_{i.oth}$ is the multiple correlation of variable i versus the remaining $p - 1$ predictors. This difference of squared multiple correlations is precisely the square of the semipartial correlation between the criterion and predictor i with the remaining $p - 1$ predictors partialled out of predictor i. It is clear from this relationship that with the currently expressed interpretation of variable importance, a variable ordering cannot be accomplished via the b^* values.

The above notion of relative variable contribution may also be utilized when some of the "predictors" are actually powers of predictors or products (i.e., "interactions") with other predictors. In such a case, what would be compared are full-model and restricted-model error sum-of-squares (SSE) values, where the restricted model contains no "predictor" involving the variable of interest. For example (J. H. Ward, personal communication, April 1985), consider a full model with X, X^2, Z, and XZ as "predictors," one restricted model with Z as the lone predictor, and a second restricted model with X and X^2 as "predictors." Let S_f be the SSE for the full model, and S_1 and S_2 be the SSEs for the two restricted models. Define, further, an F value comparing the full model (with five parameters) to each restricted model (with two and three parameters, respectively) by $F(X) = (S_1 - S_f)/(5\text{-}2)$, and $F(Z) = (S_2 - S_f)/(5\text{-}3)$. The sizes of these ratios indicate the relative importance of X and Z.

The meaning given here to variable "importance" pertains to the relative contribution of variables to predictive accuracy (as measured by R^2, or adjusted R^2). Other meanings of importance have been considered by substantive researchers and methodologists. One meaning was discussed (and denounced) in an earlier section of this chapter—one variable is more important than a second variable in a forward analysis if the first variable was entered into the model before the second was entered, and in a backward analysis if the first variable was removed from the model after the second one was removed. A second meaning is given to variable importance when the absolute (or, squared) values of the standardized regression weights are used in ordering the variables. Currently, this meaning is generally eschewed by methodologists because of the unreliable effects that predictor intercorrelations—an aspect of multicollinearity—have on these weights (Gordon, 1968).

A third meaning of variable importance is based on the correlation between each predictor and the sample-based optimum regression composite. The predictor that is correlated highest with the composite is considered most important (see Thompson & Borrello, 1985). Supposedly, a rationale for this index is that if the correlation between a single predictor and the optimal composite is high, then that predictor would yield predictive accuracy comparable to that yielded by the optimal composite. A logical problem with this index is that the "system" of predictors is essentially ignored, since an identical ordering may be obtained by simply ordering the p predictor-criterion bivariable correlations.

A fourth approach to variable ordering in multiple regression is one suggested by Lindeman, Merenda, and Gold (1980, p. 120). The notion of interest here is that of "relative percentage contribution" of predictor i:

$$100 \cdot r^2_{Y(i.pre)}/R^2_p$$

where $r_{Y(i.pre)}$ is the semipartial correlation between the criterion Y and predictor i when those predictors entered into the model before predictor i is entered are partialled out of predictor i. For p predictors there are p! values of $r_{Y(i.pre)}$ to consider. The mean of these values might be used to indicate relative variable importance. This approach to ordering would only be feasible if p was less than, say, six. Of course, for ordering purposes, only the squared semipartial correlations need to be considered or, equivalently, the squared partial correlations as suggested by Kruskal (1987).

Another meaning of predictor importance is conveyed through a new index proposed by Green, Carroll, and DeSarbo (1978). The intuitive rationale of their index is appealing, but its apparent complexity will perhaps be discouraging to most substantive researchers. Finally, Achen (1982, pp. 68–77) presents three interpretations of variable importance, all of which are based on regression weights (standardized or unstandardized).

Descriptive Discriminant Analysis

The two aspects of discriminant analysis have been spelled out elsewhere (Huberty, 1984, 1986). Briefly, descriptive discriminant analysis (DDA) pertains to the problem of explaining and interpreting effects found via multivariate analysis of variance (MANOVA). With this analysis (DDA), the response variables play the role of criterion variables. Predictive discriminant analysis (PDA), on the other hand, pertains to the problem of group membership prediction or classification. In PDA, the response variables play the role of predictor variables.

Since the purposes of the two analyses are different, criteria and indices useful in ordering and selecting response variables and variable subsets are also different. Thus, alternatives to stepwise analyses in dealing with the selection and ordering problems will be discussed separately for the two aspects of discriminant analysis.

Contexts one may think of for descriptive discriminant analysis are one-way and two-way MANOVA. In one-way MANOVA only one set of effects would be of interest, namely, the effects of the single grouping variable (on the criterion variables). In two-way MANOVA there are three sets of effects of potential interest, one for each grouping variable, plus the interaction of the two grouping variables. Although there is a number of indices and statistics that might be used in assessing MANOVA effects (see, e.g., Timm, 1975, p. 372), focus here will be on the Wilks lambda statistic, mostly for pragmatic reasons. That is, decisions and judgments concerning variable selection and variable ordering will be based on Wilks lambda values. It is assumed at the outset that all necessary data conditions (including independence, normality, covariance homogeneity and lack of outliers) are satisfied.

Variable Selection

The two variable selection problems in regression analysis need also be addressed here: (1) finding good subsets of a fixed size, and (2) choosing the final subset. As in regression analysis, the approach to the first problem recommended here is to consider all possible subsets. For a one-way layout with a reasonable number of response variables say, 20 or fewer, the method of McCabe (1975) should suffice. The subset assessment criterion used by McCabe is the Wilks lambda statistic (labelled U by McCabe). McCabe's FORTRAN program, input for which are raw data, yields the 10 (at most) best subsets—having the 10 smallest U values—for each size, 1, 2, . . . , p-1. A number of good subsets of a given size yields some potentially useful interpretive information—just as in regression analysis.

Having run an all-possible-subsets program such as McCabe's, there still remains the question: Which subset should be chosen for final interpretation? One approach to answering this question is as follows. Select, on the basis of Wilks lambda values plus substantive grounds, the preferred subset of each size, 1, 2, . . . , p-1. Then, as in regression analysis, prepare a plot of Wilks lambda versus subset size, and conduct the "elbow test" by eyeballing methods. Sometimes the bend of the elbow is not very distinguishable. Then we must rely, as we often must in data analysis, on common sense and sound judgment or, on the comparative results of multiple analyses.

This approach is, perhaps, more sensible than attempting to conduct a number of statistical tests of differences of lambda values—tests of which have only been developed when the smaller subset is contained in the larger subset. There is, however, a statistical testing procedure that makes some sense. McKay and Campbell (1982a, pp. 15–20) describe a simultaneous test procedure that may be implemented in conjunction with results from a McCabe (1975) analysis. Aitkin (1974) alluded to the STP in the context of regression analysis—the basic idea is to compare each subset test statistic (Wilks lambda from a McCabe analysis) against a single critical value, that based on all p response variables. Although this is an intuitively sensible approach, the heavy computational burden is expected to deter most researchers from using it.

This typically is the extent of the variable selection problem viewed by most social and behavioral researchers, and even by some methodologists. There are, however, applications of variable selection techniques that are not limited to main effects in the one-way layout as discussed above. Some applications are now discussed that have potential use to researchers who consider other designs and more specific research questions.

An alternative to McCabe's best-subsets program is a program written by McHenry (1978). Technicalities aside, the basic difference between the use of these two programs pertains to the type of input information used. Whereas the input for McCabe's program is raw data, input for McHenry's program consists of matrices. Input needed for a one-way layout design is a pxk (p is the number of response variables, k is the number of criterion groups) hypothesis sums-of-squares-and-cross-products (SSCP) matrix, H, plus a pxp within-group (or, error) SSCP matrix, E. These matrices may be obtained by using the SAS GLM program, or the SPSS-X procedure MANOVA. A limitation of the McHenry program, relative to the McCabe program, is that only one subset of each possible subset size is printed. The McHenry program "usually, but not invariably" (p. 291) finds the best (in the sense of smallest Wilks lambda value) subset. For a number of one-way layout analyses conducted by the current author, the best subsets obtained using the McHenry program were identical to the best subsets obtained using the McCabe program.

Now consider the two-way layout, or two-way MANOVA, situation. In an A-by-B MANOVA context, one is potentially interested in studying three sets of effects, A, B, and the AB interaction. It is in this context that the McHenry program is particularly helpful. If the "subtotals" (or "cell," if you like) effects are of interest, then subsets that best separate the cells may be determined, where the H matrix is based on the cell effects. If, however, only the AB effects (or, say, the B effects) are of interest, variable selection may focus on these effects only, where the H matrix is based on the AB (or the B) effects.

In some research situations, a focus may be placed on some particular contrast effects (see Huberty & Smith, 1982). The question then is: The variance of what variable subsystem may be accounted for by the contrast of interest? An answer may be obtained using the McHenry program with the H matrix being determined by the contrast, along with the E matrix based on the complete layout. Multiple contrasts may, of course, be considered, leading to potentially different best subsets; a compromise of good subset candidates obtained from multiple runs of the McHenry program may then be made.

Contrasts of interest may be specified prior to data collection, or may be based on the data themselves. The latter "post-hoc" contrasts may be determined by examining group means in the usual (ANOVA-related) way. Or, post-hoc contrasts may be determined by examining group separation attributable to constructs underlying the data. These constructs are reflected in linear discriminant functions (LDFs). In a three-group situation, the separation of Group 2 versus

Groups 1 and 3 may be attributed to the leading LDF whereas the separation of Group 1 versus Groups 2 and 3 may be attributed to the second LDF. The question then arises: May fewer than p variables be used to describe (and explain?) the separation attributable to some construct(s)? Without variable relevance being specified in advance, a reasonable approach to variable selection is to use all-possible subsets as suggested above. That approach seems preferable to one based on, for example, examining standardized LDF weights.

An excellent review of and source of references on many issues and techniques related to variable selection in descriptive discriminant analysis is given by McKay and Campbell (1982a). They also mention some of the problems in the ordering of variables, a recommendation for which is given next.

Variable Ordering

An interpretation of variable importance in the descriptive discriminant analysis context is very similar to that discussed earlier for the regression analysis context. The index of relative contribution to grouping variable effects recommended here may take either of four forms. One form is a "partial lambda" value. For a response variable, say, X_i, a lambda value is found that reflects the contribution of X_i in addition to, or partialing out, the remaining p-1 variables. The smaller this partial lambda value, the more "important" the variable. The second form is the lambda value for the p-1 variables with X_i removed. The larger this lambda value, the more "important" the variable. Roughly, what is claimed is that if the most important variable is deleted from the set of p response variables, the extent of "separation" is decreased the most. The third form is a "partial F" (or, F-to-remove) value, which is a transformation of the partial lambda value. The fourth form is another transformation of the partial lambda value, namely, the complement of the partial lambda. In SAS (STEPDISC) terminology, this latter index is called a "squared partial correlation." One or more of these index values may be obtained from the three computer program packages. They will yield identical variable orderings. [See Huberty, 1984, for greater detail.]

As discussed and illustrated by Huberty and Smith (1982), the F-to-remove index for variable ordering may also be utilized in a two-way layout. That is, variable importance may be assessed relative to A effects, to B effects, and to AB effects. It may be substantively informative to discover that variables highly important in terms of, say, A effects are relatively unimportant in terms of B effects.

This partial-type index is considered preferable to some other indices suggested by methodologists and textbook authors. A univariate mean-square or F value completely ignores the remaining p-1 variables, and thus seems inappropriate for assessing relative variable contribution. [On the other hand, however, the independence of an F value for X_i from F values of other variables *may* be considered an attractive feature—see the caveat section below.] Another index commonly used in a two-group situation is the absolute value of the ''standardized'' linear discriminant function weight. Since a resultant LDF is considered optimal for the available data set, and these weights are partial weights, this index has some intuitive appeal. A basic problem with this index is that a weight for a variable may be low (in absolute value) because of its (high) correlation with another variable. Possible imprecision of these weights (due to variable intercorrelations) is also well recognized. In a two-group situation, these weights may be transformed by taking variable intercorrelations into consideration; this transformation (see Huberty, 1984, p. 161), however, yields an index equivalent to the F-to-remove index. Furthermore, how to implement the weight index in a multiple-group situation, where there are two or more LDFs, is open to question. Still another index sometimes considered is a correlation between the LDF (in a two-group situation) and each response variable. While useful for labeling or naming an LDF, the use of this index in ordering variables implies a fuzzy meaning of variable importance, especially when there are two or more LDFs. Even when there are only two groups, the use of this index is of questionable value. It can be shown (Huberty, 1972) that a variable ordering yielded by these structure correlations will be identical to the ordering based on p univariate F values. This result is in tune with that mentioned in the Variable Ordering subsection for Regression Analysis.

Predictive Discriminant Analysis

The classification or allocation of experimental units to criterion groups/populations is basic to predictive discriminant analysis. The rule used to make the group assignments may be equivalently based on a variety of statistics, all of which typically incorporate scores on a number of response variables, here called predictor variables. The form of the statistic depends upon available information about the populations, data conditions, data distribution form, and costs of misclassification—for details, see, for example, Huberty (1975b, pp. 566–575), and McKay and Campbell (1982b, pp. 30–32).

The design typically considered for a predictive discriminant analysis context is a one-way layout. So we have, say, k criterion groups and p predictor variables. This is ''like'' a one-way MANOVA situation, except the roles of the two types of variables (grouping and response) are reversed. A predictive discriminant analysis situation with two-groups is equivalent to a multiple regression analysis where the criterion is a dichotomous variable. Unlike MANOVA and regression analysis where the indices of ''goodness'' are the Wilks lambda, say, and the squared multiple correlation coefficient, respectively, the index of goodness in predictive discriminant analysis, the percent of correct classifications, may be lower if the number of response variables is increased. That is, a reduction in the number of predictors involved in a classification rule can yield an increase in the percent of correct classifications. Furthermore, the deletion of predictors can be beneficial in reducing the number of doubtful cases, those units that might be considered "outliers" (membership in any group is questionable) or "fence riders" (membership is about equally likely for more than one group)—see Huberty (1984, pp. 168–169) and McKay and Campbell (1982b, p. 34).

Thus, in addition to considering the goals of parsimony and of reduced cost of subsequent data collection, it behooves the researcher to consider reducing the number of predictors so as to obtain a more efficient classification rule.

Variable Selection

An excellent review of the variable selection problem in predictive discriminant analysis is given by McKay and Campbell (1982b). Although "there is plenty of scope for further investigation of variable selection procedures for allocation problems" (McKay & Campbell, 1982b, p. 40), very little has been reported in the 1980s. The most relevant work in this area has been done by J. D. F. Habbema and his colleagues in The Netherlands (Habbema & Hermans, 1977; Hermans & Habbema, 1976; Hermans et al., 1982). The two important aspects of this work are: (1) the criterion for variable selection is the minimization of the classification error rate (percent of incorrect classifications); and (2) probabilities for classification of experimental units are based on a nonparametric density estimation approach (i.e., no probability model, such as multivariate normal, is assumed; rather, the probability model employed is determined by the sample data themselves).

That the criterion of error rate minimization (or, "hit-rate" maximization) be employed in a predictive discriminant analysis context is, of course, very appropriate. A very practical problem for the researcher is the lack of widely available computer software that incorporates this criterion in a clearly acceptable manner. Although the Hermans et al. (1982) forward selection program is available, its circulation is quite limited, its optimality features have not been studied to any great extent, and it is fairly expensive to run. As with variable selection in regression analysis and descriptive discriminant analysis, the ideal approach would be an all-subsets one. It is, at the current time, expected that such an approach is very difficult to program, especially to be able to isolate a set of subsets whose corresponding hit rates are not significantly different among themselves but which are significantly higher than for all other subsets. "Such a procedure is likely to be difficult to obtain; the theoretical problems are severe and the computational requirement is prohibitive" (McKay & Campbell, 1982b, p. 40).

So, until the ideal variable selection procedure has been proposed and reasonably efficient computer software becomes available, some less-than-optimal or ad-hoc procedures will have to suffice. Two possible procedures that have some appeal will now be discussed. One ad hoc procedure involves the use of description-oriented techniques of the type described in a previous section of this paper. This procedure is the one in common use in the applied literature. Its acceptability is usually justified on the grounds that maximizing group separation is tantamount to maximizing classification accuracy. This approach may be appropriate under the following conditions: (1) when prior probabilities of group membership are equal; (2) when the requirements for the separation criterion are met (e.g., similar covariance matrices for the Wilks lambda criterion); and (3) when the consideration of doubtful cases is ignored. [McKay and Campbell (1982b) review some half-dozen studies that compare various description-oriented techniques for variable selection when classification accuracy is the criterion of interest—in all of these studies doubtful cases are ignored.] The issue of the usefulness of group separation as a criterion for variable selection for classification purposes is, at this point, unresolved (see, however, McLachlan, 1980; Morris & Huberty, 1987). As McKay and Campbell (1982b, p. 40) queried, "To what extent can the well-developed descriptive techniques be used with confidence in the allocation context?"

In addition to the potential loss in using a separation criterion for allocation purposes, there is another problem with this procedure. As pointed out by Morris (1981) in the regression context and by Huberty, Wisenbaker, and Smith (1987) in the allocation context, it is most desirable to consider a cross-validation method or formula in estimating true proportions of correct classifications (or, true hit rates) for the various selected variable subsets. [See, also, Murray, 1977.] This is not at all a consideration made in description-oriented variable selection techniques.

The second ad hoc procedure is based exclusively on allocation notions. The procedure to be discussed is a forward selection procedure à la Habbema and Hermans (1977); it was initially studied by Smith (1984). Unlike employing a distribution-free classification rule as did Habbema and Hermans, this procedure involves the use of a normal-based rule. And it can be carried out via a computer program in one of the popular program packages, BMDP7M. The user must specify very small F-to-enter and F-to-remove limits (or, use FORCE = 1 in the DISC paragraph) so that the selection method based on lambda has no effect on the final results. Only the last step of the analysis is of interest, where all of the predictors have been entered and none have been removed. Printing of some of the stepwise output may be suppressed.

For a data set with p predictor variables, at least $p(p + 1)/2$ runs need to be made. For each run, the cross-validation method, leave-one-out (L-O-O; Huberty et al., 1987), is employed. An L-O-O analysis is an "external" analysis; that is, the units used in constructing the classification rule are different from those being allocated to the groups to determine the hit rates. The L-O-O external analysis is easy to obtain via BMDP7M. In the first run, total-group L-O-O hit rates are determined for each of the predictors individually. The predictor with the largest hit rate is chosen as the best subset of size one. The second run of

BMDP7M is used to determine L-O-O hit rates for each pair of predictors which includes the best singleton. The pair of predictors with the largest hit rate is chosen as the "best" subset of size two. The process of selecting "best" subsets of each size based on L-O-O hit rates continues until a subset of size p − 1 is selected. The subsets evaluated at each step always include the subset chosen at the previous step.

A potential decision problem may result with this procedure. It is expected that with some data sets, more than one subset of a given size may yield the same (and higher than all others) hit rate. Smith (1984, pp. 53–54) suggests a reasonable solution to the problem: consider multiple subsets of the next larger size with the higher(est) hit rate determining the chosen subset of the given size and possibly the next larger size. At times, some random process (e.g., a coin flip) is needed to select subsets with tied hit rates.

Having carried out the p(p + 1)/2 runs for this procedure, the researcher still must decide which subset size should be retained for final interpretation purposes. Just as in the regression and descriptive discriminant analysis contexts, an informal approach seems reasonable. A plot of (external) total-group hit rate versus subset size may be examined, keeping in mind the (external) hit rate yielded by the complete set of predictors. In some research situations, it may be preferable to consider the hit rate for a particular group (e.g., college drop-outs only as opposed to drop-outs and graduates; learning disabled children only as opposed to an aggregate of learning disabled, emotionally disturbed, and "normal" children) rather than the total-group hit rate. No matter which hit rate is used as a criterion, knowledge of predictors, knowledge of group definition, cost of data collection, and good sound judgment or common sense should be very helpful in deciding upon a final subset.

More detailed analyses of classification accuracy may also be made at the various steps by taking into consideration any possible doubtful cases. These are the "outliers" and "fence-riders" alluded to earlier. It is always advisable to keep in close contact with one's data!

As emphasized earlier in this chapter, any step-type analysis cannot be expected to necessarily determine the *best* subset of any given size. Of course, it would be desirable to consider all possible subsets of each size. At this point in time, no computational shortcut is available for determining hit rates (with or without cross-validation) for all possible subsets, as there is in a separation context. Thus the above forward selection procedure is recommended for practical reasons, and might be considered a viable first step in attacking the variable selection problem in a classification/allocation context.

Variable Ordering

In descriptive discriminant analysis a recommended index for variable ordering is, for variable X_i, the Wilks lambda for the p − 1 variables with X_i removed. A similar type index is recommended in predictive discriminant analysis. First, an external (L-O-O) classification analysis is carried out with all p predictors. Then, p classification analyses are made by deleting, in turn, each of the p predictors. The hit rates yielded by the p subsets of size $p - 1$ indicate an ordering of importance of the predictors. The most important predictor is the one which, when deleted, is associated with the largest drop in classification accuracy relative to that yielded by all p predictors. The least important predictor is the one with which is associated the smallest drop (or, largest increase) in classification accuracy.

The hit rates considered in assessing classification accuracy may be either total-group or separate-group hit rates. In some research situations it may be desirable to obtain variable orderings relative to classification accuracy for each group, or for one particular group. That some predictors are relatively important for allocating units to one group but not so important for allocating units to other groups may be informative.

The ordering of predictors may be determined by making one run using the BMDP7M program—specifying JACKknife in the DISCRiminant paragraph—with multiple analyses. It should be noted that the BMDP7M program prints classification results for each step. But these are irrelevant for variable ordering purposes in predictive discriminant analysis since the criterion used at each step is not classification accuracy.

THREE CAVEATS

As is well known, there are many issues pertaining to the analysis of empirical data. There are, too, philosophical differences in approaches to data analysis. It is not the intent here to discuss all such issues and differences, but is merely to point out a few warnings related to the selection and ordering of response variables in some domains of multivariate data analysis. The discussion of some fairly particular caveats regarding model specificity and sample specificity is followed by a brief discussion of the adaptation of an analysis approach to the selection and ordering problems.

Model Specificity

This caveat pertains to the collection of response variables to be considered. Variable selection and ordering results, at least by the methods discussed in this chapter, clearly depend on the collection of variables studied. This is one reason why thorough study and sound judgment are called for in choosing variables at the outset. As many relevant variables (relevance being based on substantive theory) as feasible need to be chosen for inclusion in the initial system (see Huberty & Morris, 1989), and as many irrelevant variables as possible need to be excluded. This is an easier-said-than-done situation, of course. Limited knowledge and resources sometimes preclude the researcher from including all relevant variables and from excluding all irrelevant variables. Herein lies the problem, and where *Caveat 1* applies: The final variable subset selected, and the ordering of variables in this subset should be discussed only with all accompanying variables (and measurement scales used) in mind. A decided-upon final subset of q variables out of an initial set of p variables may not be a "best" subset if one or more variables were to be added to, or deleted from, the initial set. Furthermore, a variable that is considered very important (by whatever index) in, say, a three-variable situation, may be relatively unimportant (by the same index) in a four-variable situation. See Wonnacott and Wonnacott (1981, pp. 181–183, 501–507) and Berry and Feldman (1985, pp. 18–26) for further discussion of the model specificity problem.

To illustrate the latter point, it was recently claimed that race, in the company of three other variables, was very important in accounting for agricultural extension agent wages (Koretz, 1985). It was pointed out and accepted by a court, however, that other variables should have been taken into consideration and could very well account for wage disparities.

Not only should the variables themselves be kept in mind, but how they were measured must be considered as well. Consider a set of p variables that includes the variable, Intelligence. The method (individual or group, for example) and theory considered in measuring Intelligence may in fact have a bearing on how this variable shows up in the selection and ordering results.

Generally speaking, there is no apparent reason why all p variables should be considered as possible "deletees." That is, if response variables are judiciously chosen to begin with, and are reasonably limited in number, there may be no variable selection problem at all. In particular, this may be the case when dealing with the so-called structural or causal models. With these models the partialling approach to variable ordering suggested above may be invalid (see Lewis-Beck, 1978; Pedhazur, 1982, pp. 177–188).

Sample Specificity

As well as considering the variables (and how they are measured), one should consider the (design) sample of experimental units in drawing conclusions about variable selection and ordering. Strictly speaking, results of selecting and ordering variables should only be considered descriptive for the sample of units on hand. Thus, *Caveat 2*: Inferences about "best" subsets and variable importance to other units should be made with great caution. The "best" variable subset for one sample of units may be far from the best for other samples. The greater the ratio of sample size to number of response variables, the more reasonable are the implied generalizations. A large such ratio alone, however, does not insure valid generalizations. Valid generalizations may be obtained only to the extent that the pattern of response variable intercorrelations for non-design sample experimental units follow the pattern present in the design sample.

To enhance the validity of one's conclusions regarding variable selection and ordering, some type of ''external analysis'' should be conducted. That is, separation and prediction indices/rules based on one set of data should be assessed using another set of data. One way of accomplishing this is to employ a ''hold-out'' (or, test) sample. Preferable, perhaps, is to employ a resampling strategy such as jackknifing or bootstrapping.

The extent of sample specificity of conclusions about variable selection and ordering according to procedures recommended earlier needs to be studied. Such studies would probably involve some type of data simulation. Only limited results have been published (e.g., Huberty, 1975a; Morris, 1979; Wisenbaker, 1985); very little mention is made bout across-sample stability for selection and ordering procedures in the studies reviewed by McKay and Campbell (1982a, 1982b).

Data Exploration

Rather than relying so much on the use of the computer to carry out our analyses in *one fell swoop,* Tatsuoka (1982) states:

> Instead, we should play with the data sufficiently to develop a feel for them, especially at the outset, but also later when we should pause to take stock of what has been done thus far and to see if we are doing the best analyses for our purpose. And finally, when our originally intended analyses have been completed, we need not stop there. The results may suggest further hypotheses that appear interesting and theoretically plausible. We should not hesitate to pursue them by conducting further analyses (p. 1781).

A similar position is taken by Kempthorne (1975, p. 327): ''Should there be one definitive analysis of a set of data? To be brief, no. A variety of ex-post-facto analyses may be informative.''

Tatsuoka (p. 1782) makes another point that is particularly appropriate in analyses for variable selection and ordering when he quotes R. A. Fisher: ''statistics is quantified common sense.'' Thus *Caveat 3:* Data should be carefully examined, using multiple analyses and good sound judgment.

Data exploration may be fruitfully done in the preliminary, intermediate, and final stages of the analysis process. Variable *screening* in the preliminary stage (following data listing and editing) is quite appropriate in choosing variables for further analysis. For example, a variable may be deleted from further consideration in regression analysis and both discriminant analyses contexts if it is very highly correlated with another variable. In a MANOVA context, if a variable, by itself, yields nothing but ''noise,'' it perhaps could be deleted. The same might be said for the regression context (see Pedhazur, 1982, pp. 228–229). ''Noise'' in a predictive discriminant analysis context might be interpreted as a near-zero hit rate. If in doubt, analyses with and without a questionable variable could be carried out.

Consider an example of how multiple analyses might be useful in the intermediate stage. Suppose one is uncertain as to what interpretation of variable importance is most appropriate for a given research situation; in a multiple-group situation, for example, one might be interested in group separation as well as group-membership prediction. Then multiple analyses incorporating alternative variable ordering indices might be considered. Another example where multiple analyses may be helpful for variable selection/ordering is in a predictive discriminant analysis context. Murray (1977, p. 250) suggests splitting the total sample into a number of sub-samples, finding the ''best'' subset for each sub-sample. The number of times that a given variable appears in the best subsets across the sub-samples will give a measure of the utility of that variable for future classification. This suggestion is, of course, directly related to the sample specificity problem.

Finally, in the near-final stages of a data analysis, various ''diagnostics'' should be considered. As Neter et al. (1985, p. 409) state, ''Analysis of outlying and influential observations is a necessary component of good regression analysis.'' Residual analyses in regression can also provide useful information. For a detailed discussion of the study of residuals, outliers, and influential data points in regression analysis, see Chatterjee and Hadi (1986) and Myers (1986). The search for outliers and fence-riders while conducting a predictive discriminant analysis, also, should strongly enhance the quality of prediction results.

The recent development of computer software for multivariate data analysis graphics should facilitate data exploration. The recent (March 1986) Eighteenth Symposium on the Interface of Computer Science and Statistics at Fort Collins, Colorado, included the presentation of a topic entitled, ''Cognistics: Tools for Looking at Data Sets with Many Variables,'' by Paul Tukey.

When discussing data analysis strategies, words such as ''might'' and ''perhaps'' and ''reasonable'' are used with some frequency. To the current writer this is obviously quite acceptable. To suggest a flow-chart of steps that will cover data analysis for all, say, regression studies borders on being ludicrous. Obtaining a final analysis with one run via a computer program package simply will not, for most if not all empirical investigations, do the job. Allen and Cady (1982, p. xv) state it succinctly: ''. . . data analysis should be approached with an objective well in mind, but there is seldom a rigid sequence of steps than can be applied. The data analyst should allow the findings at each stage to influence the direction through subsequent stages.'' Some ''data snooping'' will often be called for. Invariably in the conduct of data analysis, the researcher will have to rely on common sense, personal values, sound judgment, reasonableness, and the like. Neter et al. (1985, p. 409) state that the analysis of outlying and influential observations is ''neither automatic nor foolproof and requires good judgment by the analyst.'' Although applied to a little different context, a quote by Tatsuoka (1982, p. 1782) applies equally well to the variable selection and ordering context: ''Let common sense and your set of values be the judge!''

An example of the use of common sense is based on a situation presented by Gordon (1968, p. 614). Suppose the outcome of dairy farm income is being predicted with attributes of cows, men, and acreage among the predictors. Even if, by some analysis quirk (measurement error?) cows were found to be unimportant, no one would claim that cows are irrelevant to dairy farm income!

Another example where common sense can play a role in data analysis and interpretation when assessing variable importance can be noted. Suppose that an F-to-remove value for variable i is $F_i = 6.13$ and for variable j is $F_j = 5.27$, and that these are clearly the two highest F values. With such index values, it doesn't seem reasonable to conclude that variable i is more important than variable j. Rather, one might state that variables i and j are the two most important variables. Other clusters of variables with comparable F values may result which would lead to a reasonable conclusion that variables within a cluster are of comparable importance.

In sum, the empirical investigator should diligently "interact" with his/her data (with and without aid of the computer); and use common sense! While I have tried to hint at a philosophy of data analysis, a more thorough discussion is given by Good (1983); a related and excellent article is that by Mulaik (1985).

DISCUSSION

As is perhaps obvious from earlier comments in this chapter, the current writer does not in general subscribe to the use of stepwise methods for the purpose of selecting or ordering response variables in either the regression or discriminant analysis contexts. The "in general" qualifier is used since there is a situation in which a stepwise analysis may be useful, as mentioned at the outset of the discussion of alternatives. This is when the pool of response variables contains, say, some 40 to 60 or even more variables. In this situation, the use of an all-possible-subsets is not feasible. [But then, would it *really* be necessary to consider such a large number of predictor variables (in the case of regression and predictive discriminant analysis) or of criterion variables (in the case of descriptive discriminant analysis) to begin with? Could not a large number of such variables be initially screened out? Or, could not a dimension-reduction preliminary analysis be carried out?] In this situation, a stepwise analysis *might* be conducted to reduce the set of variables to a manageable size. Then an all-possible-subsets analysis could be run. The thesis advanced is that researchers can very well get along *without* the use of stepwise methods in the final, or even intermediate, stage of analysis. There are better alternatives!

It might be argued that a stepwise analysis may be appropriate when the researcher has specified an ordering of response variables prior to data collection and analysis. Such an a priori ordering may be based on substantive theory, past research, or both; if so, it is assumed that the meaning of variable "importance" is clear. This may be the case in a situation calling for a so-called causal analysis. But, then, what would be the purpose of a stepwise analysis? Certainly not to determine variable ordering. Then the proposed purpose must be to determine those variables to delete from further consideration. But, how would this determination be made? Can one rely on F-to-enter values and the associated tail probabilities? The answer to the latter question is in the affirmative, since the model comparisons to be made are not conditional on the data. [These F values are essentially the same as the so-called step-down F values (Stevens, 1973), proposed some thirty years ago by S. N. Roy and R. E. Bargmann.] The answer to the determination question should be made, however, by employing a Bonferroni-type adjustment—additive or multiplicative—of the tail probabilities (see Huberty & Morris, 1989).

It would be remiss of me not to mention a few relatively recent proposals for variable selection analyses. Little discussion will be given; the usefulness of each approach is yet to be determined. Three proposals deal basically with regression analysis. McCabe (1984) suggests a principal component analysis of the predictor variable intercorrelation matrix to obtain "principal variables" that contain, in some sense, as much information (in terms of explained variation) as possible. McCabe (p. 144) concludes that, "Such an approach would most likely reinforce the empirical conclusion that there are generally many near-equivalent subsets." He goes on to state, "The final choice of variables should be left to the researcher who knows and understands the variables" (!). Another recent proposal (Bunke & Droge, 1985) attacks the regression analysis variable selection problem when the rectilinear model is inappropriate. Here, a stepwise approach may be appropriate for choosing among several linear and nonlinear models. More recently yet, Morris (1986) has developed a computer program for conducting a stepwise ridge regression analysis.

Two proposals have been made in the context of predictive discriminant analysis. Both deal with predictor variables that are measured using the nominal scale. Goldstein and Dillon (1977) have developed a computer routine for a stepwise (really, forward) variable selection procedure for use with dichotomous predictors. Another computer program for forward selection of variables has been developed by Habbema and Gelpke (1981). The latter program handles variables that are categorical or that have been categorized—ordering of categories is ignored.

A final recommendation is made regarding the conduct of variable selection and ordering analyses and the reporting thereof. If there is to be a reduction of the number of post-screened set of variables, selection should be done *prior* to determining an ordering of variable importance. The ordering should be based on the finally-determined subset of variables. That is, selection first, ordering second. Not only should the selection and ordering procedures and indices used be clearly spelled out, but all three variable sets should be described: (1) the initially considered collection; (2) the post-screened collection; and (3) the final subset used for interpretation. The descriptions should include variable names, measurement scales used, and numbers of variables in each collection.

REFERENCES

Achen, C. H. (1982). *Interpreting and using regression.* Beverly Hills, CA: Sage.

Aitkin, M. A. (1974). Simultaneous inference and the choice of variable subsets in multiple regression. *Technometrics, 16,* 221–227.

Allen, D. M., & Cady, F. B. (1982). *Analyzing experimental data by regression.* Belmont, CA: Lifetime Learning.

Bendel, R. B., & Afifi, A. A. (1977). Comparison of stopping rules in forward "stepwise" regression. *Journal of the American Statistical Association, 72,* 46–55.

Berry, W. D., & Feldman, S. (1985). *Multiple regression in practice.* Beverly Hills, CA: Sage.

Box, G. E. P. (1966). Use and abuse of regression. *Technometrics, 8,* 625–629.

Bunke, H., & Droge, B. (1985). A stepwise procedure for the selection of nonlinear regression models. *Statistics, 16,* 35–45.

Chatterjee, S., & Hadi, A. S. (1986). Influential observations, high leverage points, and outliers in linear regression. *Statistical Science, 1,* 379–416 (with comments).

Costanza, M. C., & Afifi, A. A. (1979). Comparison of stopping rules in forward stepwise discriminant analysis. *Journal of the American Statistical Association, 74,* 777–785.

Darlington, R. B. (1968). Multiple regression in psychological research and practice. *Psychological Bulletin, 69,* 161–182.

Draper, N. R., & Smith, H. (1981). *Applied regression analysis.* New York: Wiley.

Efroymson, M. A. (1960). Multiple regression analysis. In A. Ralston & H. S. Wilf (Eds.), *Mathematical methods for digital computers* (pp. 191–203). New York: Wiley.

Goldberger, A. S. (1964). *Economic Theory.* New York: Wiley.

Goldstein, M., & Dillon, W. R. (1977). A stepwise discrete variable selection procedure. *Communications in Statistics, A6,* 1423–1436.

Good, I. J. (1983). The philosophy of explaratory data analysis. *Philosophy of Science, 50,* 283–295.

Gordon, R. A. (1968). Issues in multiple regression. *The American Journal of Sociology, 73,* 592–616.

Green, P. E., Carroll, J. D., & DeSarbo, W. S. (1978). A new measure of predictor variable importance in multiple regression. *Journal of Marketing Research, 15,* 356–360.

Habbema, J. D. F., & Gelpke, G. J. (1981). A computer program for selection of variables in diagnostic and prognostic problems. *Computer Programs in Biomedicine, 13,* 251–270.

Habbema, J. D. F., & Hermans, J. (1977). Selection of variables in discriminant analysis by F-statistic and error rate. *Technometrics, 19,* 487–493.

Harris, R. J. (1985). *A primer of multivariate statistics.* Orlando, FL: Academic Press.

Hermans, J., & Habbema, J. D. F. (1976). Manual for the ALLOC discriminant analysis programs. Technical Report, Department of Medical Statistics, University of Leiden.

Hermans, J., Habbema, J. D. F., Kasanmoentalib, T. K. D., & Raatgeuer, J. W. (1982). Manual for the ALLOC80 discriminant analysis program. Technical Report, Department of Medical Statistics, University of Leiden.

Hocking, R. R. (1976). The analysis and selection of variables in linear regression. *Biometrics, 32,* 1–49.

Hocking, R. R. (1977). Selection of the best subset of regression variables. In K. Enslein, A. Ralston, & H. S. Wilf (Eds.), *Statistical methods for digital computers* (Vol. 3, pp. 39–57). New York: Wiley.

Hocking, R. R. (1983). Developments in linear regression: 1969–1982. *Technometrics, 25,* 219–249 (with discussion).
Huberty, C. J (1972). Regression analysis and 2-group discriminant analysis. *Journal of Experimental Education, 41,* 39–41.
Huberty, C. J (1975a). The stability of three indices of relative variable contribution in discriminant analysis. *Journal of Experimental Education, 44,* 59–64.
Huberty, C. J (1975b). Discriminant analysis. *Review of Educational Research, 45,* 543–598.
Huberty, C. J (1984). Issues in the use and interpretation of discriminant analysis. *Psychological Bulletin, 95,* 156–171.
Huberty, C. J (1986). Questions addressed by multivariate analysis of variance and discriminant analysis. *Georgia Educational Researcher, 5,* 47–60.
Huberty, C. J & Morris, J. D. (1989). Multivariate analysis versus multiple univariate analyses. *Psychological Bulletin, 105,* 302–308.
Huberty, C. J, & Mourad, S. A. (1980). Estimation in multiple correlation/prediction. *Educational and Psychological Measurement, 40,* 101–112.
Huberty, C. J, & Smith, J. D. (1982). The Study of MANOVA effects. *Multivariate Behavioral Research, 17,* 417–432.
Huberty, C. J, Wisenbaker, J. M., & Smith, J. C. (1987). Assessing predictive accuracy in discriminant analysis. *Multivariate Behavioral Research, 22,* 307–327.
Jennrich, R. I. (1977a). Stepwise regression. In K. Enslein, A. Ralston, & H. S. Wilf (Eds.), *Statistical methods for digital computers* (Vol. 3, pp. 58–75). New York: Wiley.
Jennrich, R. I. (1977b). Stepwise discriminant analysis. In K. Enslein, A. Ralston, & H. S. Wilf (Eds.), *Statistical methods for digital computers* (Vol. 3, pp. 76–96). New York: Wiley.
Kempthorne, O. (1975). Inference from experiments and randomization. In J. N. Srivastava (Ed.), *A survey of statistical design and linear models* (pp. 303–331). New York: North-Holland.
Klecka, W. R. (1980). *Discriminant analysis.* Beverly Hills, CA: Sage.
Koretz, G. (1985, December). Statistical evidence becomes a federal case. *Business Week,* p. 18.
Krishnaiah, P. R. (1982). Selection of variables under univariate regression models. In P. R. Krishnaiah & L. N. Kanal (Eds.), *Handbook of statistics* (Vol. 2, pp. 805–820). New York: North-Holland.
Kruskal, W. (1987). Relative importance by averaging over orderings. *The American Statistician, 41,* 6–10.
Kvalseth, T. O. (1985). Cautionary note about R^2. *The American Statistician, 39,* 279–285.
Lewis-Beck, M. S. (1978). Stepwise regression: A caution. *Political Methodology, 5,* 213–240.
Lindeman, R. H., Merenda, P. F., & Gold, R. Z. (1980). *Introduction to bivariate and multivariate analysis.* Glenview, IL: Scott, Foresman.
Mantel, N. (1970). Why stepdown procedures in variable selection. *Technometrics, 12,* 621–625.
McCabe, G. P. (1975). Computations for variable selection in discriminant analysis. *Technometrics, 17,* 103–109.
McCabe, G. P. (1984). Principal variables. *Technometrics, 26,* 137–144.
McHenry, C. E. (1978). Computation of a best subset in multivariate analysis. *Applied Statistics, 27,* 291–296.
McKay, R. J. (1979). The adequacy of variable subsets in multivariate regression. *Technometrics, 21,* 475–479.
McKay, R. J., & Campbell, N. A. (1982a). Variable selection techniques in discriminant analysis I. Description. *British Journal of Mathematical and Statistical Psychology, 35,* 1–29.
McKay, R. J., & Campbell, N. A. (1982b). Variable selection techniques in discriminant analysis II. Allocation. *British Journal of Mathematical and Statistical Psychology, 35,* 30–41.
McLachlan, G. J. (1980). On the relationship between the F test and the overall error rate for variable selection in two-group discriminant analysis. *Biometrics, 36,* 501–510.

Morris, J. D. (1979). On selecting the best set of regression predictors. *Journal of Experimental Education, 48,* 100–103.

Morris, J. D. (1981). Updating the criterion for regression predictor variable selection. *Educational and Psychological Measurement, 41,* 777–780.

Morris, J. D. (1986). Calculating a stepwise ridge regression. *Educational and Psychological Measurement, 46,* 151–155.

Morris, J. D., & Huberty, C. J (1987, April). *Stepwise variable selection in classification problems.* Paper presented at the annual meeting of the American Educational Research Association, Washington, DC.

Mulaik, S. A. (1985). Explanatory statistics and empiricism. *Philosophy of Science, 52,* 410–430.

Murray, G. D. (1977). A cautionary note on selection of variables in discriminant analysis. *Applied Statistics, 26,* 246–250.

Myers, R. H. (1986). *Classical and modern regression with applications.* Boston: Duxbury.

Neter, J., Wasserman, W., & Kutner, M. H. (1985). *Applied linear statistical models.* Homewood, IL: Irwin.

Norusis, M. J. (1985). *SPSSX advanced statistic guide.* New York: McGraw-Hill.

Pedhazur, E. J. (1982). *Multiple regression in behavioral research.* New York: Holt, Rinehart and Winston.

Pope, P. T., & Webster, J. T. (1972). The use of an F-statistic in stepwise regression procedures. *Technometrics, 14,* 327–340.

Smith, J. C. (1984). *A comparison of four predictor selection methods in linear classification.* Unpublished doctoral dissertation, University of Georgia, Athens.

Stevens, J. P. (1973). Step-down analysis and simultaneous confidence intervals in MANOVA. *Multivariate Behavioral Research, 8,* 391–402.

Tabachnick, B. G., & Fidell, L. S. (1989). *Using multivariate statistics.* (2nd ed.). New York: Harper & Row.

Tatsuoka, M. M. (1982). Statistical methods. In H. E. Mitzel (Ed.), *Encyclopedia of educational research* (pp. 1780–1808). New York: Free Press.

Thompson, B. (1984). *Canonical correlation analysis.* Beverly Hills, CA: Sage.

Thompson, B., & Borrello, G. M. (1985). The importance of structure coefficients in regression research. *Educational and Psychological Measurement, 45,* 203–209.

Thorndike, R. M., & Weiss, D. J. (1983). An empirical investigation of step-down canonical correlation with cross-validation. *Multivariate Behavioral Research, 18,* 183–196.

Timm, N. H. (1975). *Multivariate analysis.* Monterey, CA: Brooks/Cole.

Wilkinson, L. (1979). Tests of significance in stepwise regression. *Psychological Bulletin, 86,* 168–174.

Wisenbaker, J. M. (1985, April). *The bootstrap applied to assessing the stability of predictor subsets arising from forward selection.* Paper presented at the annual meeting of the American Educational Research Association, Chicago.

Wonnacott, T. H., & Wonnacott, R. J. (1981). *Regression: A second course in statistics.* New York: Wiley.

Younger, M. S. (1985). *A first course in linear regression.* Boston: Duxbury.

ITEM RESPONSE THEORY:

ADVANCES IN ACHIEVEMENT AND ATTITUDE MEASUREMENT

Robert L. McKinley and Craig N. Mills

One of the most important methodological advances in psychological measurement in the past half-century has been the development of item response theory, or IRT. IRT, which is sometimes called latent trait theory, comprises a set of powerful procedures for scaling both stimuli and respondents through the application of nonlinear, probabilistic models that describe the stimulus-respondent interaction in terms of nonobservable, or latent, variables. Through the use of these latent variables, or traits, it is possible to reduce, or to avoid altogether, many of the problems that are often encountered when analyzing psychological assessment instruments. In addition, IRT provides several new and extremely useful statistics, not available with other measurement theories, that provide the researcher with the potential to exercise significantly greater flexibility and control in the construction and analysis of scaling instruments, be they achievement tests or instruments for assessing attitudes or personality traits.

In more traditional attitude scaling procedures, such as those developed by Thurstone (1927), Guttman (1950), and Likert (1932), as well as in classical test theory (see, for example, Magnussen, 1966), the response to a stimulus by a given respondent is modeled as a function of some set of parameters that are

Advances in Social Science Methodology, Volume 1, pages 71–135.

ISBN: 0-89232-736-7

specific to the given set of stimuli and respondents. In other words, in these methodologies the important variables tend to all be group statistics derived for a given instrument. If different respondents are used, stimulus parameter values will change. If different stimuli are used, respondent scores are changed.

Consider as an example a 20-item test of mathematics knowledge. Typically, an examinee is assigned a score which is a function of the number of items answered correctly by the examinee. Items on the test are assigned proportion-correct item difficulty statistics based on the proportion of examinees correctly responding to each item. If the test is administered to two groups of different average math skills, or if the test is readministered to the same group after learning takes place, the proportion-correct item difficulties will take on different values. Likewise, if an examinee is administered two tests of different average difficulty, two different scores will result.

The same situation arises when a pollster attempts to gauge changes in the popularity of a political figure over time without using the same question. For instance, in one poll the question might be asked, ''Do you approve of the job the candidate is doing?'' In a subsequent poll, the question is asked, ''If the election were held today, would you vote for this candidate?'' The percentages responding ''yes'' are compared for the two questions to determine whether there has been any change in popularity, the assumption being that, if there is no change, the percentages will be the same. However, for this to be an acceptable procedure, it must first be determined whether, if there were no change, the percentages would, in fact, be the same. Likewise, in order to compare scores on two math tests, it must first be determined that, given no change in math knowledge, an examinee will score the same on the two tests.

In IRT, the problems just described, the dependency of item statistics on the sample of respondents and the dependency of respondent statistics on the set of stimuli, are, in theory, eliminated. Item statistics are presented in terms of the relationship between the item and the underlying variable being measured. That is, rather than reporting item difficulty as the proportion of correct responses to the item by a particular group of respondents, item difficulty is reported as a point on the underlying variable scale. In its simplest case, item difficulty in IRT is reported as the point on the scale where the probability of obtaining a particular response is 0.5.

The processes by which IRT procedures are applied are rather complicated, and require a knowledge of fairly advanced calculus. Fortunately, it is not necessary to be intimately acquainted with the mathematical details of IRT in order to use IRT methodology. Procedures for applying IRT have already been developed, and are available in the form of widely available computer programs. Therefore, it is only necessary to have knowledge of the basic concepts and procedures of IRT in order to apply its methods. The purpose of this chapter is to acquaint the reader with those basic concepts and procedures, and to provide examples of how and when they might be applied. For that reason, this chapter has been written with a minimum of references. For those readers who are interested in further information, a topical list of supplemental readings is provided at the end of the chapter.

The basic concepts and some of the important assumptions of IRT are presented and discussed in the first section of this chapter. In the second section, the basic IRT models for binary response data are presented, while in the third section models for polychotomous response data are introduced. A number of important applications of IRT are described in the fourth section. The fifth section provides information useful for assessing the extent to which IRT is applicable to a set of data by testing some of the assumptions of the theory, and the final section includes a brief discussion of some of the directions IRT might take in the future. At the end of the chapter there is a relatively complete set of suggesting readings.

IRT BASICS

Scoring

Before proceeding with a discussion of the basics of IRT, it is first necessary to distinguish between two different contexts—binary or dichotomous scoring, and polychotomous scoring. In binary scoring, a score of 1 is assigned to a respondent if a desired behavior or trait is present, and a score of 0 is assigned if the behavior or trait is absent. This type of scoring is typically used with multiple-choice or true-false tests of aptitude or achievement, as well as with agree-disagree type attitude and opinion items.

In polychotomous scoring, a different score is assigned to each possible response. For example, in a Likert-type attitude item, it might be reasonable to assign a score of 1 for a response of "strongly agree," a score of 2 for a response of "agree," a score of 3 for "neutral," and so forth.

For any item, the probability of the respondent being assigned one of the possible scores is 1.0. With binary items, for example, the respondent will be assigned a score of 1 (correct) or 0 (incorrect). If the probability of a score of 1 is equal to P, then the probability of a score of 0 is equal to $Q = 1\text{-}P$. Thus, it is necessary to model only the probability of a correct response. Once that probability is computed, the probability of receiving a score of 0 can be computed by subtracting the probability of a score of 1 from 1.0. Similarly, in the case of polychotomous scoring, it is necessary only to model the probability of obtaining all but one of the possible scores. The probability of the remaining score can be computed by summing the probabilities of the modeled scores, and subtracting the sum from 1.0. In general, if there are k possible scores, it is necessary to model k-1 scores.

Modeling polychotomous response data is, in general, much more complex than modeling binary data. Therefore, the explanations of the concepts and principles of IRT will be presented initially from the perspective of binary scoring. Generalizations of these concepts and principles to the polychotomous case will be presented subsequently.

Models

At the heart of IRT is the notion that a mathematical formula can be used to describe the relationship between the item response variable and the respondents' status on the trait of interest. The specification of such a formula, or model, as it is generally called, includes two components—a distributional form, and a set of parameters.

The two most popular distributional forms are the cumulative normal distribution, and the logistic distribution. Initial work focused on the normal distribution, which has a more solid theoretical foundation, but most of the subsequent work has involved the logistic distribution, which is computationally less complex and yields quite similar results.

Normal Ogive Models

There are several different possible derivations of the basic normal ogive model. The derivation presented here is based on the following assumptions.

1. For each item there is a continuous latent response variable, Y, for each possible value on the scale of interest (called the θ-scale).
2. Each item has a threshold value, b, such that a score of 1 is obtained by respondents with $Y > b$, and a score of 0 is obtained by respondents with $Y < b$.
3. For each value on the θ-scale, the Y distribution is normal, with a mean of μ and a standard deviation equal to σ.

The Y variable can be thought of as the score a respondent would receive on the item if it were possible to score the item on a continuous scale. For example, consider the following multiple-choice item designed to assess the respondent's knowledge of U.S. geography.

Which of the following states is farthest north?

a. Iowa
b. Kentucky
c. Florida
d. Kansas

A respondent might have a pretty good idea that the answer is not Florida or Kentucky, but might have only a hazy notion where Iowa and Kansas are located. While this respondent might well receive a score of 0 on this item, by no means is the respondent totally ignorant of the subject at hand. Thus, the respondent's observed item score, x, might be 0, while the respondent's latent score, Y, might be somewhere near the middle of the range of possible values.

This situation is illustrated in Figure 1, which shows the distribution of Y for a particular value of θ. Also shown is the item threshold, b, and the observed item scores for the regions on either side of b. From Figure 1 it is clear that the probability that our hypothetical respondent will receive a score of 1 is equal to the probability that the respondent's latent score, Y, is greater than the item threshold, b. Since we have assumed that Y is distributed normally, we can compute this probability by finding the area under the normal curve to the right of b. This can be done either by integrating over the normal density function or, alternatively, looking up the area in a table of the normal distribution. Of course, many tables are constructed such that we would need to find the area to the left of $-b$.

If a table is used, it will probably be necessary to convert b to a z-score, since most tables are for the standard normal distribution (mean of 0.0, standard deviation of 1.0). Thus, we would want to enter the table with $z = (b-\mu)/\sigma$, or -z

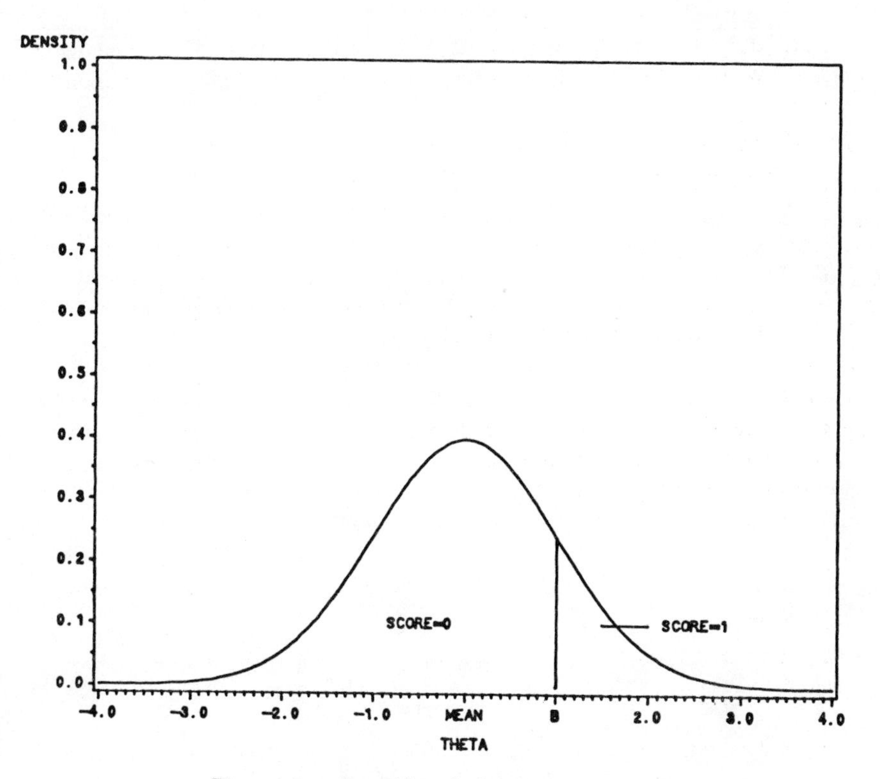

Figure 1. Conditional distribution of Y.

$= (\mu\text{-b})/\sigma$. The area obtained in this way is often denoted as $\Phi(\text{-z})$, or $\Phi((\mu\text{-b})/\sigma)$, where Φ indicates the cumulative normal distribution.

If it is further assumed that the conditional distribution of Y given θ is centered on θ (has a mean $\mu = \theta$), then -z can be written as $(\theta\text{-b})/\sigma$. Additionally, if we substitute $a = 1/\sigma$ into the equation, we obtain the basic normal ogive model, given by

$$P_i(\theta_j) = \Phi(a_i(\theta_j\text{-}b_i)), \tag{1}$$

where $P_i(\theta_j)$ is the probability of a score of 1 for respondent j on item i, θ_j is the status of respondent j on the trait of interest, a_i is the dispersion parameter for item i and is inversely related to the variance of the normal distribution, and b_i is the threshold parameter for item i.

Figure 2 shows the normal ogive for Eq. (1) obtained for a = 1.0 and b = 0.0. This curve, called an item characteristic curve, or ICC, is obtained by repeated applications of Eq. (1) using different values of θ. Each application involves computing a z-score and integrating the normal distribution from $-\infty$ to -z.

To illustrate this, imagine that an examinee with $\theta = 0.75$ is administered the

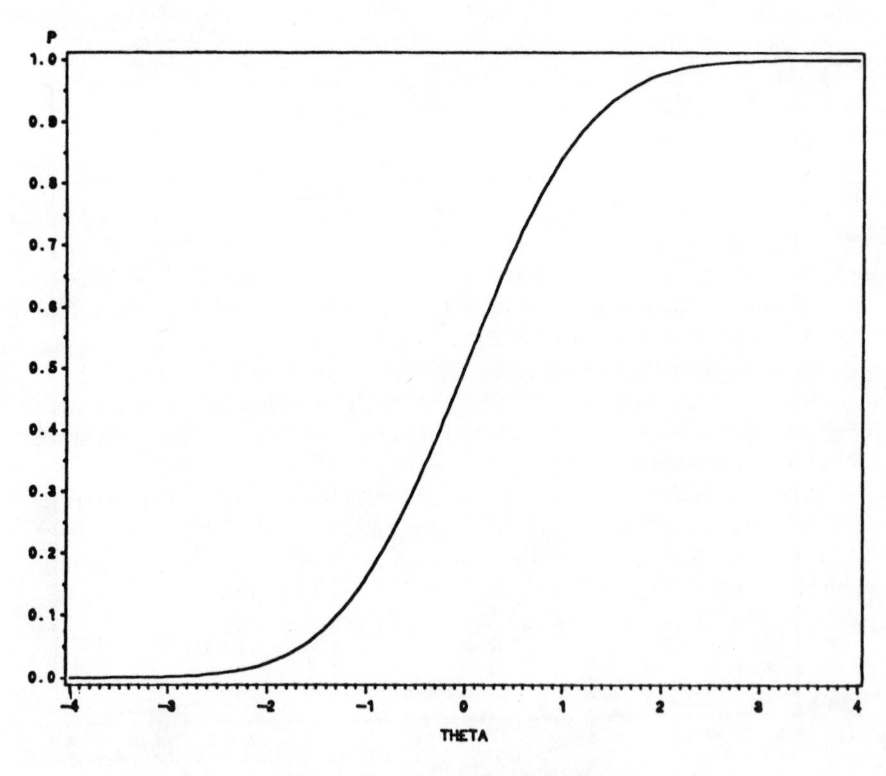

Figure 2. Normal ogive ICC.

item described above. If the values of the item and person parameters are inserted into Eq. (1), a z-score of 1.0(0.75-0.0) = 0.75 is obtained. From a table of the normal distribution it can be determined that the area to the left of a z = 0.75 is about 0.77. Thus, we would conclude that this examinee had a probability of 0.77 of getting this item correct.

A couple of important characteristics of the curve shown in Figure 2 should be noted. First, the ICC rises at an increasing rate until it reaches the point on the θ-scale equal to b, and thereafter it rises at a decreasing rate. The point where it changes from an increasing to a decreasing rate of climb is called the point of inflection, and represents the point where the ICC is steepest. For the normal ogive model, this occurs at the point where $P_i(\theta_j) = 0.5$. At this point the slope of the ICC is equal to $0.3998a_i$ (0.3998 is the square root of 2π).

Logistic Models

The ICC shown in Figure 2 was obtained through repeated integrations over the normal distribution. This process is both difficult and time-consuming. Because of this, it has become increasingly popular to use an alternative to the normal ogive model, the logistic model, which not only is much simpler to use, but yields remarkably similar results. The logistic model is given by

$$P_i(\theta_j) = \frac{\exp(Da_i(\theta_j - b_i))}{1 + \exp(Da_i(\theta_j - b_i))} \tag{2}$$

where exp(x) denotes 2.718 raised to the power of x, D = 1.7, and the remaining terms are as previously defined. The D term is added to increase the similarity of the logistic ICC to the normal ogive ICC.

If we imagine that the examinee in the example for the normal ogive model is again administered the same item (a = 1.0, b = 0.0), we can obtain the probability of a correct response by inserting the parameter values into Eq. (2). The numerator of the ratio in Eq. (2) is exp (1.7(1.0)(0.75-0.0) = exp(1.275) = 3.5787, and the denominator is 4.5787. This yields a probability of a correct response equal to 0.78. Thus, the result is very similar to the result obtained using the normal ogive model.

Figure 3 shows the logistic and normal ogive ICCs obtained for the same item. As can be seen, the two curves are almost indistinguishable. In fact, they never differ by more than 0.01. This similarity, coupled with the computational simplicity of the logistic model (no integration or use of tables) makes the logistic model a rather attractive alternative to the normal ogive model.

Parameters

The specification of a distributional form, normal ogive or logistic, identifies only a class of ICCs, not the actual shape of the curve. Recall, for example, that

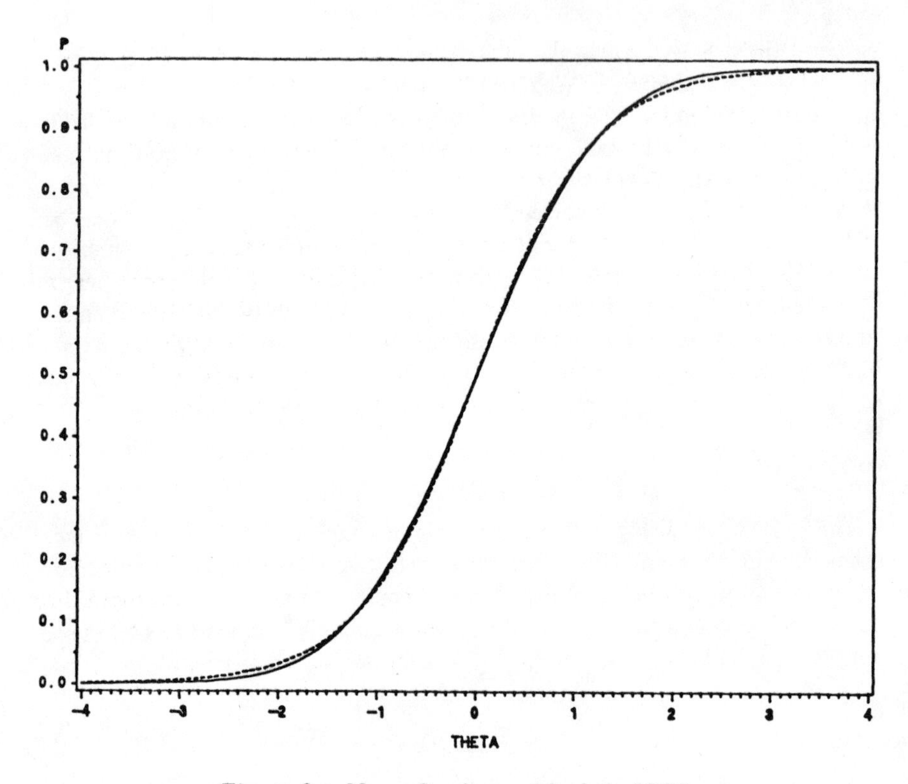

Figure 3. Normal ogive and logistic ICCS.

there are many forms of the normal distribution, depending on the values taken on by the normal distributions' two parameters, the mean and the standard deviation. Likewise, there can be many forms of the normal ogive or logistic ICCs depending on the values taken on by their parameters.

In their most general form, the normal ogive and logistic ICCs have four parameters—three item parameters and a respondent parameter. The respondent parameter, usually referred to as θ, represents the respondent's location on the scale of interest. For example, if the trait being measured is vocabulary ability, θ represents the respondent's position on the vocabulary ability scale. Thus, in this context θ is an examinee ability parameter. If, however, the trait being measured is political orientation, θ might represent the respondent's location on the liberal to conservative continuum, depending on how political orientation is defined. In this context, θ is certainly not an ability parameter. Rather, it represents the respondent's level of attitude or belief.

The three item parameters are the item threshold parameter, the item dispersion parameter, and the item guessing parameter. As was previously indicated, the item threshold parameter, b, indicates the location of the item on the scale of interest. Thus, an easy vocabulary item would have a low b-value, while a very difficult item would have a high b-value. In the context of attitude measurement, a high b-value might indicate that only respondents with extremely positive attitudes would agree with the item, while a low b-value might indicate a statement with which even respondents with negative attitudes would agree. Figure 4 shows ICCs for three items differing only in b-value. As can be seen, the effect of increasing the b-value is to shift the ICC to the right.

It was also pointed out earlier that the item dispersion parameter, a, is related to the slope of the ICC at its steepest point, which occurs at $\theta = b$. The a-parameter, often called the item discrimination parameter, indicates how well an item discriminates among different levels of θ. Note that the steeper the ICC is, the greater the change in the probability of a correct response for a given change in θ. Figure 5 shows ICCs for three items with the same b-values, but differing in a-values. As can be seen, the higher the a-value, the steeper the slope of the ICC.

The item guessing parameter, c, actually has little to do with guessing. Rather, it simply indicates the lower asymptote of the ICC. It is called the guessing parameter because it usually only takes on values other than 0.0 when guessing is

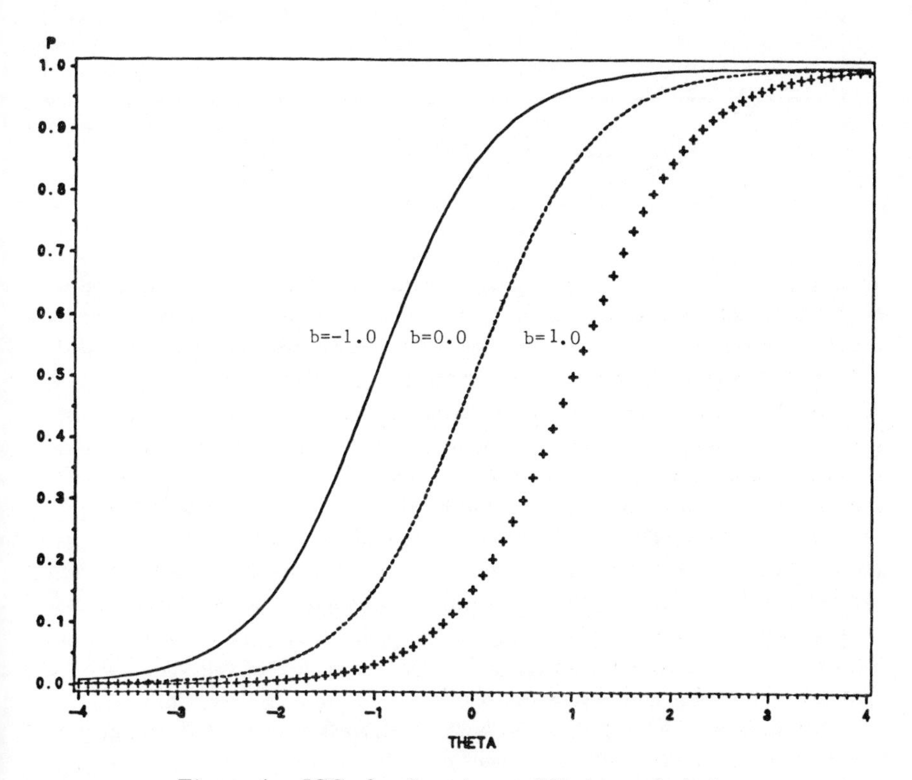

Figure 4. ICCs for three items differing only in b.

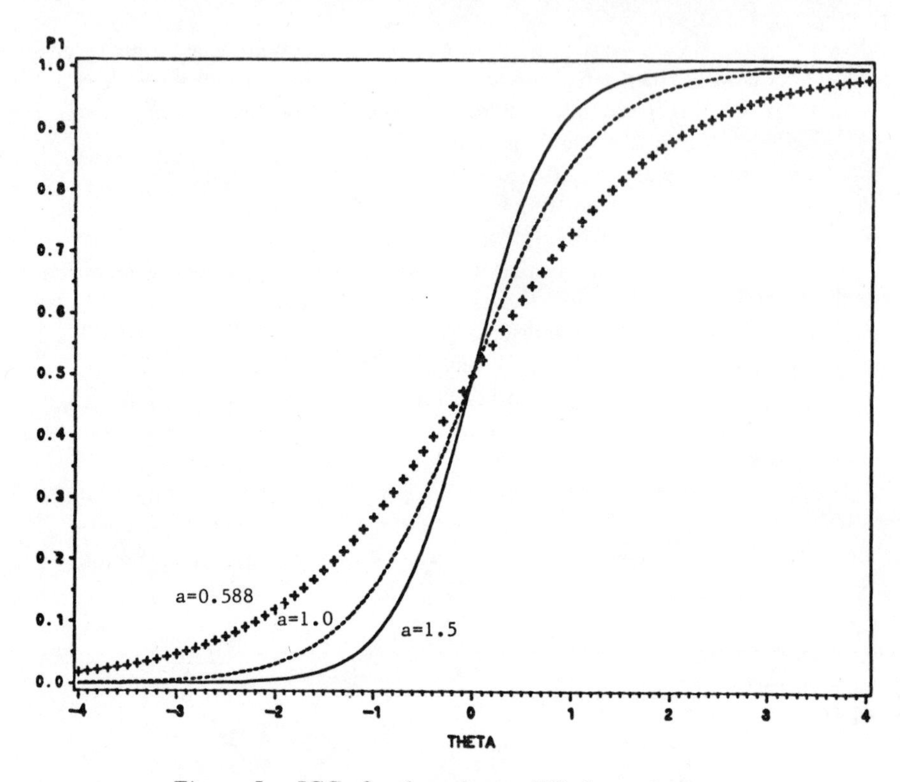

Figure 5. ICCs for three items differing only in a.

a factor, such as in the case of true-false or multiple-choice tests of knowledge. In the ICCs shown in Figure 4 and Figure 5, c = 0.0. In Figure 6, ICCs are shown for three items having the same a- and b-values, but differing in c-values.

Taken together, θ, a, and b combine to form the z-score which was discussed in conjunction with the normal ogive model. As was discussed earlier, this z-score is used in computing the ICC. The c-parameter does not contribute to the computation of z. Rather, it is used to modify the value of the ICC computed from the z-score and the appropriate distribution.

In terms of the range of values taken on by these parameters, in theory there are no limits, except that c-value must fall between 0.0 and 1.0, inclusive. In binary models, a-values must also be positive. In practice, there do appear to be some natural constraints on the ranges of the parameters, and there are some constraints that are sometimes needed for the estimation of the values of the parameters. For instance, in some models it is common practice to limit a-values to be less than or equal to 2.0, while in other models a-values are constrained to be between −1.0 and 1.0. The values of the c-parameter are generally restricted to be between 0.0 and 0.5. The range of values for b is usually unrestricted,

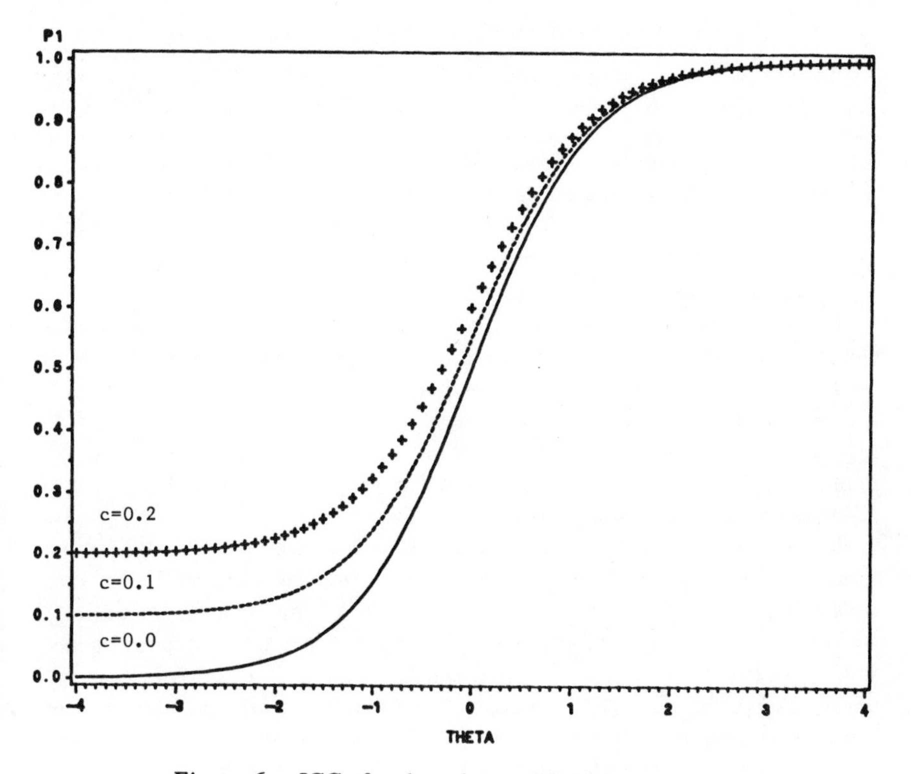

Figure 6. ICCs for three items differing only in c.

though most values seem to fall between plus and minus 4.0. The values taken on by θ are often unrestricted also, but as was the case with b-values, θ-values typically fall between plus and minus 4.0.

Parameter Invariance

One of the most important aspects of IRT centers on a property of IRT parameters called invariance. Parameter invariance is, in fact, at the heart of most of the power of IRT, and is largely responsible for most of the advantages gained from the use of IRT.

Parameter invariance refers to the fact that the true values taken on by the item parameters of an IRT model for a particular item do not depend on the characteristics of the respondents, and the true value of the person parameter of an IRT model for a particular respondent does not depend on the characteristics of the instrument. Contrast this to more traditional item and person parameters—item-total biserials, item proportion-correct difficulties, and person number-correct scores. Each of these three statistics actually describes the relationship between an item and a group of respondents, between a respondent and an instrument, or between an item and an instrument. None of them stands alone.

For example, consider the case of item proportion-correct difficulties. This item statistic, meant to indicate the difficulty of a test item, is computed as the proportion of respondents correctly answering an item. If an item is given to two groups of respondents differing in average ability, two quite different values are obtained for the same item. The same is true of number-correct scores for respondents. The same respondent receives two quite different scores if given two instruments varying in average item difficulty.

Because of the sample and instrument dependency of these traditional item statistics, in many applications their use would require procedures that are rather complex and cumbersome. IRT item and person parameters, on the other hand, are not sample or instrument dependent. A respondent will receive the same θ, regardless of the average difficulty level of the instrument. The same is true for item a- and b-values. Because of this invariance, many new and useful procedures for measurement are available.

However, one limitation on this parameter invariance property of IRT models should be noted. Although the values of the item parameters obtained for an item from different groups of respondents *theoretically* are the same, in practice they are often not the same. The differences observed in the actual values obtained stem from two basic causes. The first cause is estimation error. Since we can never observe the true values of these latent variables, we generally must be satisfied with estimates of their values. Because we are estimating the values of the parameters, the values we obtain will tend to differ from the true values and each other by some amount of error. The amount of error tends to be a function of sample size so, naturally, the larger the sample size the better.

The other source of differences between estimates of a parameter from different samples has to do with the arbitrary nature of the θ-scale. Consider Eq. (2). This equation provides us with the expected value of the response to a given item, conditional on the values taken on by the item and person parameters. If θ were equal to 1.0, b were equal to -1.0, and a were equal to 1.5, the probability of a correct response would be equal to 0.99. Thus, we are well into the upper asymptote of the curve. Now, if we subtract 1.0 from both θ and b, so that $\theta = 0.0$ and $b = -2.0$, and we recompute P, we find that P once again equals 0.99. The expected or predicted response to the item is the same. This is because, in terms of θ and b, P depends not on the actual values of the parameters, but on the difference between their values. That is, what matters isn't the actual values of θ and b, but what values θ-b takes on.

In a similar fashion, if we multiple θ and b by 2.0, but divide a by 2.0, we obtain the same value for P. This is because the value of P depends on the value taken on by the exponent of the model, not the values taken on by the individual parameters. Therefore, as long as we hold the value of the exponent constant, we can perform any linear transformation we wish on the parameters without changing the ICC. In practice, this means we can set the mean and standard deviation of the θ-scale to whatever values we want.

Two major approaches are typically taken to setting the mean and standard deviation of the θ-scale. Both involve setting the scale during the estimation process. The first approach is to set the mean of the θs to 0.0, and the standard deviation to 1.0. The other approach is to set the mean and standard deviation of the b-values to 0.0 and 1.0, respectively. Whichever approach is taken, there are a couple of rules which must be followed. First, whatever scaling is done to the b-values must also be done to the θ-values. Second, adding or subtracting a constant from the bs and θs in order to adjust the scale mean does not alter the a-values. Third, any time the bs and θs are multiplied by a constant in order to set the standard deviation, the a-values must be divided by the same constant.

Because two respondent groups may have quite different true distributions, standardizing the scale by setting the mean and standard deviation of θ to 0.0 and 1.0 for both groups will have the effect of making the two sets of item b-value estimates appear to be different, even though they are for the same items. In a similar fashion, scaling the b-values will make two estimates of the same θ appear to be different. Because of this, IRT model parameters are said to be invariant only within a linear transformation. Therefore, any time two estimates of the same parameter are compared, it is first necessary to make sure they are on the same scale. This problem will be discussed in greater detail later, in the equating section.

Basic Assumptions

Unidimensionality

Almost all currently used IRT models require the assumption that θ comprises a single component. That is, in procedures based on these IRT models, it is assumed that there is only one respondent trait or characteristic being measured. If this assumption is met, then the ICC can be represented by a simple curve drawn in two dimensions. In such cases, the IRT model is said to be unidimensional. If θ has two or more components, the ICC becomes a function that can only be represented by surfaces drawn in multiple dimensions. In these cases, the IRT model is said to be multidimensional. Needless to say, unidimensional models are a great deal easier to work with than are multidimensional models. Because of this, much of the available IRT methodology is based on unidimensional models. More complex (i.e., multidimensional) models will be discussed in the final section of the chapter.

While unidimensional models are easier to use, there are hazards involved in their use. Predictions of respondent behavior obtained using a unidimensional model will be accurate only if the stimulus measures only a single trait. For example, knowing an examinee's vocabulary ability does not allow us to accurately predict the examinee's response to a stimulus that measures not only vocabulary, but also mathematics. For example, consider the following item.

> Bill travels west for 3 miles, then south for 4 miles. If he then returns to his initial location via a route comprising a straight line, what is the total distance he will have traveled?
>
> a. 5
> b. 7
> c. 12
> d. 25

It seems clear that this item has more than one important component. In order to correctly respond to this item (without guessing), the respondent must first be able to read and comprehend the stem of the item. Simply comprehending the stem is not sufficient, of course. It is also necessary to apply the Pythagorean Theorem, or a related algorithm, for obtaining the length of the hypotenuse of the right triangle formed by Bill's route. Thus, there appears to be a verbal and/or reading comprehension component to the item, as well as algorithmic and computational components. Respondents with high math computation ability might still fail to correctly respond to the item if the stem is not comprehended. Likewise, high reading comprehension ability does not guarantee a correct response if computational skills are deficient. Finally, neither reading comprehension skills nor computational skills will compensate if the examinee can not come up with the proper algorithm for solving the problem. Thus, it would seem likely that it would be difficult, if not impossible, to model examinee responses to this item using only a single examinee parameter.

To further illustrate, consider a two-part attitude scale designed to measure respondents' attitudes toward the use of corporal punishment in child-rearing. In the first part of the instrument, respondents are asked to agree or disagree with a set of statements about corporal punishment. In the second part of the instrument, several complex situations that might arise in child-rearing are described, and respondents are asked to indicate what they consider to be the most appropriate parental response to the situation. Responses to the first part might be adequately modeled using a unidimensional IRT model, in which the single respondent parameter represents the respondent's attitude toward corporal punishment. However, in the second part of the instrument, modeling responses effectively might require consideration of the respondents' reading comprehension ability. A respondent who favors corporal punishment, but does not properly comprehend the situation being described, might provide a response seemingly inconsistent with the responses given in the first part of the instrument. Thus, to adequately model responses to the instrument as a whole, it might be necessary to use two respondent parameters. The longer and more complex the descriptions in the second part are, the more necessary a second respondent parameter would be.

Conditional Independence

Another fundamental assumption of virtually all IRT models is that, for a given respondent, responses to different stimuli are conditionally independent (the word conditional indicates the independence of item responses is conditional on it being the same examinee responding to all items or, alternatively, that it be examinees with the same θ). The assumption that knowing the response to one stimulus provides no information about the response to another stimulus beyond what was already known from the respondent's θ allows the responses of a single individual to different stimuli to be modeled separately. That is, when predicting the response to a stimulus by a given individual, it is not necessary to consider the individual's responses to other items. This permits the model to be much simpler than would be the case if the probability of a particular response to a stimulus depended not only the respondent's θ, but also on what the responses to the other stimuli were.

To illustrate the importance of conditional independence, consider the use of the following two items to assess attitudes of doctors toward the value of preventative medicine. Assume the items are scored 1 for a response of "yes," and 0 otherwise.

1. Have you ever given patients advice on preventative health practices?

   a. yes
   b. no

2. Do you often see positive results from your preventative health practices advice?

   a. yes
   b. no

It would seem reasonable to assume that doctors who value preventative medicine would: (a) be more likely to give preventative health practice advice, and (b) be more likely to attribute positive results to that advice. Thus, it might seem as though the responses of a doctor to these two items could be accurately predicted if the attitude of the doctor were known. However, there is a serious complication. In order to predict the response to the second question, it is necessary to know not only the doctor's attitude toward preventative medicine, but also how the doctor responded to the first item. Even a doctor who highly values preventative medicine will respond "no" on the second item if the doctor has never given preventative health advice. Remember, a doctor who values preventative medicine will be more likely to give such advice, but there certainly is no guarantee.

Similarly, in the math test example discussed earlier, knowing an examinee's math ability would not be sufficient for predicting the examinee's responses to word problems, since reading comprehension ability is also required. The examinee's responses to other word problems might provide a great deal of information about how the examinee will respond to the next word problem beyond what is provided by knowledge of the examinee's math ability. Therefore, the examinee's responses to the word problems are not conditionally independent.

Monotonicity

In the preventative medicine example used earlier, it was suggested that it was reasonable to assume that a doctor who values preventative medicine is more likely to give preventative health practices advice than a doctor who values preventative medicine less or not at all. Thus, the more a doctor values preventative medicine, the more likely the doctor will respond 'yes' when asked whether such advice is given. The higher the value, the more probable the response. Likewise, in the case of a vocabulary test, the higher the examinee's vocabulary ability, the more likely it is that the examinee will respond correctly to a vocabulary item.

This relationship between the respondent's status on the trait being measured and the probability of a correct response occurring can be seen in Figures 2 through 6. Notice that the ICC doesn't always increase at the same rate, but it never decreases. It is an important assumption of IRT that the probability of a correct response will never decrease as θ increases. This property is called monotonicity, and the curves shown in the figures are said to be monotonically nondecreasing.

Information

Item Information

One of the most useful statistics yielded by IRT is called item information. Item information is an indicant of the degree to which a particular item contributes useful information about a respondent's θ. Thus, item information can be useful in selecting an item matched closely to a particular respondent's ability, or to develop an instrument that provides a great deal of information at a particular point (or points) on the θ-scale.

Item information is computed as a function of the slope of the ICC at θ. If the ICC is steep at a particular value of θ, then the item is contributing useful information. However, if the ICC is relatively flat at a particular value of θ, then the item does not contribute much information about θ. In other words, in regions of the scale where the ICC is flat, great changes in θ are accompanied by very small changes in the probability of a correct response. Thus, the item does not help discriminate among examinees with relatively large differences in θ, so long as they are in the region of the scale where the ICC is flat.

Figure 7 shows a plot of the information yielded by an item at various points along the θ-scale. The ICC for the item is the logistic curve shown in Figure 3. A comparison of these two figures reveals that, where the ICC is steep, the item yields very high information. But where the ICC is relatively flat, the item yields very low information. Thus, examination of an item information curve such as is shown in Figure 7 can reveal a great deal about how an item will function—for which respondents it will function well, and for which respondents it will not function well.

Figure 8 shows item information curves for two items which have the same b- and c-values, but differ in a-values. Figure 9 shows item information curves for two items with the same a- and c-values, but different b-values. An examination of these two figures indicates that the b-value has a great effect on where along the θ-scale an item will yield information, while the a-value has a significant effect on how much information is yielded. In general, increasing the a-value increases the maximum of the information curve, but decreases the range over which the information is yielded. Thus, an item with a high a-value may provide a great deal of information about respondents who are located at a particular point along the

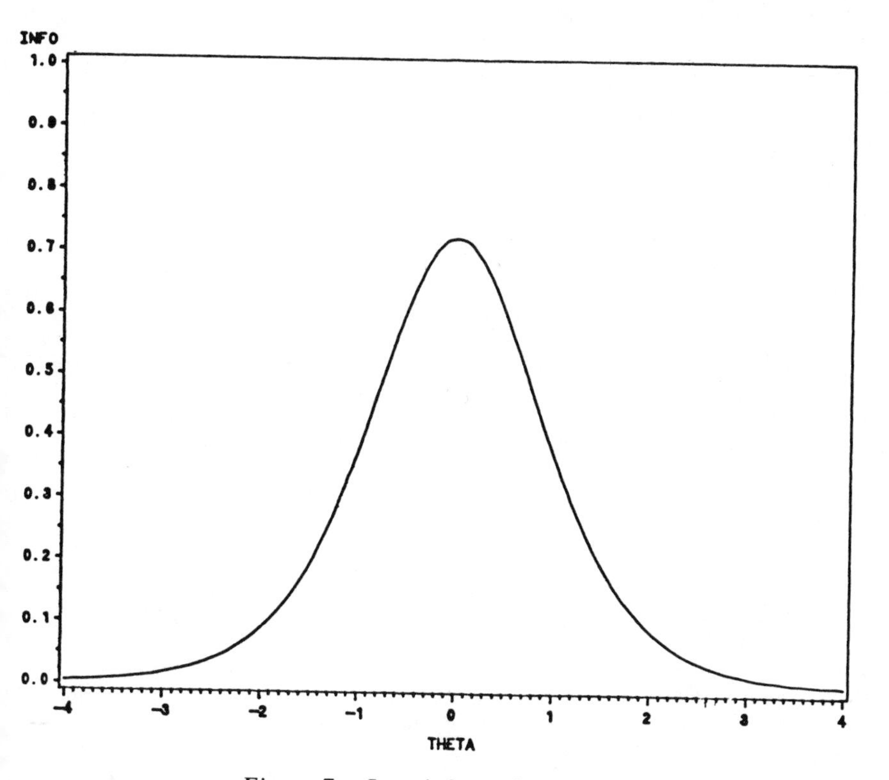

Figure 7. Item information curve.

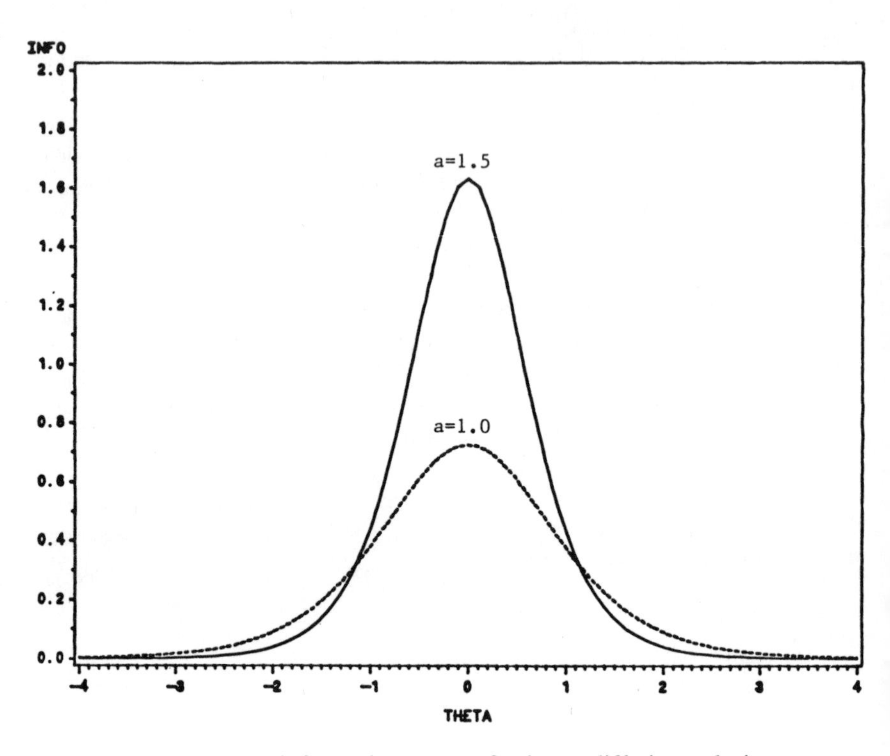

Figure 8. Item information curves for items differing only in a.

scale, while providing little information for respondents located elsewhere on the scale.

Figure 10 shows item information curves for items with the same a- and b-values, but with different c-values. Comparing these information curves reveals that increasing c has the effect of lowering information. It also makes the information curve asymmetric, since the effect is more pronounced at the low end of the θ-scale where more guessing is likely to occur.

Test Information

Curves such as are shown in Figure 7 can also be obtained for a test as a whole. It is a convenient property of IRT information that test information can be obtained by summing the item informations. Thus, for any value of θ, the information about that θ yielded by the test can be obtained by computing item information at that value of θ for each item, and summing the results over items. Because of this summative property, it is possible to use the test information curve as a guide in selecting items to produce tests with specified measurement properties.

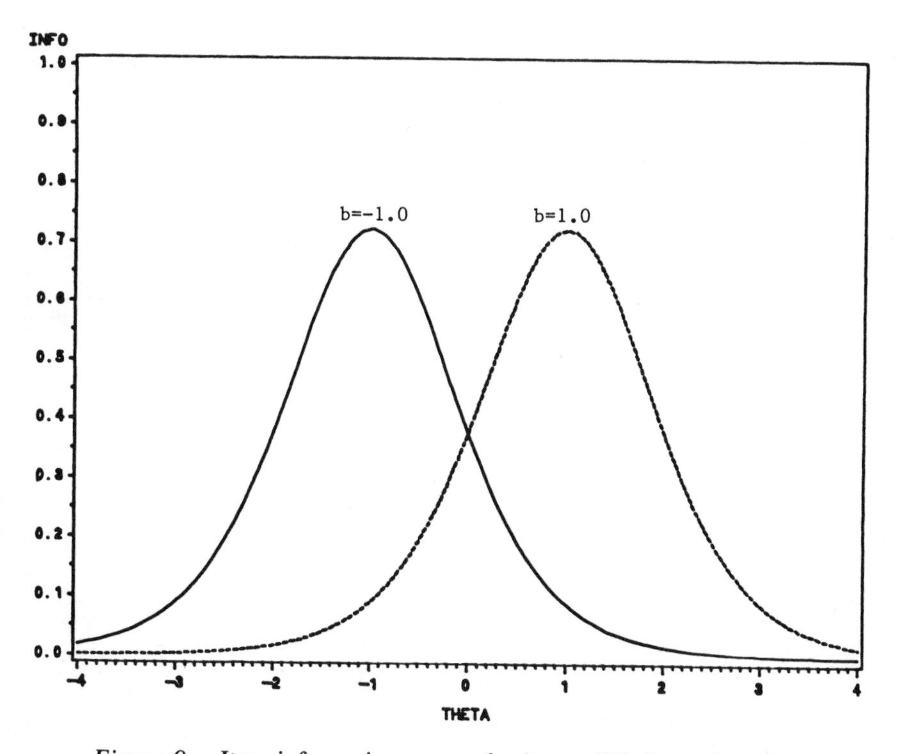

Figure 9. Item information curves for items differing only in b.

Test information can be thought of as a measure of the accuracy of the measurement of θ. In fact, test information at a particular value of θ is equal to the inverse of the square of the standard error of θ. Thus, test information can be considered an indicant of the quality of a test for measuring different ranges of the θ-scale.

Figure 11 shows a test information curve for a test containing items with a wide spread of b-values (curve A), along with a test information curve for a test containing only items with moderate b-values (curve B). Curve A is relatively flat, indicating this test would yield fairly good measurement across the scale. The peaked, narrow curve in Figure 11 indicates a test which would measure well in the middle of the range, but not well in the extremes.

Figure 12 shows a useful way of comparing the test information curves for two sets of items. The curve shown in Figure 12, called a relative efficiency curve, represents the ratio, at any value of θ, of the test informations yielded by the two sets of items. From this type of curve it is very easy to see how two test forms compare in terms of how well θ can be estimated in different ranges of the scale. In this particular instance, the relative efficiency curve was obtained by dividing curve A by curve B. This produced a value greater than 1.0 at the extremes,

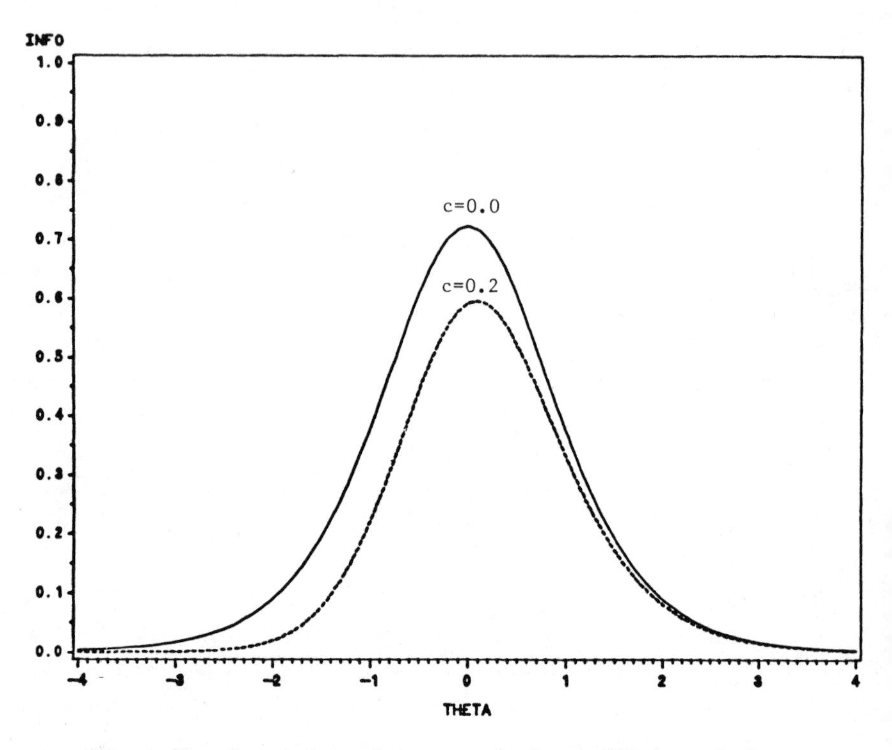

Figure 10. Item information curves for items differing only in c.

where the test with a spread of b-values provides more test information, and a value less than 1.0 in the middle of the scale, where a test with only moderate b-values would provide the most information. Thus, from Figure 12 it can readily be seen, for any range of the scale, which test would be preferable.

True Score

It was indicated earlier that the ICC provided the expected value of the response to a particular item at different levels of θ. Similarly, if test scores are obtained by summing item scores, then the expected value of the test score for a particular level of θ can be obtained by summing the expected values of the individual items. That is, the expected value of the test score for a given value of θ is computed as

$$\tau_j = \sum_{i=1}^{n} P_i(\theta_j), \tag{3}$$

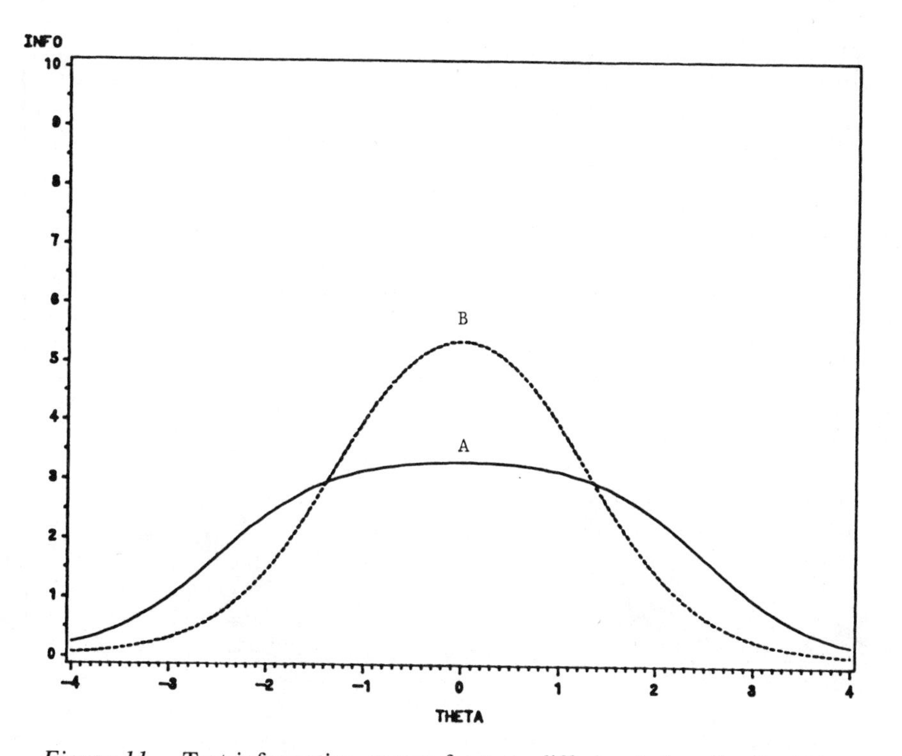

Figure 11. Test information curves for tests differing in b—distribution.

where τ_j is the expected test score, or true score, for respondent j, $P_i(\theta_j)$ is the probability of a correct response to item i by respondent j, and n is the number of items on the test. In practice, of course, Eq. (3) is evaluated using estimated parameters rather than true parameters. In these circumstances, the resulting value is called the respondent's estimated true score.

If Eq. (3) is applied to numerous values across the θ-scale, and the resulting values are plotted against θ, the resulting curve is called a test characteristic curve, or TCC. The TCC, then, is a visual representation of the nonlinear transformation of θ to the number-correct score scale. Such a plot is illustrated in Figure 13.

In many instances, Eq. (3) will be modified by dividing the sum of the Ps by the number of items. This places the estimated true scores on the proportion-correct score scale. This transformation is useful in some applications, but in general the number-correct score scale is more readily interpretable, since it is more familiar to most users.

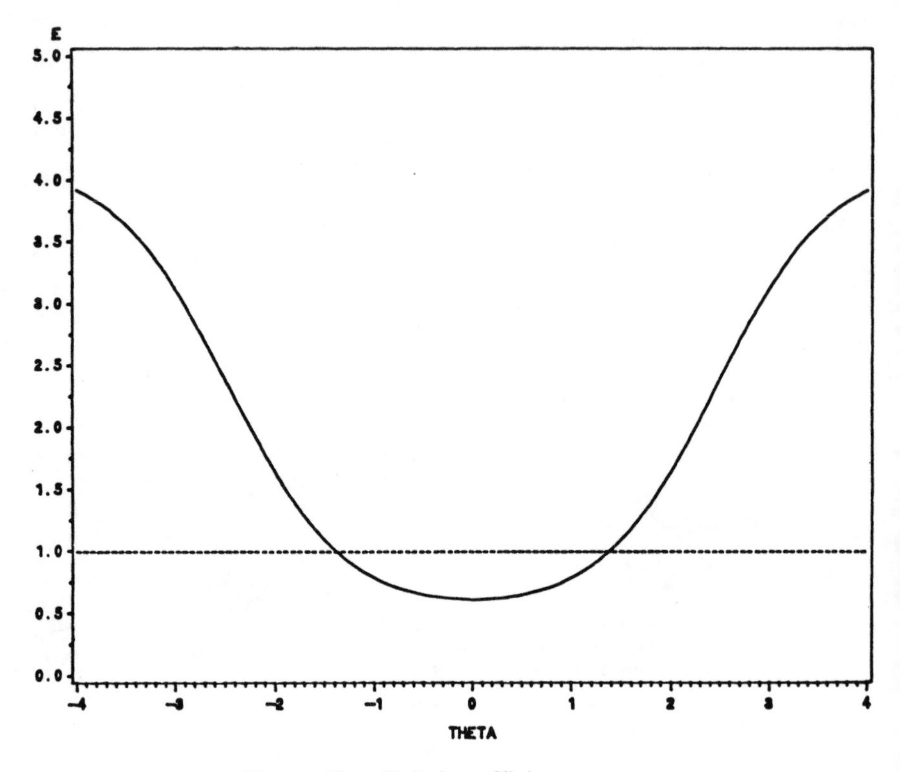

Figure 12. Relative efficiency curve.

BINARY MODELS

In the previous section of this chapter, the basic normal ogive and logistic models were introduced and discussed briefly. In this section, some important variations on the basic logistic model will be presented, and their important characteristics will be discussed. Most of the same variations also exist for the normal ogive model. However, very little has been done to apply any normal ogive models other than the basic model already described. On the other hand, a great deal of work has been done on different variations of the basic logistic model, and a great deal of controversy surrounds the issue of which variation should be used under various measurement conditions. Therefore, most of the discussion presented in this section will focus on the logistic models.

Some researchers elect to consider only selected measurement parameters. In the first three parts of this section, the three most common model variations, the one-, two-, and three-parameter models, will be presented. In the fourth portion of this section the three models will be compared. The final portion of this

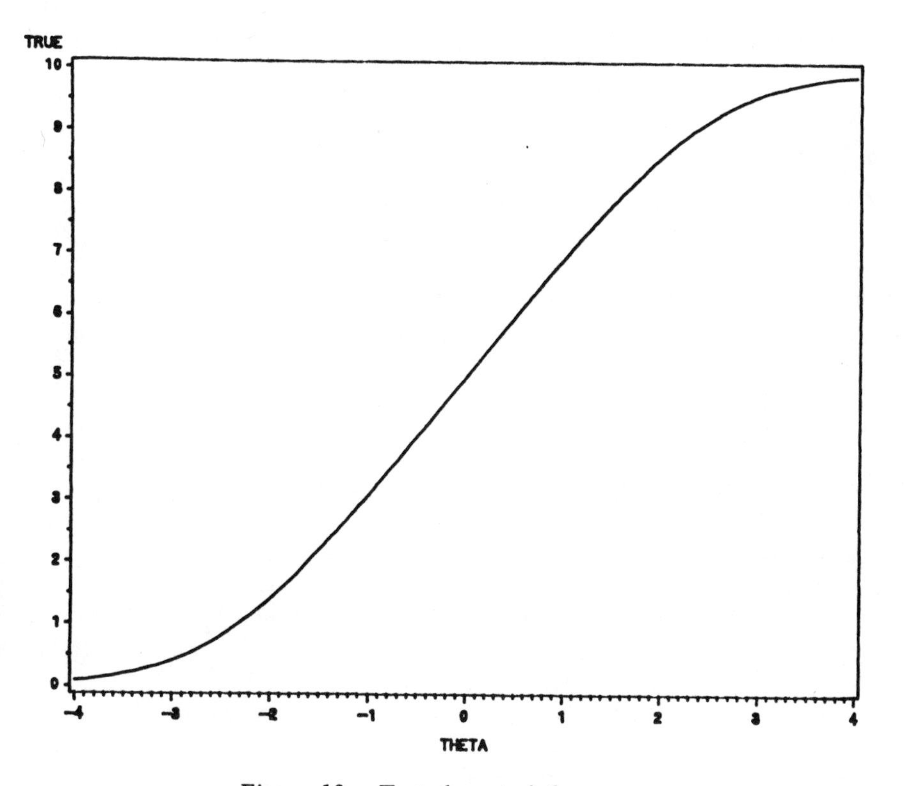

Figure 13. Test characteristic curve.

section pertains to the problem of estimating the parameters of these models. No attempt will be made to provide the mathematical or statistical details for the estimation algorithms. Rather, the discussion will focus on the availability of computer programs for different models.

One-Parameter Logistic Model

Model

The simplest logistic model, the one-parameter logistic (1PL) model, is given by

$$P_i(\theta_j) = \frac{\exp(D(\theta_j - b_i))}{1 + \exp(D(\theta_j - b_i))} \tag{4}$$

where exp(x) means 2.718 raised to the power of x, and the remaining terms are as previously defined. For all practical purposes, the 1PL model can be considered to be the same as the basic logistic model presented in Eq. (2), with the added constraint that all item a-values equal to 1.0.

In another important variation, the a-value is set equal to 1/1.7, and the sign of the b-value is reversed. This yields an exponent for Eq. (4) equal to $\theta_j + b_i$, since Da_i now equals 1.7 times 1/1.7, or 1.0. The b-value in this variation is called an item easiness parameter. It has the same interpretation as before, except a negative number signifies a difficult item instead of an easy item. In this form, the model is called the Rasch model, after a Danish statistician who developed it independently of the general class of logistic models.

Proponents of the Rasch model claim that it has some very attractive properties which make it preferable to the other two variations discussed above. Perhaps the most important of the properties attributed to this model is the separability of the item and person parameters. That is, it is in theory possible to estimate the b-parameter for a set of items without knowing the respondents' θs. Because of this separability property, the item and person parameter estimates for the Rasch model may be unbiased. Equally important, they can be obtained with a relatively small sample size. However, it should be pointed out that recent research has cast doubts on the validity of some of these claims (Divgi, 1986).

A disadvantage of the Rasch model is that it requires the assumption that all items are equally discriminating, an assumption which is almost never met in reality. The proponents of the Rasch model, on the other hand, would argue that the model is quite robust to the violation of this assumption, and that instruments should be constructed so as to contain equally discriminating items, anyway. Proponents of the other models, on the other hand, argue that this is neither practical nor desirable.

Information

Item information for the 1PL model is given by

$$I_i(\theta_j) = D^2PQ, \tag{5}$$

where $I_i(\theta_j)$ is the item information for item i at θ_j, $Q = 1\text{-}P$, and P is computed from Eq. (4). The maximum value taken on by $I_i(\theta_j)$ is 0.72, which occurs when $\theta_j = b_i$. Thus, when evaluating the adequacy of an item for measuring at a particular θ level, it is helpful to compare the obtained item information with the theoretical maximum of 0.72. An item yielding an information value near 0.72 is measuring about as well as possible, while an item with information well below 0.72 is far from optimal.

Because item information for the 1PL model depends only on b, it is quite easy to see that to optimize measurement, items with b-values as close as possible to the respondent's θ should be administered. For example, consider a respondent with math ability of $\theta = 1.0$. In order to accurately determine this respondent's ability, we would want to administer items that were moderate in difficulty—that is, items with b-values in the vicinity of $b = 1.0$. Imagine that we had two items available to use, one with $b = 0.0$, and one with $b = 1.5$. The first item should be a little too easy for the respondent, while the second item should be a little too difficult. The probability of a correct response by this respondent to these two items is 0.731 for the first item and 0.378 for the second item.

In order to determine which of the two items would provide the most information about the respondent's ability, we apply Eq. (5). Thus, we find that the information yielded by the first time at $\theta = 1.0$ is 0.57, and for the second item the information yielded is 0.68. From these values it can be seen that the second item yields slightly more information and, in fact, is fairly near the theoretical maximum. Of course, knowing the characteristics of the 1PL model, we could have determined this by simply determining which item's b-value is closer to 1.0. This process is not so simple for more complex models, however. Nor is it quite so simple when, rather than choosing between two items, it is necessary to select the best set of items from a large bank, as would happen in practice.

Two-Parameter Logistic Model

Model

The two-parameter logistic (2PL) model is formed by altering the exponent of Eq. (4) to include the a_i term. Thus, the 2PL model is given by

$$P_i(\theta_j) = \frac{\exp(Da_i(\theta_j - b_i))}{1 + \exp(Da_i(\theta_j - b_i))} \tag{5}$$

where all the terms are as previously defined. This is the same model as was described in the previous as the basic logistic model.

The 2PL model is attractive in the sense that it does not require the assumption of equal item discrimination parameters. However, it has the disadvantage of requiring much larger sample sizes for estimation of the parameters. Perhaps more important, because the item and person parameters interact multiplicatively, they no longer have the property of separability. Thus, in order to estimate the item parameters, it is also necessary to estimate the person parameters. This results in estimates which are neither unbiased nor efficient. Moreover, estimation of the a-parameter can be quite problematic at times, resulting in the need to add arbitrary constraints to the parameter, such as an artificial minimum and maximum.

Information

Item information for the 2PL model is given by

$$I_i(\theta_j) = D^2 a_i^2 PQ, \tag{6}$$

where P is computed from Eq. (5), and all other terms are as previously defined. The maximum value of item information for the 2PL model is $0.72a_i^2$, which again occurs at $\theta_j = b_i$.

For the 2PL model, the information yielded by an item depends on both the a- and b-parameters. Because of this, it is much more difficult to determine what items will yield the best measurement for a particular θ. Items with b-values closer to θ do not necessarily yield more information than items with b-values farther away if their a-values are lower. Thus, item selection requires the construction of information plots, rather than the simple examination of b-parameters adequate for the 1PL model.

Consider, for example, that we again have a respondent with $\theta = 1.0$, and that we once again must choose between two items. If the first item has a = 1.5 and b = 0.0, and the second item has a $\theta = 0.75$ and b = 1.5, simply choosing the item with the closer b-value results in the selection of the second item, which in this case is the wrong answer. If, instead, we apply Eq. (6), we find that the information yielded by the first item is 0.437, while the second item yields an information value of 0.369. From this it can be seen that the second item is not the best choice. The high a-value of the first item makes it the better choice, even though the b-value is farther from the ability value. Thus, the need for considering both a- and b-values when using the 2PL model is clear.

Three-Parameter Logistic Model

Model

The three-parameter logistic (3PL) model is given by

$$P_i(\theta_j) = c_i + (1 - c_i)\frac{\exp(Da_i(\theta_j - b_i))}{1 + \exp(Da_i(\theta_j - b_i))}, \tag{7}$$

where, again, all the terms are as previously defined. This model, certainly the most complex of the logistic models currently in use, is both blessed with many advantages, and cursed with many disadvantages.

The greatest advantage of the 3PL model over the other models is that it allows for nonzero probabilities of correct responses to multiple-choice and true-false items for respondents with very low θs. This is very useful, since it takes into account the possibility of guessing. Neither the 1PL nor the 2PL model accounts for guessing. In the case where guessing occurs, this would certainly bring into question the appropriateness of the simpler models.

On the other hand, estimation of the lower asymptote is very difficult, and often creates additional problems in the estimation of the a-value. Not only are the sample sizes required for estimation of the 3PL model quite large, but it is also necessary that a fair portion of the respondents have low θs. Otherwise, no information as to the lower asymptote will be available, and it will not be possible to estimate the c-value.

Information

Item information for the 3PL model is given by

$$I_i(\theta_j) = D^2 a_i^2 P^2 \frac{1 - c_i}{c_i + \exp(Da_i(\theta_j - b_i))}, \tag{8}$$

where P is computed from Eq. (5), and all of the remaining terms are as previously defined. The maximum value of item information for the 3PL model is a somewhat complex function of the c-value, and will not be presented here. Item selection most certainly requires the construction of item information plots for the 3PL model. In general, though, selecting items that yield the most information will involve trade-offs among close b-values, high a-values, and low c-values.

Model Comparison

It should be pointed out at this point that there are some fundamental differences among these models in terms of how they represent the trait being measured. Most important among these differences is the manner in which the inclusion of a discrimination parameter affects the results obtained. If the instrument is not unidimensional or unifactoral, and most, if not all, measurement devices will contain at least some minor factors, the 1PL model yields a θ-estimate that tends to represent a composite of respondent scores on whatever factors are present in the instrument. In the 2PL and 3PL models, however, θ tends to represent the respondent score on the largest factor present. This difference occurs because the a-parameter tends to take on large values for items measuring the dominant factor, and low values for items measuring secondary factors. In the 1PL model all items are weighted equally, regardless of what factor is measured by the items.

As a practical consequence, the 1PL model is susceptible to contamination by superfluous factors, while the 2PL and 3PL model tend to purify the data by eliminating the effects of extraneous factors. If the secondary factors are important, on the other hand, the 1PL model faithfully reflects this structure, while the 2PL and 3PL models tend to omit information about these secondary factors. Of course, all three models require the assumption that the data are unidimensional, so if there are important secondary factors, it is probably not appropriate to use any of the models.

In order to illustrate the differences in the parameters of these models, parameter estimates were obtained for the 1PL, 2PL, and 3PL models for the same data. The resulting item parameter estimates are shown in Table 1. The test information curves for the three models are shown in Figure 14. For these data, item parameter estimates were obtained using the MARGIE program (McKinley, 1986).

From Table 1 it can be seen that, overall, the b-values for the three models are

Table 1. Item Parameter Estimates for 1PL, 2PL, and 3PL Models

	1PL	*2PL*		*3PL*		
Item	*b*	*a*	*b*	*a*	*b*	*c*
1	−4.1	2.0	−2.1	1.4	−2.6	0.1
2	−0.6	0.2	−2.0	0.0	−19.0	0.1
3	0.9	0.6	1.0	1.2	1.0	0.1
4	−0.1	0.5	−0.2	0.7	0.4	0.2
5	1.4	1.0	1.1	1.1	1.1	0.0
6	0.1	0.4	0.2	0.6	0.7	0.2
7	−1.4	1.1	−1.1	2.0	−0.4	0.4
8	0.0	0.6	0.0	0.6	0.3	0.1
9	0.3	0.5	0.4	1.0	0.8	0.2
10	−0.6	0.7	−0.6	0.8	−0.3	0.2
11	−0.8	1.5	−0.6	1.3	−0.6	0.0
12	−0.4	0.2	−1.0	0.2	−0.2	0.1
13	−2.6	1.2	−1.9	1.1	−1.9	0.1
14	−0.9	0.5	−1.1	0.5	−0.8	0.1
15	0.7	0.7	0.7	0.9	0.8	0.1
16	1.0	0.5	1.2	1.0	1.3	0.1
17	1.4	1.1	1.1	1.3	1.1	0.0
18	−1.0	0.7	−1.0	0.7	−0.8	0.1
19	−0.5	0.9	−0.4	0.8	−0.4	0.0
20	−0.6	0.3	−1.2	0.3	−0.6	0.1
21	−0.3	1.1	−0.6	1.2	−0.5	0.1
22	0.3	0.4	0.4	0.4	0.8	0.1
23	−0.9	1.1	−0.7	1.0	−0.7	0.0
24	−1.6	0.9	−1.3	1.0	−1.1	0.1
25	0.9	0.6	1.0	1.3	1.1	0.1
26	−0.2	0.7	−0.2	1.0	0.2	0.2
27	−2.8	0.8	−2.4	0.7	−2.5	0.1
28	0.3	0.3	0.6	0.5	1.3	0.2
29	0.5	0.5	0.6	1.5	1.0	0.2
30	−0.3	0.5	−0.4	0.6	−0.0	0.1

fairly similar. The correlation of the b-values for the 1PL and 2PL models was 0.91, while a correlation of 0.55 was obtained between the b-values for the 1PL and 3PL models. The 2PL and 3PL model b-values had a correlation of 0.76. The a-values for the 2PL and 3PL models had a correlation of 0.69.

A close examination of the values in Table 1 reveals a great deal about the relationships among these three models. For instance, it can be seen in Table 1 that, when the 2PL a-value is very close to the constant a-value used for the 1PL model, the b-values for the two models are very similar. However, when the 2PL a-value is higher than the 1PL constant a-value, the 2PL b-value is closer to 0.0

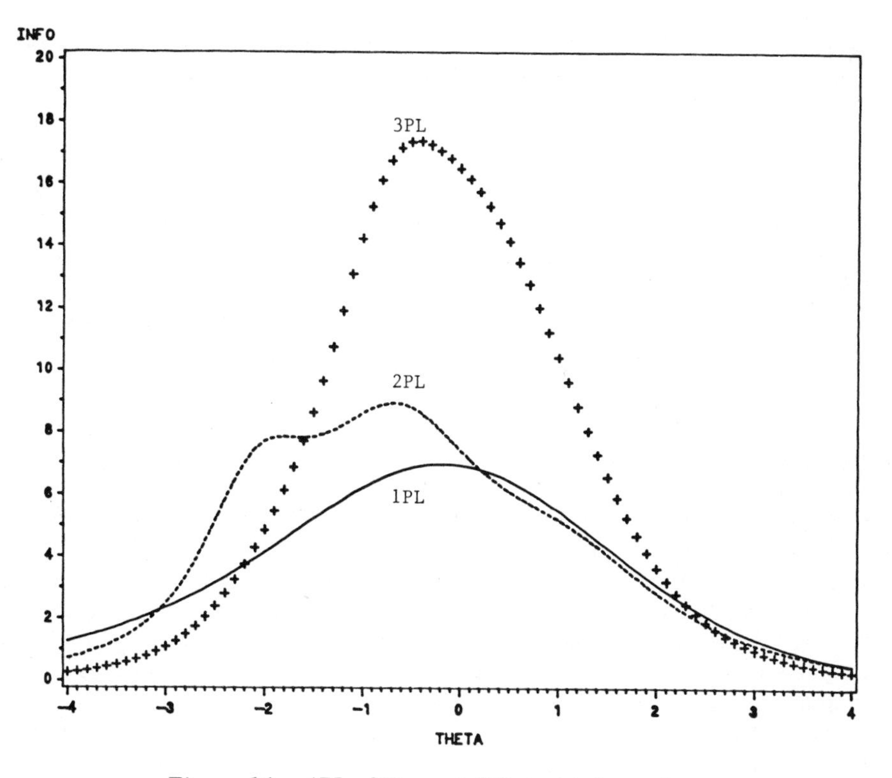

Figure 14. 1PL, 2PL, and 3PL test information.

than the 1PL b-value, and when the 2PL a-value is lower than the 1PL constant a-value, the 2PL b-value is farther away from 0.0. This is because increasing the a-value contracts the θ-scale, and lowering the a-value stretches the scale.

Comparing the estimates for the 2PL and 3PL models, it can be seen that, where c is quite close to 0.0, the 3PL a- and b-values are quite similar to the a- and b-values for the 2PL model. However, as the value of c increases, the value of b tends to increase, as does the value of a. The b-value shift to the right occurs because, when guessing is not taken into account, the item appears to be easier than it is. Correcting for guessing reveals the greater difficulty of the item. The effect of guessing on item discrimination is a well-known result. Guessing tends to decrease item discrimination, so correcting for guessing tends to inflate the a-value. Of course, these results are relevant only when guessing is a possibility, and when binary models are used.

An examination of the test information curves in Figure 14 is also revealing. The two most noticeable features of these curves is the lack of smoothness of the 2PL and 3PL curves, and the fact that the 2PL and 3PL curves are somewhat higher than the 1PL curve. Both of these features are the result of the inclusion of the a-parameter. The effect of the inclusion of the c-parameter is to somewhat lower the curve at the lower end of the scale.

Estimation

Needless to say, in order to make use of the information provided by IRT methodology, it is first necessary to estimate the values of the parameters of the model employed. In some cases, this is not terribly difficult, as is the case with the Rasch model. It is possible to estimate both item and person parameters for the Rasch model using a desktop calculator (see, for example, Wright & Stone, 1979). In most other cases, estimation of model parameters is quite difficult (see, for example, Wingersky, 1983, for a discussion of an estimation algorithm for the 3PL model).

Algorithms

There are many different algorithms for estimating the parameters of IRT models. The four most commonly used types of procedures are the joint maximum likelihood procedures, unconditional maximum likelihood procedures, marginal maximum likelihood procedures, and Bayesian procedures. The unconditional maximum likelihood procedures are limited to use with the 1PL model, but the other procedures can be used with two- and three-parameter models also. The program mentioned above, MARGIE, utilizes a marginal maximum likelihood procedure.

Until recently, the most often used procedures were based on the joint maximum likelihood approach to parameter estimation. In this approach, item and person parameters are estimated jointly, usually by holding item parameters constant at some provisional values while estimating person parameters, and then holding the person parameters constant at the newly estimated values while estimating the item parameters. This type of cycling is continued until the procedure converges. Convergence is usually defined as the point at which the probability of observing the response data, conditional on the most recent parameter estimates, is maximized.

Despite the great popularity of joint maximum likelihood estimation procedures, there are some important limitations on the procedures which should be mentioned. The most important of these limitations is the failure of the procedure to yield estimates for some parameters. This occurs most frequently for respondents who have the same response for all items, such as when an examinee correctly answers all items or incorrectly answers all items, and for items that have been answered the same way by all respondents. In these cases, the maximum likelihood estimator of the parameter of interest takes on a value of infinity, and the procedure breaks down. Other instances where the procedure breaks down are more rare, and usually involve respondents with wildly erratic and inconsistent responses.

In recent years, marginal maximum likelihood procedures have become increasingly popular, although their use is still far below the level of use of the joint maximum likelihood procedures. The increase in their popularity has been primarily a result of new estimation procedures that have been developed recently, coupled with a desire to avoid the problems encountered with joint maximum likelihood estimation. These new procedures, which involve estimating item parameters by specifying and integrating over the θ distribution, greatly reduce the expense of the estimation process, and make it possible to use the marginal maximum likelihood approach with much longer tests. The item parameter estimates which result can be used in any of a variety of estimation procedures to obtain ability estimates. Until recently, the available marginal maximum likelihood procedures were quite costly, and really not practical with tests longer than 20 items, a problem still encountered with unconditional maximum likelihood procedures.

Bayesian procedures are just now becoming available for use, which at least partially explains why this approach is not used widely. The Bayesian approach to parameter estimation tends to be quite complex, and will not be described here. It will be sufficient to say that this approach holds great promise, but a great deal of research must yet be done before the use of Bayesian procedures becomes widespread.

Programs

Given the great complexity of most of the estimation algorithms available for use, it is fortunate that there are a number of computer programs available for estimation of the parameters of most of the models discussed so far. Table 2

Table 2. Computer Programs for IRT Parameter Estimation

Program	*Authors*	*Models*
ANCILLES	Urry	3PL
BICAL	Wright & Mead	1PL
BILOG	Bock & Mislevy	1PL,2PL,3PL
LOGIST	Wood, Wingersky & Lord	1PL,2PL,3PL
MARGIE	McKinley	1PL,2PL,3PL
MAX	Wright & Panchapakesan	1PL
MAXLOG	McKinley & Reckase	2PL
NORMOG	Kolakowski & Bock	2PNO

provides some summary information about the most popular of these programs. Listed in the table are the names of the programs, the authors of the programs, and the models for which the programs can be used. Note that several of these programs can be used for more than one model.

Sample Size Requirements

Another important consideration that must be made in the application of IRT models regards sample size. As has been mentioned previously, estimation of model parameters requires an increasing number of respondents as model complexity increases. It is generally recommended that there be at least 300 respondents for the 1PL model. For the 2PL model the required sample size increases to 700, and for the 3PL model at least 1000 respondents are needed.

POLYCHOTOMOUS MODELS

Two basic types of polychotomous IRT models will be discussed in this section—nominal response models, and graded response models. Each type has several variations, some of which are very different, and some of which differ only in subtle ways. No attempt will be made here to sort out all of the variations. Rather, only a broad overview of the general models will be presented.

Nominal Response Models

Probably the most important application of nominal response IRT models is to extract useful information from multiple-choice distractors. It is occasionally the case, for instance, that important information about a respondent's ability level can be obtained by examining which wrong alternative the respondent selects. Consider, for example, the following item designed to assess the respondent's knowledge of history.

Which U.S. president signed the Emancipation Proclamation?

a. G. Washington
b. A. Lincoln
c. U. Grant
d. A. Johnson

The basic assumption is, of course, that a respondent who answers the item correctly has more knowledge of history than a respondent who selected some other option. However, it may be possible to obtain more information from this item. For example, it might be reasonable to assume that option "a" would be selected by only those respondents who know Washington was a U.S. president, but who either don't know what the Emancipation Proclamation was, or don't know when it was signed. A respondent who knows considerably more about the document and when it was signed would not be likely to respond "a." On the other hand, a respondent who knows that the Emancipation Proclamation dealt with slavery, but who doesn't know for sure who signed it, might respond "c" or "d."

In such a case as this, it would seem appropriate and useful to model responses to each option as a function of θ, rather than simply modeling the correct response. Such a procedure yields a curve for each option. These curves are calling operating characteristic curves, or OCCs. Figure 15 shows a set of OCCs that might be obtained for the response options described above.

The horizontal axis of Figure 15 is θ, as has been the case with figures depicting ICCs. Now, however, the vertical axis is not the probability of a score of 1. Rather, it is the probability of observing response x_{ij}, where the subscript i denotes item i, and the subscript j denotes option j of item i.

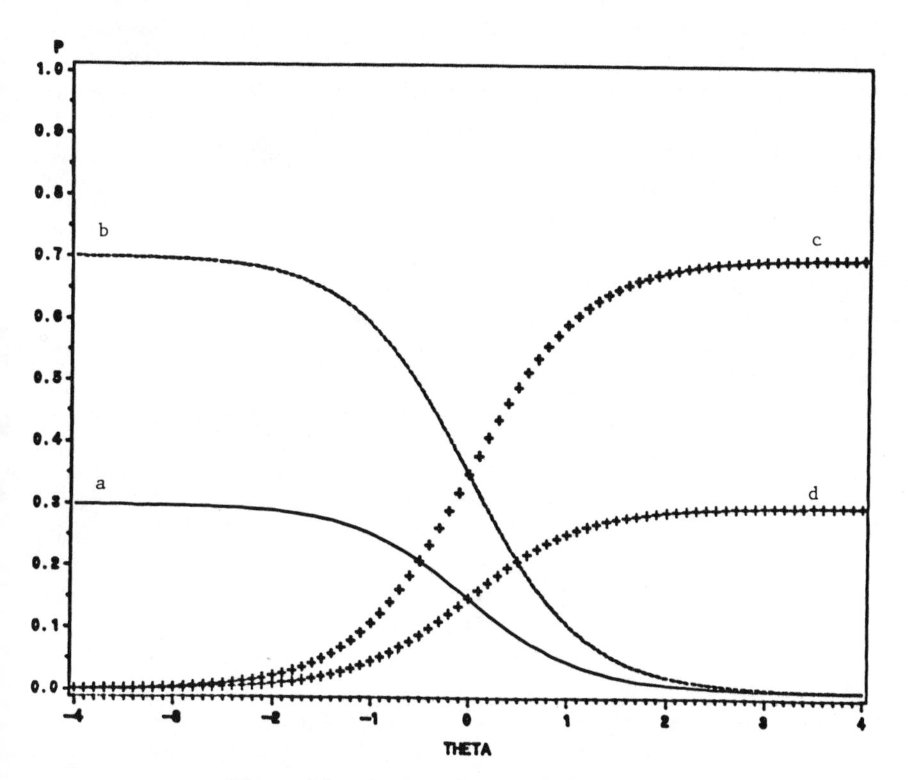

Figure 15. Option characteristic curves.

There are a few important characteristics of the set of OCCs shown in Figure 15 that should be noticed. First, at any point on the scale, the sum of the probabilities of the options equals 1.0. Second, clearly the monotonicity property, which was so important for binary models, does not hold for an individual OCC, which in the nominal response model are allowed to have negative a-values. However, it is still presumed to hold for the OCC for the correct response. In addition, since the OCCs must always sum to 1.0 at any point on the scale, it is not actually necessary to model all the options. If all but one of the options are modeled, the OCC for the remaining option can be computed as 1.0 minus the sum of the other OCCs. Finally, it should be noted that the location parameter for an option no longer occurs at the point where $P = 0.5$. Indeed, for many options P will never be as high as 0.5. Instead, the option location parameter will simply indicate a point of inflection which, in many cases, will be the highest point attained by the OCC.

Based on the set of OCCs shown in Figure 15, it would appear that for respondents with very low θs, option "a" is slightly more attractive than the other options. The other three options are about equally attractive. As θ increases from very low to moderate, the attractiveness of Washington as an option decreases, and the attractiveness of the other three options increases. The probability of response "c," Grant, increases quickly, then decreases quickly, reflecting the fact that respondents with a little knowledge of history are likely to familiar with Grant's name, and that he was associated with the Civil War. However, respondents with a little more knowledge of history know that he did not sign the Emancipation Proclamation.

The OCC for option "d," Johnson, changes little until fairly high levels of θ are reached. It then increases rapidly for a short stretch, and then decreases. This might occur because only respondents with a fair amount of knowledge of history would know that Johnson was president shortly after the Civil War, and thus would find Johnson an attractive option. This situation is sometimes indicated by the expression, "a little knowledge can be a dangerous thing."

The model which produced the OCCs shown in Figure 15 is called a nominal response model. It is formed by treating each of the options as a distinct outcome and modeling it separately. In this way, information can be obtained from each option. The information obtained from each option can be obtained in much the way it is obtained for an ICC—option information is a function of the slope of the OCC at a particular level of θ. Item information, then, is the sum of the option informations, and test information is the sum of the item informations.

The nominal response model is given by

$$P_{ik}(\theta_j) = \frac{\exp(Da_{ik}(\theta_j - b_{ik}))}{\Sigma\exp(Da_{ik}(\theta_j - b_{ik}))}, \tag{9}$$

where $P_{ik}(\theta_j)$ is the probability of observing a response of option k to item i by examinee j, a_{ik} and b_{ik} are the item parameters for item i for option k, and the summation in the denominator is over options. Notice that, because we are modeling all of the options, there is no need for the lower asymptote parameter. The formula for option information is relatively complicated, and will not be presented here.

Figure 16 shows the option information curves obtained using the nominal response model for a hypothetical item. Figure 17 shows the item information curves for this item using the nominal response model and a binary response model. As can be seen, in all cases the information is higher for the nominal response model.

It should be pointed out that, in a nominal response model, there is no assumption that the options are ordered as they were in the example above. The reason the model is called a nominal response model is that no order properties are assumed. If an item is constructed so that the options are ordered, it is usually desirable to take a somewhat different approach.

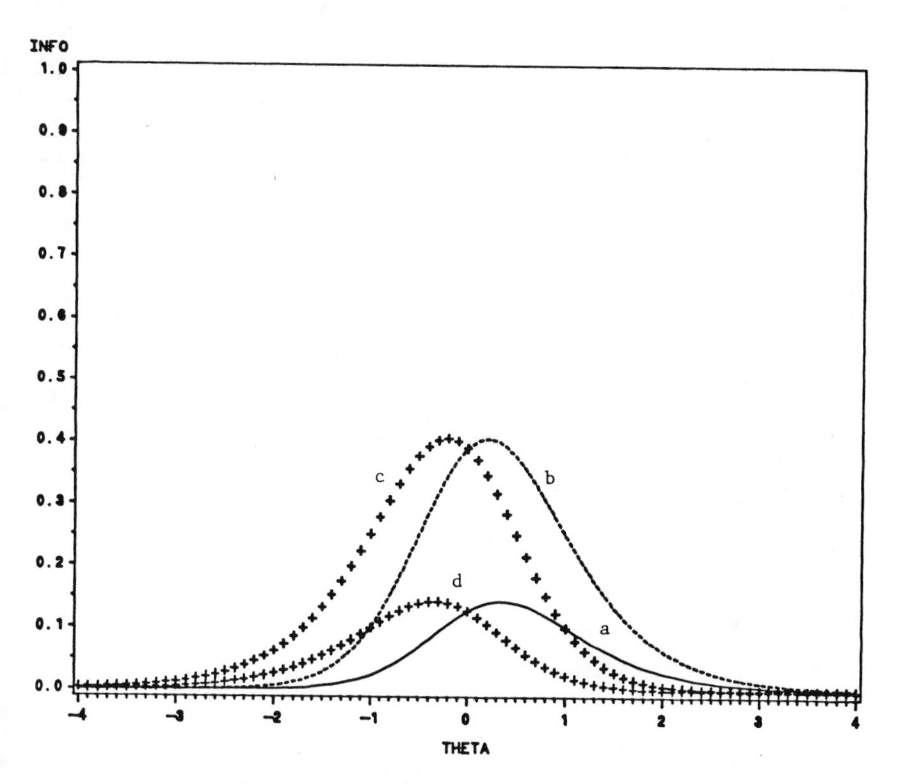

Figure 16. Option information curves.

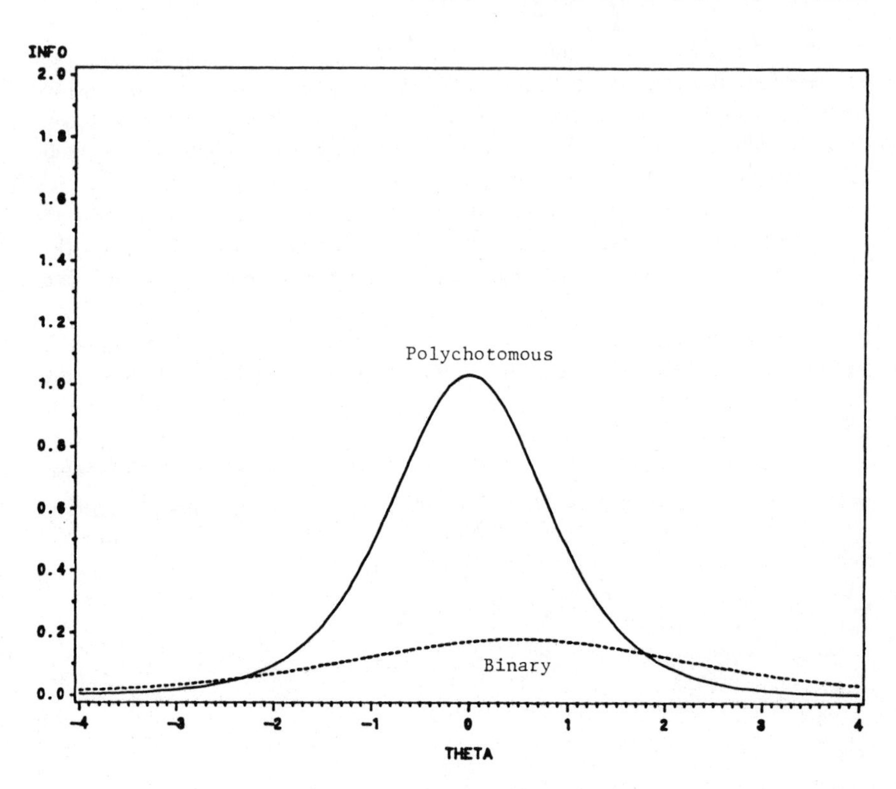

Figure 17. Binary and polychotomous item information.

Graded Response Models

It is sometimes desirable to use an item format in which the different response options represent different values along the scale of interest. Take, for example, the following item from a scale designed to assess the relative importance of different news sources.

How often do you watch the evening news on television?

a. Never
b. Rarely
c. Occasionally
d. Frequently
e. All the time

The presumption here is, of course, that someone who relies a great deal on television for news will respond "e," while someone who relies on some other source will respond "a."

The item just described requires treatment that differs somewhat from the item described for the nominal response model. The reason for this lies in the nature of the response options. In the nominal response case, the options represented discrete alternatives from which to choose. In the graded response case, however, the response alternatives are cumulative. That is, they don't really represent different concepts or entities. Rather, each successive option represents the same thing as the preceeding option, only a little bit more of it. Thus, someone who watched the news on television occasionally watches television on rare occasions plus a few more.

This situation produces a set of option chracteristic curves like those shown in Figure 18. In Figure 18, curve a represents the probability of responding at least never, curve b represents the probability of responding at least rarely, and so forth. In order to determine the probability of responding at least but not more than rarely, it is necessary to compute the probability of responding at least rarely, and subtracting it from the probability of responding at least occasionally.

Once this subtraction process is completed, the probabilities of responding in each category are shown by the OCCs in Figure 19. These curves can then be

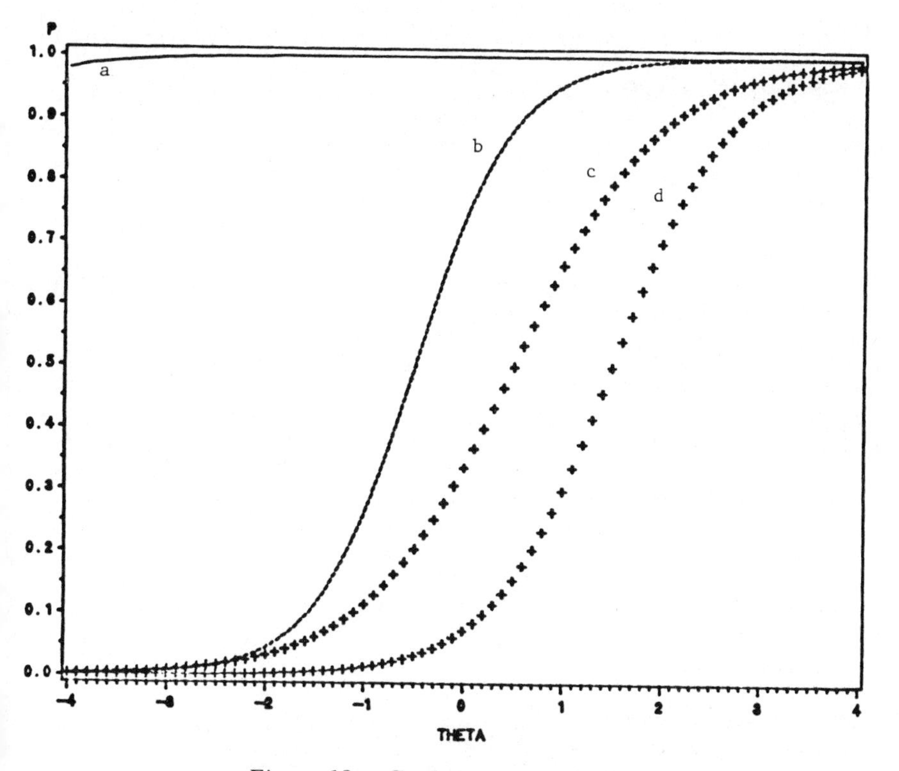

Figure 18. Graded response OCCs.

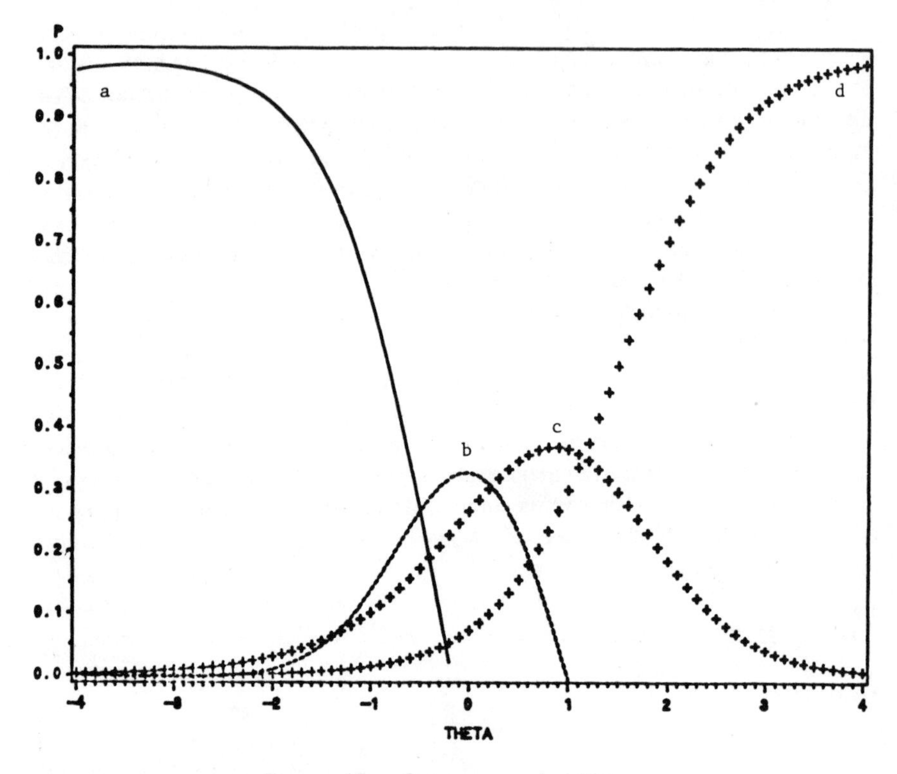

Figure 19. Category probabilities.

used to obtain option information curves, which again can be summed to obtain an item information curve.

Estimation

There are several programs available for estimating the parameters of various polychotomous models. Some of these programs, their authors, and the models for which they can be used are shown in Table 3.

Table 3. Computer Programs for Polychotomous Response Models

Program	*Authors*	*Models*
CREDIT	Masters	1PL graded
LOGOG	Kolakowski & Bock	2PL nominal
PARTIAL	McKinley	1PL graded

APPLICATIONS

It should be clear at this point that IRT has applicability to a wide range of fields, including aptitude and achievement testing, attitude scaling, and personality assessment. In each of these fields IRT can be used to improve test development, scoring, equating, and analysis, and can even be used to improve test administration. The general approach to applying IRT in each of these situations does not depend on the model selected, and can be presented in a generic fashion that applies to all models. Exceptions for particular models will be noted during the discussion.

Test Construction

The advantages of utilizing item and test information curves for test construction purposes have already been mentioned. The use of information curves, it was pointed out, allows the test developer to target the regions of the scale where precise measurements are desired, to avoid wasting items in regions where precise measurements are not needed. The way in which this is accomplished will be illustrated for two quite different testing applications—mastery testing, and ability testing.

Mastery Testing

Table 4 shows the 1PL b-values for a set of 20 vocabulary items to be used in construction a 5-item mastery test. Mastery is to be determined using a cut-score of 60 percent correct, or a raw score of 12 on the item bank. There is no need or desire to accurately measure the vocabulary ability of the examinee. All that is desired is to determine on which side of the cut-score the examinee is.

Table 4. Hypothetical Item Bank

Item	*b*	*Information*	*Item*	*b*	*Information*
1	0.42	0.72	11	−0.72	0.33
2	−1.96	0.05	12	0.74	0.66
3	−0.12	0.60	13	0.22	0.71
4	−0.41	0.47	14	−0.59	0.39
5	−0.08	0.62	15	0.39	0.72
6	−0.43	0.46	16	1.03	0.54
7	0.85	0.62	17	0.74	0.66
8	0.10	0.68	18	−0.74	0.32
9	0.99	0.56	19	0.24	0.71
10	0.24	0.71	20	0.14	0.69

Under these conditions, the goal of test construction is to select 5 items from the bank that will yield information in the region where the decision is to be made, and that do not waste information in irrelevant regions of the scale. This situation is illustrated in Figure 20, which shows the desired, or target, information curve for the mastery test. As can be seen, the curve is quite narrow, and is peaked at θ_c, which represents the value of θ that yields a true score of 12. Of course, at this point, we have no idea what the value of θ_c is, but we can fairly simply and quickly obtain a fair idea as to what it will be.

If we compute the true score for our item bank at different levels of θ, and then plot those values by θ, we have the TCC composed of the ICCs for all the items in the bank, which is shown in Figure 21. From this curve, we can tell that the θ that corresponds to a score of 12 is a little greater than 0. It is actually about 0.388.

Now, if the items we select for our 5-item mastery test are to yield their maximum information at $\theta = 0.388$, and the maximum information for an item occurs at $\theta = b$, then it stands to reason that the items that yield the most

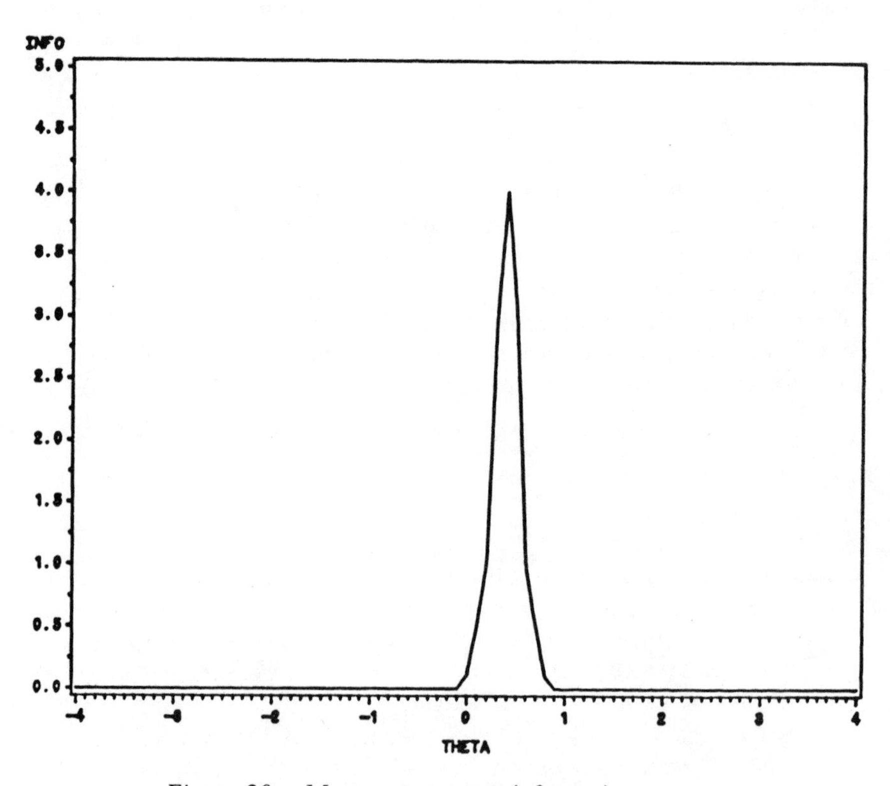

Figure 20. Mastery test target information curve.

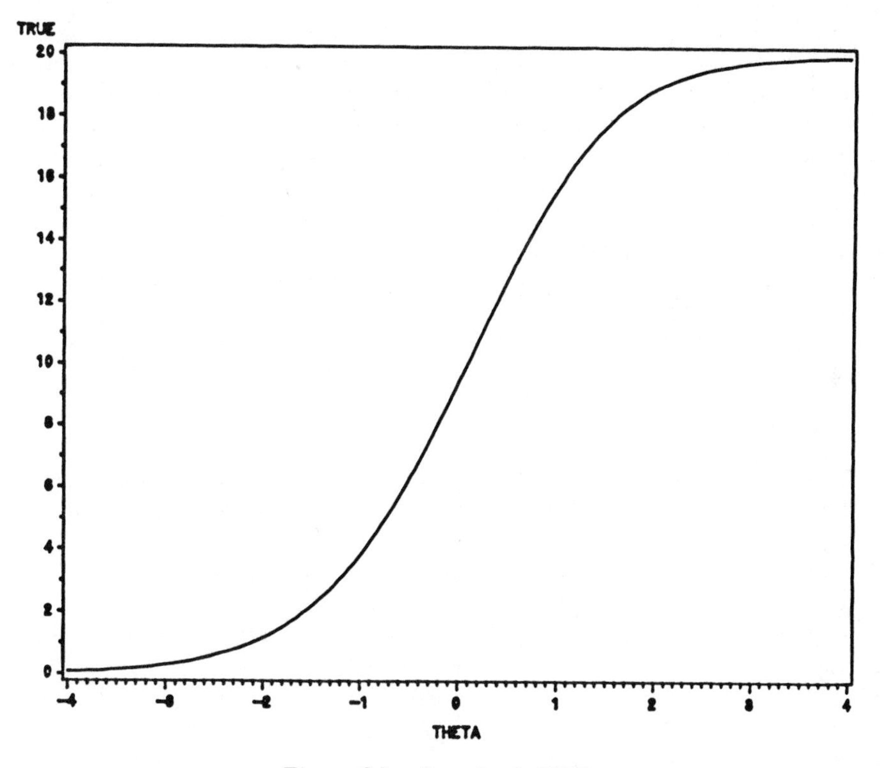

Figure 21. Item bank TCC.

information at the cut-score are the items with b-values closest to 0.388. The second column of numbers in Table 4 are the informations yielded by each item at $\theta = 0.388$. Based on these data, we would select items 1, 10, 13, 15, and 19 for our 5-item mastery test. Figure 22 shows the test information curve for these items.

Ability Testing

In the example above, the goal of measurement was to determine whether an examinee was above or below a specified cut score. In such a case, precision of measurement is required only in the vicinity of the decision point. However, it is very often the goal of measurement to obtain a precise measure of a trait for all respondents, regardless of status. In this situation, the target information curve would look like the example shown in Figure 23.

In Figure 23, the target information curve is relatively flat, indicating that θ can be fairly well estimated across the scale. In order to obtain a curve such as is shown in Figure 23, it is necessary to select some items that yield information at

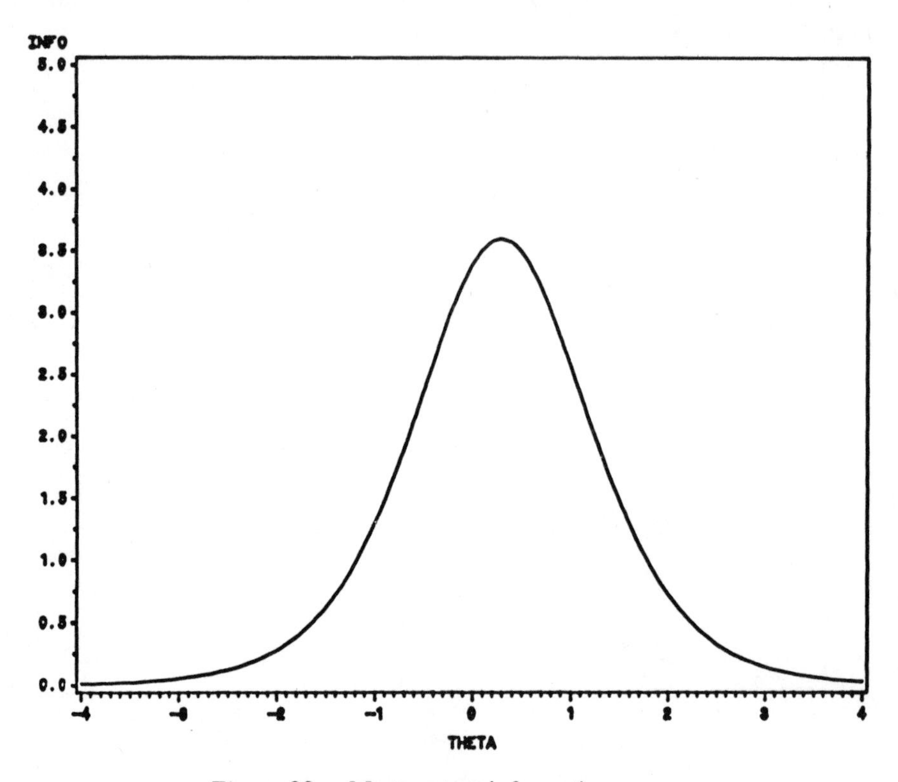

Figure 22. Mastery test information curve.

the low end of the scale, some items that yield information in the middle of the scale, and some items that yield information at the upper end of the scale.

Take, for example, a 5-item test comprised of items 2, 5, 16, 17, and 18. These items yield their maximum informations at θ equal to -1.96, -0.74, -0.08, 0.74, and 1.03. This produces the test information curve shown in Figure 24. As can be seen, the test yields at least some information across the ability range. Of course, it would be foolish to attempt accurate measurement across a broad range of ability with only 5 items, but this example does serve to illustrate the general principles involved.

Equating

Frequently alternate forms of an instrument are developed, either to increase security, or to enable the assessment of instrument reliability and validity. In such instances, every attempt is made to develop forms which yield comparable scores. That is, a respondent should receive the same score, regardless of which form is received.

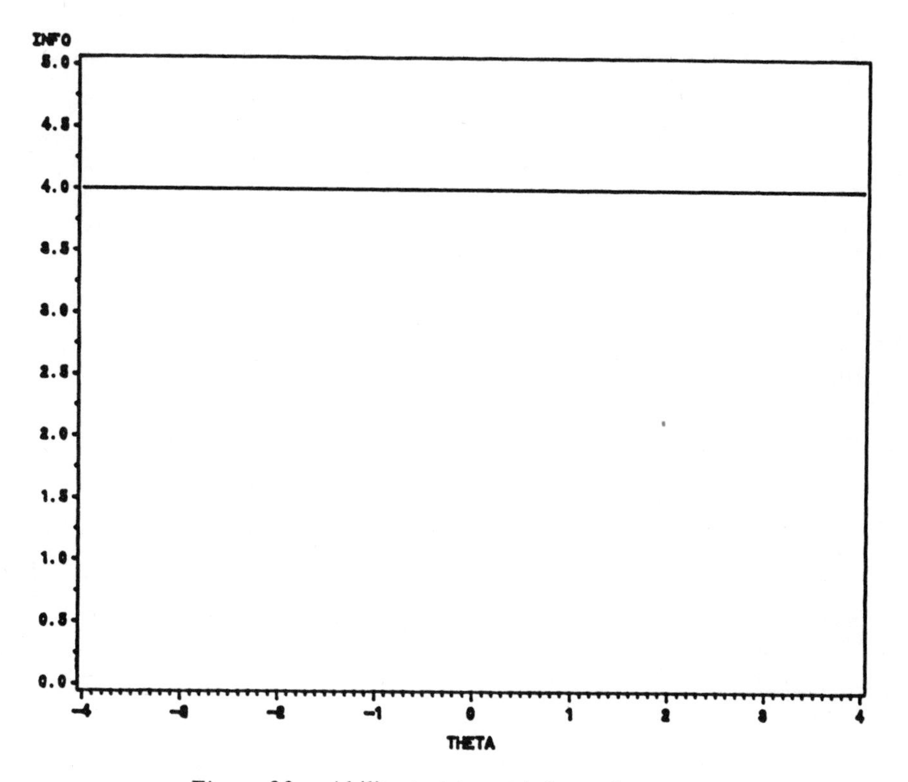

Figure 23. Ability test target information curve.

In practice, it is almost impossible to construct alternate forms that are sufficiently parallel as to yield comparable scores and, as a result, it is necessary to equate the score scales of the two forms. There are a number of procedures for equating different forms of an instrument, but they all tend to be rather complicated. Fortunately, the equating process becomes much more simple when IRT is employed.

The basic approach to IRT equating hinges on the invariance property of the model parameters. Because IRT parameters are invariant within a linear transformation, as was pointed out earlier, ability estimates for the same respondent obtained from different forms should vary only in scale. Thus, all that is necessary for equating of two forms is to find the linear transformation that places the ability estimates from the two forms on the same scale. One way this can be done is through the use of the common item data collection scheme.

In the common item data collection scheme, different forms of an instrument are constructed so as to have some items in common. The two forms are then administered to different groups of respondents, and the resulting response data are used to estimate the model parameters. This process produces two sets of

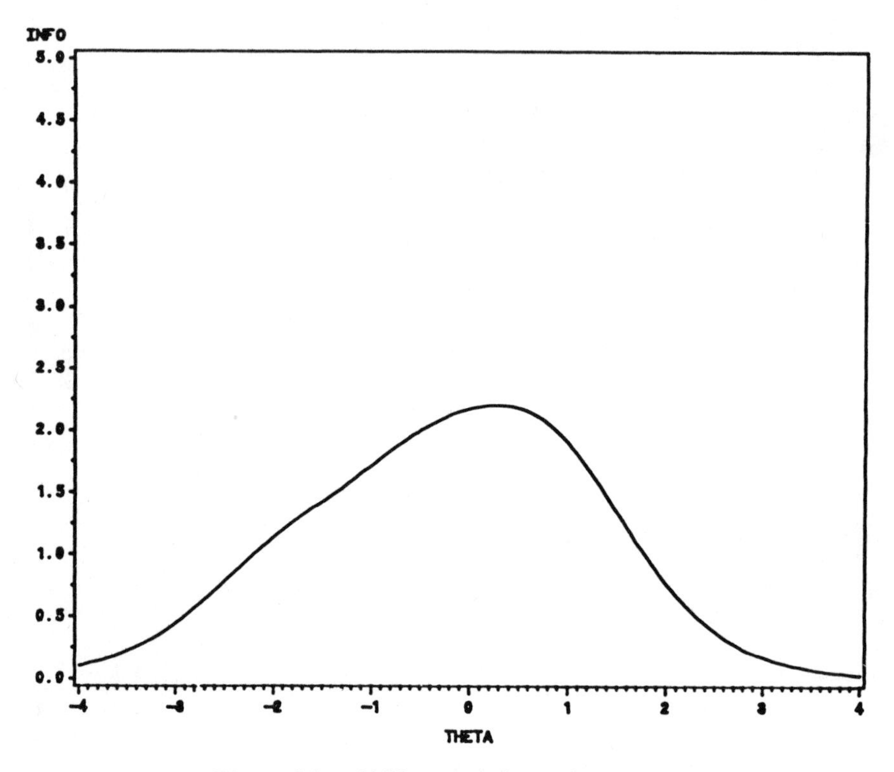

Figure 24. Ability test information curve.

item parameter estimates for some items, since they appear on both forms. If the respondent groups have identical ability distributions, the two sets of item parameter estimates will be on the same scale, and should differ only by errors in estimation. If, however, the ability distributions differ, the item parameter estimates for the common items obtained from the two groups will be on different scales. Thus, a comparison of the means and standard deviations of the two sets of b-parameter estimates for the common items provides all the information necessary for equating the two scales.

As an example, imagine that two 10-item forms of a test were constructed in such a way that there were 5 items in common to the two, and that the two forms were each administered to 500 examinees. Also imagine that the forms were calibrated using the 1PL model, resulting in the b-value estimates shown under the columns headings "Form A" and "Form B" of Table 5.

It can be seen from the table that Items 1 through 5 were unique to Form A, Items 11 through 15 were unique to Form B, and Items 6 through 10 were in common to the two forms. It can also readily be seen that the respondents who

Table 5. Hypothetical 1PL Model Calibration Results

	b-values		
Item No.	*Form A*	*Form B*	*Form B'*
1	−1.0		
2	0.5		
3	1.2		
4	0.2		
5	−0.5		
6	−1.2	−0.6	−1.2
7	−0.2	0.5	0.0
8	0.6	1.2	0.7
9	0.3	0.6	0.1
10	0.0	0.8	0.3
11		−0.5	−1.0
12		1.0	0.5
13		0.8	0.3
14		−0.6	−1.2
15		−0.4	−0.9

received Form B were of lower average ability than the group receiving Form A, as reflected in the higher b-values for the common items for Form B.

In order to equate the score scales for these two forms, it is only necessary to compute the mean and standard deviation of the b-values for each form and equate them. For Form A, the common items have a mean b-value of −0.1 and a standard deviation of 0.62. For Form B, the mean and standard deviation are 0.5 and 0.6, respectively. From these values it can be determined that, to put the two sets of b-values on the same scale, the Form B values must be transformed by multiplying them by $0.62/0.6 = 1.033$, and then adding to them $-0.01\text{-}1.033\,(0.5) = -0.5265$. The same transformation is applied to all of the Form B b-values, not just those for the common items. This produces the values in Table 5 under the column heading "Form B'", which are the Form B item parameters on the Form A scale. This same transformation would then be used to scale the Form B ability estimates.

The equating procedure just described is called the major axis method of common item equating. Another simple approach, called the least squares approach, involves computing the least squares regression line for predicting the Form A b-values from the Form B b-values using only the common items. This regression equation would then be used to scale the Form B b-values, and the same transformation would be applied to the Form B θ estimates.

A third equating procedure, the maximum likelihood procedure, is more complex, and requires the use of special parameter estimation programs. Essentially, this involves the simultaneous calibration of the two forms in a single computer run. This is accomplished by coding Items 1 through 5 as "not reached" for the Form B examinees, and coding Items 11 through 15 as "not reached" for the Form A examinees. This simultaneous calibration automatically places the item parameter estimates, and therefore the ability estimates, for the two forms on the same scale using the information from the items in common to the two forms, but requires the use of a computer program that handles the "not reached" coding. At present, the most popular program for this type of equating is the LOGIST program (Wingersky, Barton, & Lord, 1982).

Finally, an equating procedure growing in popularity is the true score method (Lord, 1980). In this procedure, which actually equates raw scores rather than ability estimates, the TCC for Form A is used to determine what value of θ yields an estimated true score equal to each possible raw score. Then, for each value of θ obtained in this way, the estimated true score on Form B is computed. Since the estimated true score for Form B is computed from the same θ that yielded the corresponding raw score on Form A, the two scores are said to be equated. Of course, this requires that item parameters for the two forms be on the same scale.

In order to illustrate this procedure, consider the Form A and transformed Form B b-values in Table 5. Table 6 shows the values of θ that yield the 11 raw scores possible on the 10 items of Form A. For raw scores of 0 and 10 no estimate of θ was available, so the value was arbitrarily set to -9.0 and 9.0. No estimate could be obtained for these two scores because 0 and 10 are the asymptotes of the TCC—it literally would require infinitely low and infinitely high ability to reach these scores on the TCC. That is not to say it would require infinite ability to get a raw score of 10. It just means that a true score of 10 would never be predicted from the model for less than infinite ability.

Table 6. True Score Equating of Form B to Form A

Form A Raw Score		*Form B True Score*
0	−9.00	0
1	−1.62	1
2	−1.05	3
3	−0.65	4
4	−0.31	5
5	0.00	6
6	0.31	7
7	0.64	8
8	1.02	9
9	1.57	9
10	9.00	10

Although the θ-values reported in Table 6 could have been read, though somewhat less accurately, from the TCC, in actuality they were computed using the EQUTAU program (McKinley, 1986). This program uses a maximum likelihood estimation procedure to estimate the value of θ that maximizes the probability of obtaining a particular raw score on an instrument given the item parameter estimates.

Adaptive Testing

Adaptive testing was designed to overcome some of the problems encountered with more conventional, paper-and-pencil tests. This is accomplished by "adapting" the test to the individual in such a way that the individual receives only those items most appropriate for someone at that individual's ability level. Of course, the same principle applies to measurement of attitudes or opinions.

The first attempts at developing adaptive testing procedures utilized traditional item and test statistics, such as item-total correlations and proportion-correct item difficulties. However, the procedures developed using these statistics were only partially successful. The real power of adaptive testing was not realized until IRT-based procedures were developed.

The first step in adaptive testing is to develop and pretest a large number of items—the number required will vary depending on the nature of the test and the application. In order to pretest the items, a relatively large sample of respondents should be used, and they should not differ much from the population for which the testing is intended, since the purpose of pretesting is to obtain accurate estimates of the item parameters. The pretest data are then analyzed to obtain item parameter estimates for each item for an IRT model. These items and their item parameter estimates comprise what is known as the item bank.

Using the item bank, the test for a given individual is constructed interactively on a computer terminal or a microcomputer. This is accomplished by selecting, during the administration of the test, only items that are most appropriate for someone of the individual's estimated ability. For example, if the 1PL model is used, only items with b-values close to the individual's ability estimate are selected for administration. Prior to the administration of the first item, an initial guess as to the respondent's ability is made. After the individual responds to an item, the item is scored by the computer, and the item score is used to update the estimate of the examinee's ability. The next item is then selected for administration by matching item b-values to the updated ability estimate.

Figure 25 illustrates the adaptive testing strategy just described. This type of plot is called a convergence plot, since it illustrates how the testing procedure converges on a final ability estimate. As can be seen, the horizontal axis is the number of the item (whether it was the first item administered, the second, and so forth), while the vertical axis is the ability estimate after a given item is administered. The horizontal line halfway up the vertical axis represents the

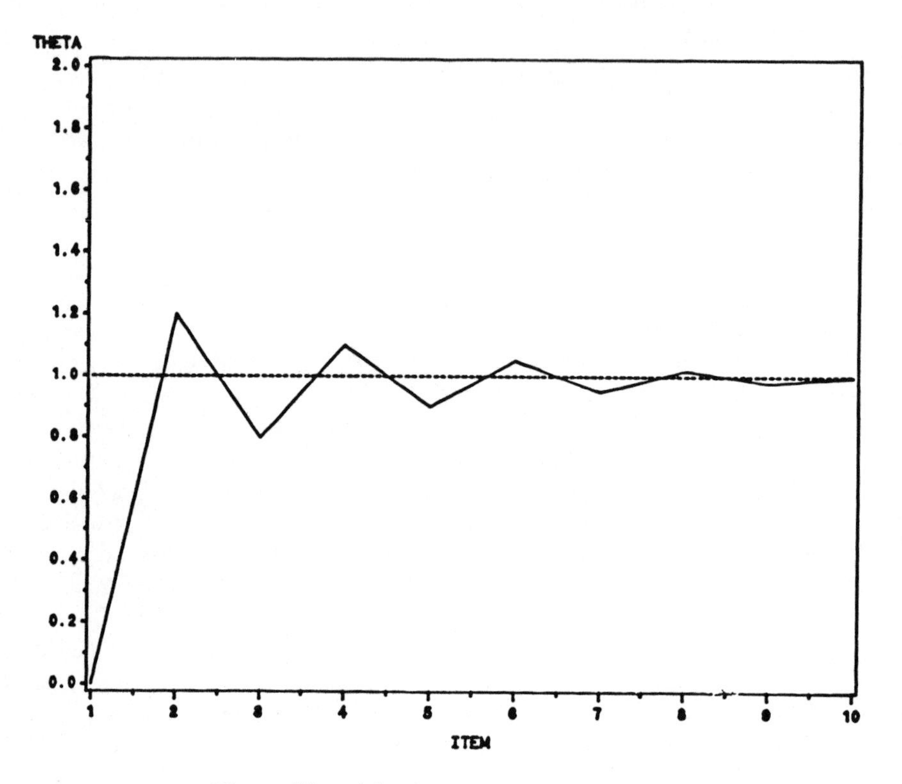

Figure 25. Adaptive test convergence plot.

examinee's true ability. The jagged line traces the pattern of ability estimates obtained for the examinee as the test progresses.

Figure 25 indicates that the initial estimate of ability, which was little more than a guess, was too low—the examinee's true ability was much higher. As a consequence, the first item administered was too easy, and the examinee responded correctly to it. On the basis of the examinee's correct response, the estimate of ability was increased. The second item selected for administration, then, was more difficult than the first item.

As indicated by the figure, the second item administered was, in fact, too difficult—the updated ability estimate was too high. As a result, the examinee responded incorrectly to the second item. This produced a third estimate of ability which was between the first and second estimates. This process continued for ten items, at which point there was a negligible change in the ability estimate from one item to the next. At this point, the testing session was terminated.

TESTING IRT ASSUMPTIONS

The use of most IRT methodology requires some rather strong assumptions about the nature of the response data. Among these are the assumption of unidimensionality, and the assumption that the item-trait relationship can be adequately described using the particular model selected for use. Because these assumptions are often not met in practice, it is essential that, prior to or during the application of IRT methods, these assumption be examined. In this section, a procedure for testing unidimensionality and two procedures for evaluating the adequacy of the model will be presented.

Unidimensionality

Probably the soundest approach to testing the assumption of unidimensionality is through the application of principal components analysis. If the response data are unidimensional, then a principal components analysis of the inter-item correlation matrix ought to yield one large eigenvalue. The other eigenvalues should all be quite small, and all of about the same magnitude.

Unfortunately, even tests which should be highly unidimensional seldom are. Instead of the pattern described above, what is typically obtained from the principal components analysis is one moderate-size eigenvalue, one or two somewhat smaller eigenvalues, and a number of very small, equal-size eigenvalues. This is due to several causes, including spurious components produced by reduced inter-item correlations due to guessing, differences in item thresholds, nonlinearity, and item ambiguity.

Fortunately, a number of research studies have found that IRT models are fairly robust with respect to the violation of the assumption of unidimensionality. That is to say, as long as the data are at least approximately unidimensional, no major problems are encountered when applying IRT methodology. Studies suggest that, in order for IRT to be appropriate, the first principal component should account for at least 30 to 40 percent of the total variance.

As a consequence, the choice usually confronting the prospective IRT user is not whether the data are unidimensional, but whether the data are close enough to being unidimensional. The presence of several minor components can be tolerated as long as they do not represent important psychological variables, and as long as the first component is sufficiently large.

One common approach to evaluating the results of a principal components analysis is to construct a ''scree'' plot. In a scree plot, eigenvalues are plotted against their corresponding component number. For instance, the first eigenvalue is plotted against the number 1, the second eigenvalue is plotted against the number 2, and so on. Such a plot is illustrated in Figure 26. The values plotted in Figure 26 are shown in Table 7.

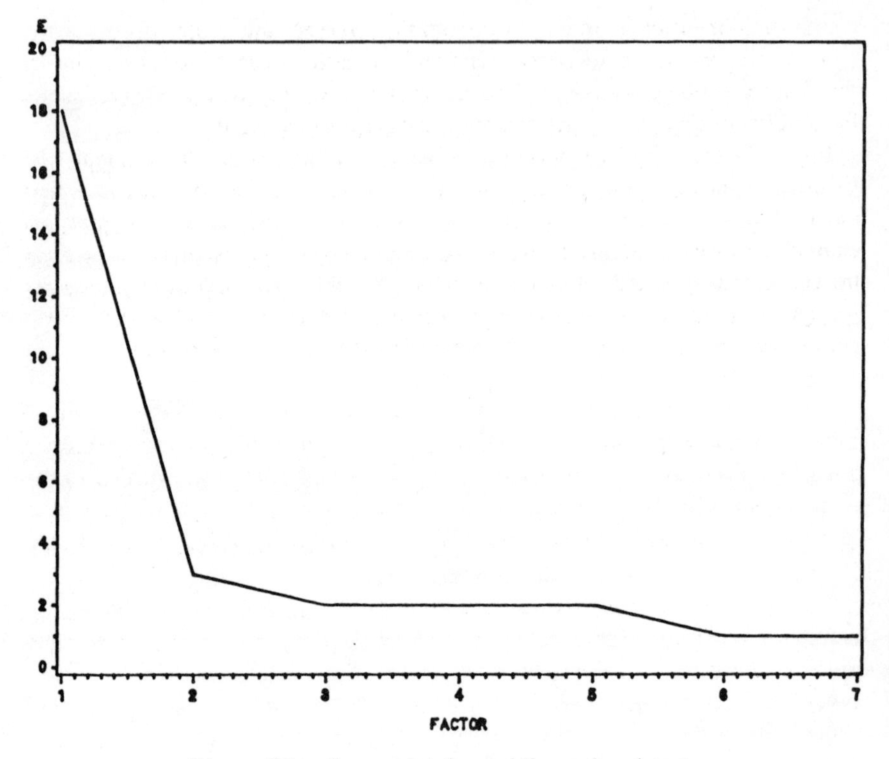

Figure 26. Scree plot for unidimensional test.

The results of the principal components analysis reported in Table 7 and Figure 26 indicate that the test is relatively unidimensional. Note that the scree plot falls quite rapidly from the first to second component, and then quickly levels off. This "elbow" is a fairly good indicator of the number of meaningful components. A simple procedure for determining whether the data are suffi-

Table 7. Eigenvalues from a Principal Components Analysis

Component	*Eigenvalue*	*Percent of Variance*
1	18.0	36.0
2	3.0	12.0
3	2.0	8.0
4	2.0	8.0
5	2.0	8.0
6	1.0	4.0
7	1.0	4.0

ciently unidimensional, then, is to determine whether this elbow occurs at the second component. Another approach that is sometimes used is to form a ratio of the first to second eigenvalues. The larger the ratio, the more evidence there is for unidimensionality. In this example, the ratio has a value of 6.

Figure 27 shows a scree plot for a test which is much less unidimensional. The values plotted in Figure 27 are shown in Table 8. As can be seen, the first eigenvalue is of the same magnitude as was the first eigenvalue in the previous example. However, in this example, the second eigenvalue is almost as large as the first eigenvalue, indicating that there are probably two important components present in the data. The elbow in the scree plot does not occur at the second component, but at the third, and the ratio of the first to second eigenvalue is only 1.2.

Before leaving this topic, a couple of important caveats regarding the use of principal components analysis to test the IRT unidimensionality assumption for binary data should be mentioned. The first of these regards the selection of the correlation coefficient to be used as input into the analysis. Common practice is to use Pearson product-moment correlations. However, if the data are binary, the

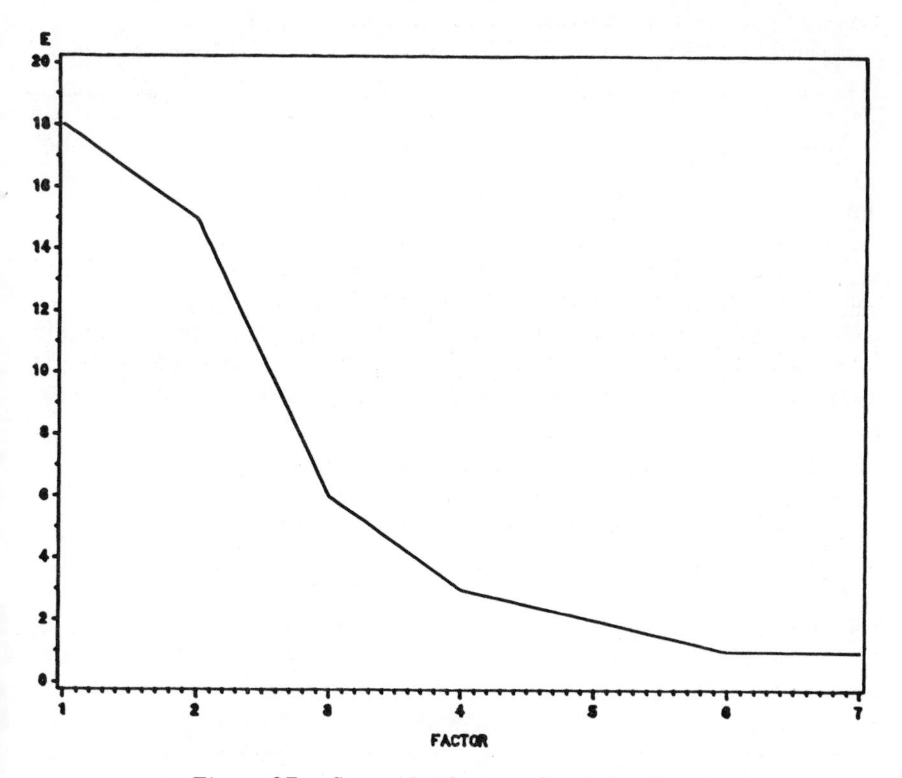

Figure 27. Scree plot for two-dimensional test.

Table 8. Eigenvalues of a Multidimensional Test

Component	*Eigenvalue*	*Percent of Variance*
1	18.0	36.0
2	15.0	30.0
3	6.0	12.0
4	3.0	6.0
5	2.0	4.0
6	1.0	2.0
7	1.0	2.0

Pearson correlation does not have a theoretical maximum value of 1.0 unless the two items for which the correlation is computed have the same proportion-correct scores. Because of this, the inter-item correlations will all be artificially reduced to the extent that items vary in difficulty and, as a result, the first principal component will be reduced. The variance lost from the first component typically shows up as a difficulty component. It is important to recognize that this component is a statistical artifact, and that it does not represent a meaningful psychological variable.

Some people try to avoid the interpretations caused by spurious difficulty components by using tetrachoric correlations, which are not subject to the same difficulty effects as Pearson correlations. This procedure sometimes is successful. However, frequently tetrachoric correlation matrices do not meet all the requirements for principal components analysis, resulting in such nonsensical outcomes as negative eigenvalues. Since eigenvalues are essentially variances, it is clearly nonsensical to have a negative value for an eigenvalue. Thus, the tetrachoric correlation approach is often not satisfactory. At present, the best approach is probably to perform the analysis using tetrachoric correlations if possible. If not, then use Pearson correlations, but examine the results to see if any important components appear to be related to item difficulty. If so, then discount that component.

Another important caveat regards the problem of guessing in true-false and multiple-choice items. Guessing has the effect of reducing the magnitude of the correlation between items, since it is, for all practical purposes, a random event. This is not to suggest that respondents guess at random. Rather, it is to point out that, to the extent that responses don't follow the patterns predicted by the principal components model, which contains no guessing parameter, error is introduced into the data.

Because guessing reduces inter-item correlations, the first component is again artificially reduced. Unlike the item difficulty problem just discussed, however, guessing rarely shows up as a separate component. Instead, it just reduces the magnitude of the larger eigenvalues.

It has been suggested that this problem can be corrected by correcting the two-way contingency table from which each correlation is computed. This could be done by assuming some constant value for the probability of guessing, and using this value to predict the number of respondents that would be in each cell of the contingency table had there been no guessing. This approach sounds promising, but research suggests it has certain serious pitfalls. One of the most serious problems with this approach is that there is no way to know what value to use for the guessing constant. It seems clear from the research that over-corrections, assuming too large of a value for guessing, is a more serious problem than the problem it is attempting to cure. On the other hand, under-corrections appear to do very little good. All things considered, if a correction for guessing is used, it seems to be better to under-correct than to over-correct.

Goodness-of-Fit

As important as the unidimensionality assumption is the assumption that the particular form of the model selected provides a reasonable description of the item-trait interaction. Even the more complex models, such as the three-parameter logistic and normal ogive models, occasionally do not provide a reasonable description of the data, due to problems such as nonmonotonicity, and the simpler models, especially the Rasch model, frequently prove to be inadequate. Thus, it is very important that the goodness-of-fit of the model to the data be examined. This can and should be done in two ways—a test of item fit, and a test of person fit.

Item Fit

One of the most commonly used methods of assessing item fit is a procedure proposed by Yen (1981). This method is essentially an application of the Pearson chi-square statistic to a two-way contingency table formed by cross-classifying examinees on the basis of whether or not they got an item correct, and on the basis of ability level. This is accomplished by first sorting respondents into categories formed by dividing the θ-scale into intervals. Intervals are formed so that roughly the same number of respondents fall into each. Typically ten categories are used, resulting in a 10 by 2 contingency table (10 θ categories, 2 item response categories).

Once the respondents have been sorted into the 20 cells of the table, the expected and observed proportion-correct score for each cell is computed. Observed proportions are computed by simply counting the number of respondents in each cell getting the item correct, and dividing by the number of respondents in the cell. The expected proportion correct for a given item and a given cell is obtained by computing the average probability of a correct response for the respondents in that cell. That is, for each respondent in the cell, the probability of a correct response is computed from the IRT model by substituting the item parameter estimates for the item and the θ estimate for the respondent into the model. These probabilities are then summed over respondents, and the sum is divided by the number of respondents in the cell.

Once the expected and observed proportions are obtained for each cell, they are input into the Pearson chi-square statistic formula. The resulting statistic can be tested for significance using a chi-square table and 10-m degrees of freedom, where m is the number of item parameters estimated (1 for the Rasch model, 2 for the 2PL model, and 3 for the 3PL model). If the statistics obtained in this way are tested for significance using a Type I error rate of 0.05, then it would be expected that roughly five percent of the items on given instrument will have significant chi-squares. If the obtained percentage doesn't deviate substantially from this, then it can be assumed that the model yields adequate item fit.

Another popular procedure for evaluating the goodness-of-fit of an IRT model to data is the item-ability regression plot. In this procedure, the item parameter estimates for a given item are used to compute and plot the ICC. Then, on the same set of axes, the empirical ICC is plotted. The empirical ICC is computed by dividing the θ-scale into intervals, sorting examinees into the intervals using their ability estimates, and computing for each interval the proportion of correct

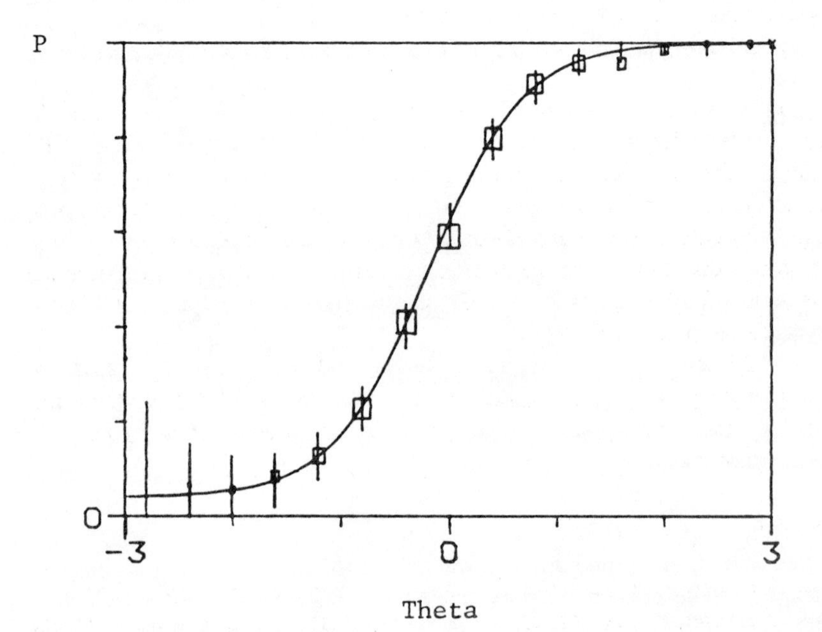

Figure 28. Item-ability regression plot showing good fit.

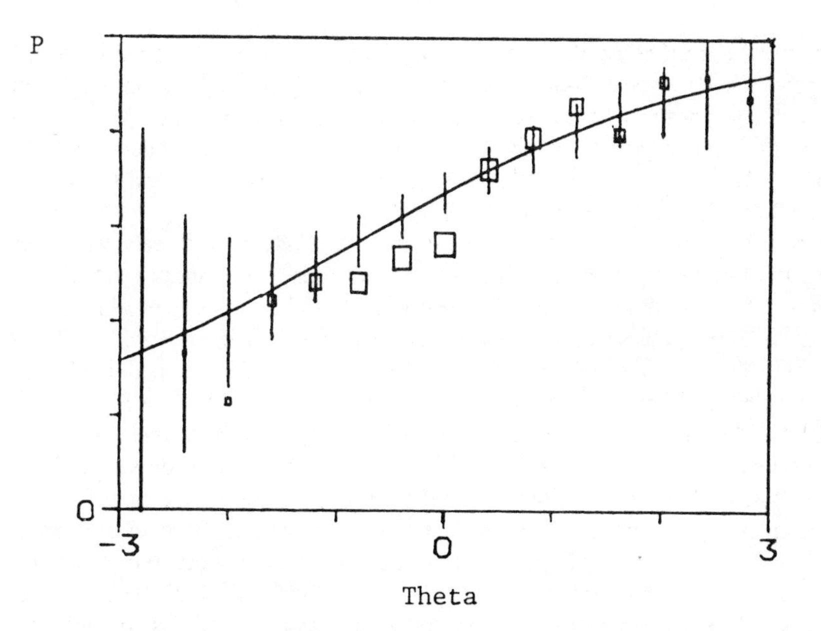

Figure 29. Item-ability regression plot showing poor fit.

responses to an item by the examinees in that interval. Thus, the empirical ICC is an empirical verification of the predictions made using the ICC computed from the model.

Figure 28 shows an item-ability regression plot for an item for which the model yielded adequate fit. The boxes represent the proportion of correct responses for the examinees in a particular interval. The size of the box is proportional to the number of examinees in the interval, and the vertical lines crossing the ICC at regular intervals are related to the standard error of a proportion from the binomial distribution. Notice that for this item all of the boxes fall within the limits defined by the vertical lines, indicating that for this item the model yielded fairly accurate predictions.

Figure 29 shows an item-ability regression plot for an item for which the model yielded poor fit. Notice that several of the boxes fall outside the limits defined by the vertical slashes. For this item, the model did not yield very accurate predictions.

Person Fit

Assessing person fit is often called appropriateness measurement. In appropriateness measurement, an attempt is made to evaluate, for each respondent, the adequacy of the IRT model as a description of that respondent's item scores. This can be done in many different ways. The procedure described here represents one of the more promising approaches.

In this procedure, the probability of a correct response is computed for each respondent for each item by inserting the item and person parameter estimates into the model. Then, for a given respondent, the likelihood of the observed responses is computed by multiplying together the individual item probabilities. For a correct response, the item probability is simply the probability computed from the model. For an incorrect response, the item probability is 1.0 minus the probability of a correct response. Once the likelihood of the set of observed responses is computed, it is standardized by subtracting its expected value and dividing the result by the theoretical standard deviation.

The statistic which results from this has a distribution which is approximately standard normal. Thus, to test whether the model fits, the probability of the obtained value of the statistic can be determined by using a table of the standard normal distribution and compared to some critical value.

FUTURE DIRECTIONS

Microcomputers

Until recently, one of the greatest limitations on the use of IRT methodology has been the need for access to a mainframe computer. However, with the advent of relatively high speed microcomputers, the process of converting IRT methods to microcomputer form has begun. Already, numerous estimation programs for the microcomputer are available for simpler models such as the 1PL model. Some programs for micros are even available already for more complex models, although the processing time for these programs is still prohibitive.

Perhaps equally important, with the increased memory and storage capacities of the new generation of micros, it is now possible to store and process on micros the large amounts of data necessary for applications of IRT such as adaptive testing and equating. Work has even begun on microcomputer test development systems.

Nonlinear Factor Analysis

It was pointed out in a previous section that the principal components analysis approach to testing the IRT assumption of unidimensionality had several serious flaws. The good news is that it looks like there may be help on the horizon in the form of nonlinear factor analysis. Recent work in this area has progressed rapidly, and it appears that, in the near future, workable procedures for performing nonlinear factor analysis will be available. This promises to be a valuable contribution to the field of IRT, and in fact will be a valuable contribution to the entire field of measurement.

Dynamic Testing

One of the greatest criticisms of the field of testing today is that it is relatively disconnected from the field of psychology. Nowhere is this more evident than in the field of achievement testing and the measurement of change. Very little progress has been made in the past century in the area of measuring change, despite the development of numerous psychological models of learning and change. One reason for this regards the instability of the structure of achievement tests when learning is occurring.

Both classical test theory and IRT assume that we know the structure of the test, and that we can count on it being stable. However, it is beyond doubt that learning on the part of respondents can change the nature of the psychological variables being measured. Consider, for example, the case of the pretest-posttest paradigm for measuring learning in a mathematics course. When a pretest is administered to novice respondents, responding tends to be a function of prior experience, general aptitude, guessing, and a host of other variables. However, on the posttest, responses will, with any luck, primarily be a function of the learning that took place in the classroom. Clearly the nature of the variables being measured has changed.

This change in the nature of the variables being measured poses an almost insurmountable measurement problem. It is necessary to somehow measure change on a variable, while at the same time taking into account the changes that occur in the nature of the variable itself. Until recently little progress has been made in tackling this problem.

Recently, however, there have been some important developments in IRT that may provide a solution to this dilemma. With the advent of multidimensional IRT, which will be discussed in the next portion of this section, it may now be possible to simultaneously model respondent behavior on the pretest and the posttest, while also accounting for the differences in the contributions to performance of the various latent traits.

In what would perhaps be an even more important development, it may soon be possible to assess the learning process itself through the use of the dynamic testing paradigm. By breaking items into a series of related subtasks, and administering different combinations of the subtasks in conjunction with instruction, it will be possible to quickly identify and address stumbling blocks in the learning process. This type of dynamic testing would provide not only a powerful measurement tool, but also a powerful learning and instructional tool.

Multidimensional Models

It has been pointed out a number of times that most IRT methodology requires the assumption of undimensionality. It has also been indicated on several occasions that very many times the assumption of unidimensionality is unreasonable. In those cases, the researcher has the choice of not using IRT, using IRT and hoping the procedures are sufficiently robust with respect to the violation of the unidimensionality assumption, or using a multidimensional IRT, or MIRT, model.

Up until this point very little has been said about multidimensional models, primarily because MIRT is still in its infancy. Few of the procedures for multidimensional models have been extensively investigated, and much of the technology for applying the procedures (such as equating techniques) are as yet undeveloped. However, there has been a growing interest in the area of MIRT in recent years, and work has begun on the development of procedures for applying MIRT models. It appears as though it will not be long before MIRT models will begin to take a more prominent role in both research and production.

Most of the recent progress in MIRT research has occurred in two areas—the development of a multidimensional two-parameter normal ogive nonlinear factor analysis model (Bock, Gibbons, & Muraki, 1985), and the development of multidimensional two- and three-parameter logistic IRT models (McKinley, 1983, 1987). Work on these procedures is still at an early stage, but has progressed to the point that estimation procedures are available. For the nonlinear factor analysis procedure, the TESTFACT program (Wilson, Wood, & Gibbons, 1984) is available. For the two-parameter logistic IRT model, the MAXLOG program (McKinley & Reckase, 1983) is available, and for the three-parameter model the MULTIDIM program (McKinley, 1987) is available.

To briefly introduce the reader to MIRT, consider the case of a test which measures two traits. For example, imagine a math test which contains some purely computational items, and some word problems. In all likelihood, such a test would measure at least two dimensions—math computation skills, and reading comprehension skills. Since the word problems measure both sets of skills, it is impossible to sort the items into unidimensional subsets. Thus, the only way in which IRT can be used with such a test is to model both dimensions simultaneously.

Figure 2 showed an ICC for modeling respondent performance on a single dimension. In two dimensions, the curve shown in Figure 2 would become a surface, such as is shown in Figure 30. This surface is obtained by plotting the probability of a correct response as a function of two variables, math ability, and reading comprehension ability, using the two-parameter logistic MIRT model.

As can be seen, the monotonicity property still holds. The surface rises as ability increases on either dimension. However, there is no longer a single point of inflection. Rather, there is a line across the surface where it intersects a horizontal plane at $P = 0.5$. In addition, it is no longer reasonable to consider the slope of the surface at a particular point. There are innumerable slopes at any point, depending on the direction traveled.

In a test with three components, the surface shown in Figure 30 would have to be extended to include an additional dimension. Such a figure, needless to say, cannot be represented in a two-dimensional drawing. It also seems clear at this

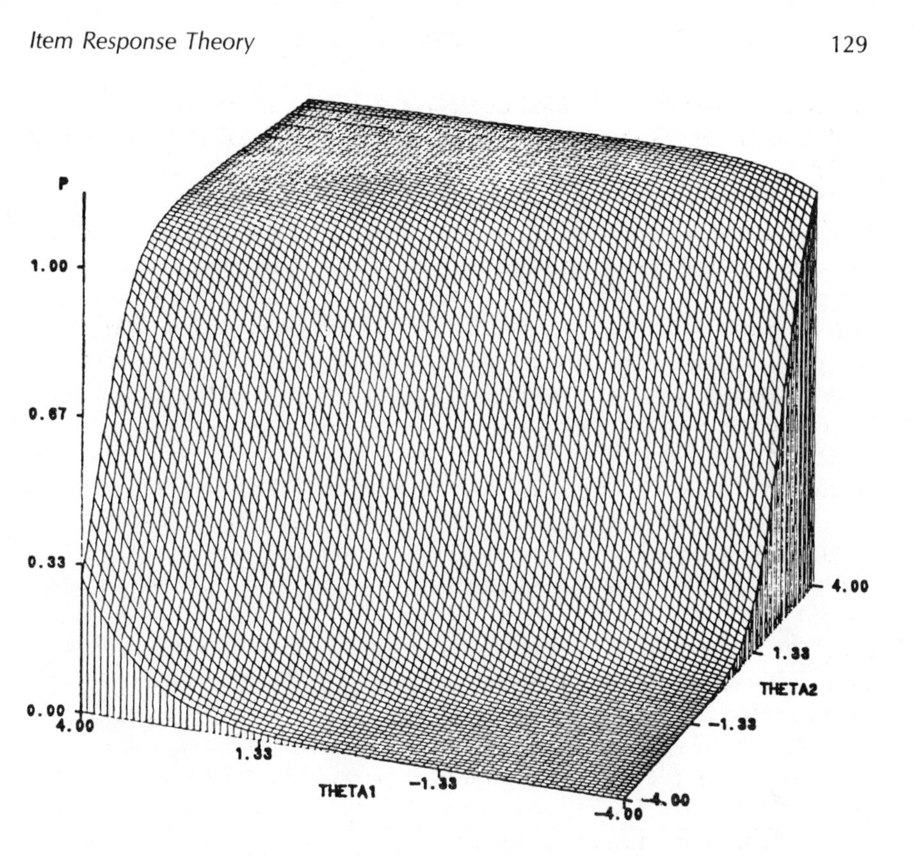

Figure 30. Multidimensional item response surface.

point that virtually all IRT concepts become increasingly complex and difficult to interpret as dimensionality increases. As a result, work on this model and similar models has progressed rather slowly. However, as indicated earlier, the work does seem to be accelerating, and soon procedures which can be used operationally may be available.

REFERENCES

Bock, R. D., & Mislevy, R. J. (1982). *BILOG: Maximum likelihood item analysis and test scoring: Binary logistic models.* Chicago: International Educational Resources, Inc.

Bock, R. D., Gibbons, R., & Muraki, E. (1985). *Full information factor analysis.* MRC Report 85-1. Chicago: National Opinion Research Center.

Guttman, L. L. (1950). The basis for scalogram analysis. In S. A. Stouffer, et al. (Eds.), *Measurement and prediction.* Princeton, NJ: Princeton University Press.

Kolakowski, D., & Bock, R. D. (1973). *LOGOG: Maximum likelihood item analysis and test scoring: Logistic model for multiple item responses.* Ann Arbor, MI: National Educational Resources, Inc.

Likert, R. (1932). A technique for the measurement of attitudes. *Archives of Psychology, 140,* 44–53.

Magnussen, D. (1966). *Introduction to test theory.* Reading, MA: Addison-Wesley.

McKinley, R. L. (1987). *MULTIDIM user's guide.* Princeton, NJ: Educational Testing Service.

McKinley, R. L. (1986). MARGIE: Marginal maximum likelihood estimation of the parameters of the one-, two-, and three-parameter logistic models. *Behavior Research Methods, Instruments, & Computers, 17,* 513–515.

McKinley, R. L. (1986). *EQUTAU: IRT true score equating.* Princeton, NJ: Educational Testing Service.

McKinley, R. L. (1983, April). *A multidimensional extension of the two-parameter logistic latent trait model.* Paper presented at the annual meeting of the National Council on Measurement in Education, Montreal.

McKinley, R. L. (1982). *PARTIAL: Maximum likelihood estimation of the parameters of the Rasch partial credit model.* Iowa City: American College Testing Program.

McKinley, R. L., & Reckase, M. D. (1983). MAXLOG: A computer program for the estimation of the parameters of a multi-dimensional logistic model. *Behavior Research Methods & Instrumentation, 15,* 389–390.

Thurstone, L. L. (1927). Psychophysical analysis. *American Journal of Psychology, 38,* 368–389.

Wilson, D., Wood, R., & Gibbons, R. (1984). *TESTFACT user's guide.* Mooresville, IN: Scientific Software.

Wingersky, M. S. (1983). LOGIST: A program for computing maximum likelihood procedures for logistic test models. In R. K. Hambleton (Ed.), *Applications of item response theory.* Vancouver: Educational Research Institute of British Columbia.

Wingersky, M. S., Barton, M. A., & Lord, F. M. (1982). *LOGIST user's guide.* Princeton, NJ: Educational Testing Service.

Wright, B. D., & Mead, R. J. (1977). *BICAL: Calibrating items and scales with the Rasch model.* Research Memorandum No. 23A. Chicago: Statistical Laboratory, Department of Education, University of Chicago.

Wright, B. D., & Stone, M. H. (1979). *Best test design.* Chicago: MESA.

Yen, W. M. (1981). Using simulation results to choose a latent trait model. *Applied Psychological Measurement, 5,* 245–262.

READINGS

Adaptive Testing

Jensema, C. J. (1974). The validity of Bayesian tailored testing. *Educational and Psychological Measurement, 34,* 757–766.

Jensema, C. J. (1977). Bayesian tailored testing and the influence of item bank characteristics. *Applied Psychological Measurement, 1,* 111–120.

McBride, J. R. (1976). *Research on adaptive testing, 1973–1976: A review of the literature.* Unpublished paper, University of Minnesota.

McKinley, R. L., & Reckase, M. D. (1984, April). *An evaluation of one- and three-parameter logistic tailored testing procedures for use with small item pools.* Paper presented at the annual meeting of the National Council on Measurement in Education, New Orleans.

McKinley, R. L., & Reckase, M. D. (1981, June). *A comparison of a Bayesian and a maximum likelihood tailored testing procedure* (Research Report 81–2). Columbia, MO: University of Missouri.

McKinley, R. L., & Reckase, M. D. (1980, April). *A successful application of latent trait theory to tailored achievement testing*. Paper presented at the annual meeting of the National Council on Measurement in Education, Boston.

McKinley, R. L., & Reckase, M. D. (1980). Computer applications to ability testing. *AEDS Journal, 13,* 193–203.

Urry, V. W. (1977). A successful application of latent trait theory. *Journal of Educational Measurement, 14,* 181–196.

Urry, V. W. (1983). *Tailored testing theory and practice: A basic model, normal ogive submodels, and tailored testing algorithms* (Report NPRDC TR 83-32). San Diego: Navy Personnel Research and Development Center.

Vale, C. D. (1981). Design and implementation of a micro-computer-based adaptive testing system. *Behavior Research Methods and Instrumentation, 13,* 399–406.

Weiss, D. J. (1974). *Strategies of adaptive ability measurement* (Research Report 74-5). Minneapolis: University of Minnesota.

Weiss, D. J. (1982). Improving measurement quality and efficiency with adaptive testing. *Applied Psychological Measurement, 6,* 379–396.

Weiss, D. J. (1983). *Computer-based measurement of intellectual capabilities* (Final Report). Minneapolis: University of Minnesota.

Appropriateness Measurement

Birenbaum, M., and Tatsuoka, K. K. (1980). *The use of information from wrong responses in measuring students' achievement* (Research Report 80-1). Urbana: University of Illinois.

Birenbaum, M., & Tatsuoka, K. K. (1983). The effect of a scoring system based on the algorithm underlying the students' response patterns on the dimensionality of achievement test data of the problem solving type. *Journal of Educational Measurement, 20,* 17–26.

Donlon, T. F., & Fischer, F. E. (1968). An index of an individual's agreement with group determined item difficulties. *Educational and Psychological Measurement, 28,* 105–113.

Drasgow, F. (1982). Choice of test model for appropriateness measurement. *Applied Psychological Measurement, 6,* 297–308.

Drasgow, F., & Levine, M. L. (1981). *Appropriateness measurement*. Paper presented at the ONR Contractor's meeting, Memphis.

Fischer, F. E. (1970). Some properties of the personal biserial index. *Journal of Educational Measurement, 7,* 275–277.

Harnisch, D. L., & Linn, R. L. (1981). Analysis of item response patterns: Questionable test data and dissimilar curriculum practices. *Journal of Educational Measurement, 18,* 133–146.

Harnisch, D. L., & Linn, R. L. (1982). *Identification of aberrant response patterns in a test of mathematics*. Paper presented at the annual meeting of the American Educational Research Association, New York.

Levine, M. V., & Rubin, D. B. (1979). Measuring the appropriateness of multiple-choice test scores. *Journal of Educational Statistics, 4,* 269–290.

Tatsuoka, K. K., & Linn, R. L. (1983). Indices for detecting unusual response patterns: Links between two general approaches and potential applications. *Applied Psychological Measurement, 7,* 81–96.

Tatsuoka, K. K., & Tatsuoka, M. M. (1982). Detection of aberrant response patterns. *Journal of Educational Statistics, 7,* 215–232.

Wright, B. D. (1977). Solving measurement problems with the Rasch model. *Journal of Educational Measurement, 14,* 97–116.

Dynamic Testing

Babad, E. Y., & Budoff, M. (1974). Sensitivity and validity of training-potential measurement in three levels of ability. *Journal of Educational Psychology, 66,* 439–447.

Carlson, J. S., & Weidl, K. H. (1979). Toward a differential testing approach: Testing-the-limits employing the Raven's matrices. *Intelligence, 3,* 323–344.

Embretson, S. (1986). *Improving the measurement of spatial ability by a dynamic testing procedure.* Paper presented at the annual meeting of the American Educational Research Association, San Francisco.

Embretson, S. (in press). The psychometrics of dynamic testing. In C. D. Lidz (Ed.), *Dynamic testing.* Beverly Hills, CA: Guilford Press.

Feuerstein, R. (1979). *The dynamic assessment of retarded performers: The learning potential assessment device, theory, instruments and techniques.* Baltimore: University Park Press.

Effects of Guessing

Carroll, J. B. (1945). The effect of difficulty and chance success on correlations between items or between tests. *Psychometrika, 10,* 1–19.

Mattson, D. (1965). The effects of guessing on the standard error of measurement and the reliability of test scores. *Educational and Psychological Measurement, 25,* 727–730.

Plumlee, L. B. (1954). The predicted and observed effect of chance success on multiple-choice test validity. *Psychometrika, 19,* 65–70.

Reckase, M. D. (1981). *The formation of homogeneous item sets when guessing is a factor in item responses* (Research Report 81–5). Columbia, MO: University of Missouri.

Equating

Angoff, W. H. (1984). *Scales, norms, and equivalent scores.* Princeton, NJ: Educational Testing Service.

Braun, H. I., & Holland, P. W. (1982). Observed test score equating: A mathematical analysis of some ETS equating procedures. In P. W. Holland & D. B. Rubin (Eds.), *Test equating.* New York: Academic Press.

Gulliksen, H. (1950). *Theory of mental tests.* New York: John Wiley & Sons.

Hicks, M. H. (1983). True score equating by fixed b's scaling: A flexible and stable equating alternative. *Applied Psychological Measurement, 7,* 255–266.

Levine, R. S. (1955). *Equating the score scales of alternate forms administered to samples of different ability.* ETS Research Bulletin No. 23. Princeton, NJ: Educational Testing Service.

Lord, F. M. (1980). *Applications of item response theory to practical testing problems.* Hillsdale, NJ: Lawrence Erlbaum Associates.

Marco, G. L. (1977). Item characteristic curve solutions to three intractable testing problems. *Journal of Educational Measurement, 14,* 139–160.

Stocking, M. L., & Lord, F. M. (1982). *Developing a common metric in item response theory* (RR-82-25-ONR). Princeton, NJ: Educational Testing Service.

Estimation

Andersen, E. B. (1972). The numerical solution of a set of conditional estimation equations. *Journal of the Royal Statistical Society, Series B, 34,* 42–54.

Bock, R. D., & Aitkin, M. (1981). Marginal maximum likelihood estimation of item parameters: An application of the EM algorithm. *Psychometrika, 46,* 443–460.

McKinley, R. L. (1985). MARGIE: Marginal maximum likelihood estimation of the parameters of the one-, two-, and three-parameter logistic models. *Behavior Research Methods, Instruments, and Computers, 17,* 513–514.

McKinley, R. L., & Reckase, M. D. (1983). MAXLOG: A computer program for estimating the parameters of a multi-dimensional extension of the two-parameter logistic model. *Behavior Research Methods and Instrumentation, 15,* 389–390.

McKinley, R. L., & Reckase, M. D. (1981). A comparison of the ANCILLES and LOGIST parameter estimation procedures for the three-parameter logistic model using goodness of fit as a criterion. *Catalog of Selected Documents in Psychology, 11,* 75. Ms. 2351.

Swaminathan, H. (1983). Parameter estimation in item response models. In R. K. Hambleton (Ed.), *Applications of item response theory.* Vancouver: Educational Research Institute of British Columbia.

Swaminathan, H., & Gifford, J. A. (1986). Bayesian estimation in the three-parameter logistic model. *Psychometrika, 51,* 589–602.

Thissen, D. B. (1982). Marginal maximum likelihood estimation for the one-parameter logistic model. *Psychometrika, 47,* 175–186.

Wainer, H., & Wright, B. D. (1980). Robust estimation of ability in the Rasch model. *Psychometrika, 45,* 373–391.

Wingersky, M. S. (1983). LOGIST: A program for computing maximum likelihood procedures for logistic models. In R. K. Hambleton (Ed.), *Applications of item response theory.* Vancouver: Educational Research Institute of British Columbia.

Wright, B. D., & Mead, R. J. (1977). *BICAL: Calibrating items and scales with the Rasch model* (Research Memorandum No. 23). Chicago: University of Chicago.

Wright, B. D., & Panchapakesan, N. (1969). A procedure for sample-free item analysis. *Educational and Psychological Measurement, 29,* 23–48.

Wright, B. D., & Stone, M. H. (1979). *Best test design.* Chicago: MESA Press.

Goodness-of-Fit

Hambleton, R. K., & Murray, L. (1983). Some goodness of fit investigations for item response models. In R. K. Hambleton (Ed.), *Applications of item response theory.* Vancouver: Educational Research Institute of British Columbia.

Kingston, N. M., & Dorans, N. J. (1985). The analysis of item-ability regressions: An exploratory IRT model fit tool. *Applied Psychological Measurement, 9,* 281–288.

McKinley, R. L., & Mills, C. N. (1985). A comparison of several goodness of fit statistics. *Applied Psychological Measurement, 9,* 49–57.

Mills, C. N., & McKinley, R. L. (1984, April). *An investigation of the adequacy of several goodness of fit statistics.* Paper presented at the annual meeting of the National Council on Measurement in Education, New Orleans.

Yen, W. M. (1981). Using simulation results to choose a latent trait model. *Applied Psychological Measurement, 5,* 245–262.

Item Response Theory

Hulin, C. L., Drasgow, F., & Parsons, C. K. (1983). *Item response theory: Application to Psychological Measurement.* Homewood, IL: Dow Jones-Irwin.

Lord, F. M. (1980). *Applications of item response theory to practical testing problems.* Hillsdale, NJ: Lawrence Erlbaum Associates.

Lord, F. M., & Novick, M. R. (1968). *Statistical theories of mental test scores.* Reading, MA: Addison-Wesley.

Multidimensional IRT

McDonald, R. P. (1982, July). *Unidimensional and multidimensional models for item response theory.* Paper presented at the 1982 Item Response Theory/Adaptive Testing Conference, Wyzata, Minnesota.

McKinley, R. L., & Reckase, M. D. (1984, May). *An investigation of the effect of correlated abilities on observed test characteristics* (Research Report ONR84-1). Iowa City: The American College Testing Program.

McKinley, R. L., & Reckase, M. D. (1983, August). *An extension of the two-parameter logistic model to the multidimensional latent space* (Research Report ONR83-2). Iowa City: The American College Testing Program.

McKinley, R. L., & Reckase, M. D. (1982, August). *The use of the general Rasch model with multidimensional item response data* (Research Report ONR82-1). Iowa City: The American College Testing Program.

Mulaik, S. A. (1972). *A mathematical investigation of some multidimensional Rasch models for psychological tests.* Paper presented at the annual meeting of the Psychometric Society, Princeton.

Reckase, M. D., & McKinley, R. L. (1984, June). *Multidimensional difficulty as a direction and a distance.* Paper presented at the annual meeting of the Psychometric Society, Santa Barbara.

Reckase, M. D., & McKinley, R. L. (1983, June). *The item difficulty concept generalized to the multidimensional latent space.* Paper presented at the annual meeting of the Psychometric Society, Los Angeles.

Reckase, M. D., & McKinley, R. L. (1983, April). *The definition of difficulty and discrimination for multidimensional latent trait models.* Paper presented at the annual meeting of the American Educational Research Association, Montreal.

Reckase, M. D., & McKinley, R. L. (1982, August). *The feasibility of a multidimensional latent trait model.* Paper presented at the annual meeting of the American Psychological Association, Washington, D.C.

Reckase, M. D., & McKinley, R. L. (1982, July). *Some latent trait theory in a multidimensional latent space.* Paper presented at the 1982 Item Response Theory/Computerized Adaptive Testing Conference, Wyzata, Minnesota.

Rasch, G. (1960). *Probabilistic models for some intelligence and attainment tests.* Copenhagen: Danish Institute for Educational Research.

Samejima, F. (1974). Normal ogive model on the continuous response level in the multidimensional latent space. *Psychometrika, 39,* 111–121.

Sympson, J. B. (1978). A model for testing with multidimensional items. In D. J. Weiss (Ed.), *Proceedings of the 1977 Computerized Adaptive Testing Conference.* Minneapolis: University of Minnesota.

Nonlinear Factor Analysis

Bock, R. D., Gibbons, R., & Muraki, E. (1985, August). *Full-information factor analysis.* MRC Report 85-1. Chicago: National Opinion Research Center.

Christoffersson, A. (1975). Factor analysis of dichotomized variables. *Psychometrika, 40,* 5–32.

McDonald, R. P. (1967). *Nonlinear factor analysis.* Psychometric Monograph.

Muthen, B. (1978). Contributions to factor analysis of dichotomous variables. *Psychometrika, 43,* 551–560.

Wilson, D., Wood, R., & Gibbons, R. (1984). *TESTFACT user's guide.* Mooresville, IN: Scientific Software.

Polychotomous Models

Andrich, D. (1978). A rating formulation for ordered response categories. *Psychometrika, 43,* 561–573.

Andrich, D. (1982). An extension of the Rasch model for ratings providing both location and dispersion parameters. *Psychometrika, 47,* 105–113.

Andrich, D. (1985). An elaboration of Guttman scaling with Rasch models for measurement. In N. Brandon-Tuma (Ed.), *Sociological methodology.* San Francisco: Jossey-Bass.

Bock, R. D. (1972). Estimating item parameters and latent ability when responses are scored in two or more nominal categories. *Psychometrika, 37,* 29–51.

Masters, G. N. (1982). A Rasch model for partial credit scoring. *Psychometrika, 47,* 149–174.

Samejima, F. (1969). Estimation of latent ability using a response pattern of graded scores. *Psychometrika Monograph No. 17.*

Sympson, J. B. (1986). *Extracting information from wrong answers in computerized adaptive testing.* Paper presented at the annual meeting of the American Psychological Association, Washington, D.C.

Testing IRT Assumptions

Divgi, D. (1980, April). *Dimensionality of binary items: Use of mixed models.* Paper presented at the annual meeting of the National Council on Measurement in Education, Boston.

McKinley, R. L., & Mills, C. N. (1985, March). *Detecting multidimensionality using a test of local independence.* Paper presented at the annual meeting of the National Council on Measurement in Education, Chicago.

McKinley, R. L., & Mills, C. N. (1984, June). *The use of analysis of residuals to assess the unidimensionality of data.* Paper presented at the annual meeting of the Psychometric Society, Santa Barbara.

Reckase, M. D. (1977). *Ability estimation and item calibration using the one and three parameter logistic models: A comparative study* (Research Report 77-1). Columbia, MO: University of Missouri.

Stout, W. F. (1984, June). *The statistical assessment of latent trait dimensionality in psychological testing* (Final Report). Urbana: University of Illinois.

Tucker, L. R., Humphreys, L. G., & Roznowski, M. A. (1986). *Comparative accuracy of five indices of dimensionality of binary items* (Technical Report No. 1). Urbana: University of Illinois.

ELEMENTS OF CLASSICAL RELIABILITY THEORY AND GENERALIZABILITY THEORY

James Algina

In general terms, the purpose of this chapter is to present selected elements of generalizability theory, a theory that guides the selection of appropriate reliability coefficients for designs for collecting test-score data. Here the term "test" is used in the broad sense of a systematic procedure for observing a sample of a person's behavior and describing it with the aid of a numerical scale. Thus, test refers to procedures such as observational schedules as well as to procedures such as multiple choice tests and attitude questionnaires.

The chapter has four major sections. The first introduces classical test theory as a point of comparison for generalizability theory. The second points out why classical reliability theory provides a basis for selection of reliability coefficients in only a narrow range of situations. The third is an overview of generalizability theory for single-facet and two-facet designs. The fourth discusses estimation of generalizality coefficients. Because of space limitations, several topics in generalizability theory are not discussed in the present chapter. These are the definition and use of standard errors of measurement, the formulation and use of predicted universe scores, and multivariate generalizability theory.

The development of generalizability theory has largely been due to Cronbach and his colleagues (Cronbach, Gleser, & Rajaratnam, 1963; Gleser, Cronbach,

Advances in Social Science Methodology, Volume 1, pages 137–169.

ISBN: 0-89232-736-7

& Rajaratnam, 1965; Rajaratnam, 1960; Rajaratnam, Cronbach & Gleser, 1965). This work culminated in the book, "The dependability of behavioral measurements: Theory of generalizability for scores and profiles" (Cronbach, Gleser, Nanda, & Rajaratnam, 1972), the most complete statement, to date, of generalizability theory. Cronbach and his colleagues, as they acknowledge, drew upon and extended the work of earlier psychometricians. Chief among these were Burt (1955), Ebel (1951), Finlayson (1951), Hoyt (1941), Lindquist (1953), Lord (1955a, 1955b), Medley, Mitzel and Doi (1956), and Medley and Mitzel (1963).

Since the publication of Cronbach et al. (1972) several expositions of selected aspects of generalizability theory have been published in journals (Algina, 1978; Shavelson & Webb, 1981; Shrout & Fleiss, 1979) and books (Brennan & Kane, 1979; Crocker & Algina, 1985, chap. 8; Gillmore, 1983; Thorndike, 1982, chap. 6; van der Kamp, 1976). Fryans (1985) published an edited volume on generalizability theory. Brennan (1983) published a monograph that is more complete than the expository pieces listed previously.

Much of the original work on generalizability theory, that has appeared since 1972, has focused on applying generalizability theory to problems other than estimating reliability of scores on individual examinees: applying generalizability theory to objects of measurement other than people (Cardinet, Tourneur, & Allal, 1976, 1981), formulation of estimation of reliability coefficients for class means (Kane & Brennan, 1977; Kane, Gillmore, & Crooks, 1976) and sampling models for validity (Kane, 1982). In addition, Brennan and his colleagues (Brennan, 1980; Brennan & Kane, 1977a, 1977b) have discussed the application of generalizability theory to formulating and estimating reliability coefficients for criterion-referenced tests.

CLASSICAL RELIABILITY THEORY

In this section certain aspects of classical reliability theory are briefly presented. The purpose is to provide a point of comparison for generalizability theory. In essence generalizability theory is a generalization of classical reliability theory. The importance of the generalization is that it permits the formulation of reliability coefficients, called generalizability coefficients in generalizability theory, that are applicable in a wider range of measurement situations than the classical reliability coefficient. A more detailed comparison is presented in the chapter section entitled "Why is Generalizability Theory Necessary?"

The particular purposes in this section are four-fold: to define the true score and error score concepts of classical reliability theory; to formulate the classical true-score model; to define the classical reliability coefficient; and to present several methods for estimating the classical reliability coefficient. In pursuing the last purpose, we present several methods that use the analysis of variance (ANOVA) to estimate variance components. It is probably true that none of these estimation procedures is widely used at present; we present them to emphasize the point that it is not the focus on variance components nor the estimation procedure that distinguishes generalizability and classical reliability theory. It is true that generalizability coefficients are typically estimated using variance components. However, classical reliability coefficients can, and probably should be estimated using such methods. The principal distinction between the two theories is the breadth of applicability of the theories.

The Classical True-Score Model and Reliability Coefficient

In this section the approach of Lord and Novick (1968) to the construction of the classical true score model is adopted. In this approach, which was originally presented by Novick (1966), the observed score for an examinee is considered a realization of a random variable—loosely speaking, a variable that takes on its values according to a set of probabilities—defined for that particular examinee and test. The justification for the random-variable characterization of the examinee's observed score is as follows. The score an examinee receives on a test is clearly only one of several that the examinee might have received. Consider, for example, an examinee about to take a cognitive test. The score the examinee eventually receives will be affected by factors such as fatigue, guessing, momentary fluctuations in attention, memory and motivation, and the like. Consequently, just prior to the time the examinee takes the test, we can conceive of the examinee as having several potential scores that will occur according to an unknown set of probabilities, that is, as a random variable. Lord and Novick (1968) refer to an examinee's distribution of potential scores as a propensity distribution. In Table 1, propensity distributions are illustrated for three hypothetical examinees.

The true score for a particular examinee is defined as the expected value of the examinee's propensity distribution. That is, the true score for the pth examinee on test i is defined as

$$T_{pi} = \epsilon(X_{pi})$$

where $\epsilon(\ )$ denotes the expectation operator. The true scores for the three examinees are displayed at the bottom of Table 1. For the pth examinee on the ith test the error score random variable is defined as

$$E_{pi} = X_{pi} - T_{pi}$$

The distributions associated with the error score random variables for the three examinees are presented in Table 2.

The observed and error score random variables defined above are not the random variables of primary interest in applications of classical test theory. Rather, the observed score random variable of primary interest is the marginal X random variable, that is, the random variable defined over all the potential observed scores for all examinees in the population. Treating the hypothetical

Table 1. Propensity Distributions for Three Hypothetical Examinees

	Examinee		
Test Score	*1*	2	3
0			.10
1			.20
2		.05	.40
3		.10	.20
4		.20	.10
5		.30	
6	.10	.20	
7	.20	.10	
8	.40	.05	
9	.20		
10	.10		
True Score	8	5	2

examinees in Table 1 as the population of interest, the marginal probability of a particular test score is the average of the probabilities that the three examinees have for that test score. For example, the marginal probability of a score of 2 is $1/3(.00 + .05 + .40) = .15$. Similarly, the error score random variable of primary interest is defined over all potential error scores for all examinees in the population. The true score random variable is defined over all examinees in the population. These three random variables are related by the classical true-score model

$$X = T + E$$

As a consequence of the construction of the random variables T and E, $\rho_{TE} = 0$. Hence,

$$\sigma_X^2 = \sigma_T^2 + \sigma_E^2$$

Table 2. Error-Score Distributions for Three Hypothetical Examinees

	Examinee		
Test Score	*1*	2	3
−3		.05	
−2	.10	.10	.10
−1	.20	.20	.20
0	.40	.30	.40
1	.20	.20	.20
2	.10	.10	.10
3		.05	

The reliability of a particular test can be defined as the squared correlation between X and T. It can be shown that

$$\rho_{XT}^2 = \frac{\sigma_T^2}{\sigma_X^2} = 1 - \frac{\sigma_E^2}{\sigma_X^2} \tag{1}$$

Alternatively, reliability can simply be defined as the ratio σ_T^2/σ_X^2.

Reliability Estimation Using Two or More Tests

Defining the reliability coefficient as ρ_{XT}^2 emphasizes that the coefficient provides information about the degree to which individual differences on X provide information about individual differences on T. The closer ρ_{XT}^2 is to one the more confident one can be that decisions or data analyses based on individual differences in X will be similar to those that would have been made on T. However, because T is an unobservable random variable, defining reliability as ρ_{XT}^2 does not provide a method for estimating reliability. This problem is solved by assuming a second test form, X′, on which each examinee has the same propensity distribution as he or she had on X. Thus $T = T'$. The measurements obtained using such test forms are called parallel measurements. The correlation between X and X′ is

$$\rho_{XX'} = \frac{\sigma_{TT'} + \sigma_{TE'} + \sigma_{T'E} + \sigma_{EE'}}{\sigma_X \sigma_{X'}}$$

Because of the assumption that an examinee has equal propensity distributions on X and X′ and because of the construction of T and T′ it can be shown that $\sigma_{TT'} = \sigma_T^2 = \sigma_{T'}^2$, $\sigma_X^2 = \sigma_{X'}^2$ and that $\sigma_{TE'} = \sigma_{T'E} = 0$. Upon making the additional assumption that for each examinee E and E′ are uncorrelated, we find

$$\rho_{XX'} = \frac{\sigma_T^2}{\sigma_X^2} = \frac{\sigma_{T'}^2}{\sigma_{X'}^2}$$

Consequently if two test forms that are parallel can be identified, there is a way to estimate the reliability of both X and X′.

If two test forms yield parallel measurements then ρ_{XT}^2 can be estimated by admimistering the tests to a sample of examinees and calculating $\hat{\rho}_{XX'}$, the Pearson product moment correlation between scores on X and X′. An alternative procedure is to treat the data as arising from an examinee-by-forms two-factor design. A two-way ANOVA is conducted and the resulting mean squares are used to estimate the variance components, σ_T^2 and σ_E^2. The estimated variance components are then substituted in

$$\rho_{XT}^2 = \frac{\sigma_T^2}{\sigma_T^2 + \sigma_E^2} \tag{2}$$

Table 3. Computational Formulas and Expected Mean Squares for a Two-Factor ANOVA of Scores on Parallel Tests

SV	*df*	*SS*	*MS*	*EMS*
Persons (p)	$n_p - 1$	$n_p\Sigma(X_{p_p^F} - X_{PF})_2$	$SS_p/(n_p - 1)$	$\sigma_E{}^2 + n_p\sigma_T{}^2$
Forms (f)	$n_f - 1$	$n_f\Sigma(X_{P_f^f} - X_{PF})^2$	$SS_p/(n_f - 1)$	$\sigma_E{}^2$
Residual (r)	$(n_f - 1)(n_p - 1)$	$\Sigma\Sigma(X_{pf} - X_{PF})^2 - SS_P - SS_i$	$SS_r/(n_p - 1)(n_f - 1)$	$\sigma_E{}^2$

Table 3 displays the computational formulas and expected mean squares (EMS) on which the variance-components estimation for parallel forms is based. The degrees of freedom for forms and the residual are shown for the general case of n_f, rather than two, parallel test forms. In the formulas for sums of squares, X_{pf} denotes the score of examinee p on form f, X_{Pf} denotes the mean score on form f, X_{pF} denotes the mean score for examinee p across the n_f forms and X_{PF} denotes the mean of all $n_p n_f$ scores earned by all n_p examinees on all n_f forms. The EMS for forms does not include a component due to variation in test means because parallel tests have equal population means. Using the EMS it can be shown that

$$\sigma^2{}_E = \frac{(n_p - 1)(n_f - 1)EMS_r + (n_f - 1)EMS_f}{n_p(n_f - 1)}$$

and

$$\sigma_T{}^2 = (EMS_p - \sigma_E{}^2)/n_f$$

By substituting mean squares (MSs) for EMSs, equations for calculating $\hat{\sigma}_E{}^2$ and $\hat{\sigma}_T{}^2$ are obtained. These estimates can then be substituted in (1).

In the event that X and X′ are not parallel, the EMS in Table 3 are no longer correct. The appropriate EMSs are presented in the section on generalizability theory. For the present purposes, note only that when X and X′ are not parallel, MS_r is an estimate of a variance component $\sigma_e{}^2$ which is larger than $\sigma_E{}^2$. Consequently, a lower bound to $\rho_{XT}{}^2$ can be estimated by using $1 - \hat{\sigma}_e{}^2/\hat{\sigma}_X{}^2$. In this expression $\hat{\sigma}_e{}^2 = MS_r$ and $\hat{\sigma}_X{}^2$ is sample observed score variance on test X.

Reliability Estimation Using a Single Form

The theory developed above is sometimes impractical to apply because there is only a single form available. In this case it is still possible to estimate reliability provided that the forms can be divided into separately scoreable parts such that when the subpart scores are added up the total score on the test is obtained. Usually this is accomplished by dividing the test items in half and scoring each half, or by scoring each item.

There is an extensive literature on methods for estimating reliability from a single test. However, it is probably fair to say that two methods are in principal use today. In the first, scores on separate halves (A and B) of the test are correlated to obtain $\hat{\rho}_{AB}$. This correlation is then adjusted because it is a correlation between half-length tests. The adjustment is accomplished using the Spearman-Brown prophecy formula

$$\hat{\rho}_{SB} = \frac{2\hat{\rho}_{AB}}{1 + \hat{\rho}_{AB}}$$

If the half tests are parallel, $\hat{\rho}_{SB}$ is an estimate of ρ_{XT}^2. If not, it is an estimate of a lower bound to ρ_{XT}^2. A second common procedure is equivalent to treating the subpart scores as arising from an examinee by subpart factorial design. The subparts may be based on any division of the test into equal parts, including dividing the tests into items. The following function of the MSs is then calculated.

$$\hat{\alpha} = \frac{(MS_p - MS_r)}{MS_r}$$

This procedure was developed by Hoyt (1941). The coefficient is denoted as α because coefficient α (Cronbach, 1951) can also be applied to such subpart scores scores and yields the same results as Hoyt's procedure. KR-20, developed by Kuder and Richardson (1937), can only be applied to dichotomously scored subparts, and yields the same result as Hoyt's procedure applied to dichotomously scored data. It is well known that $\hat{\alpha}$ is an estimate of ρ_{XT}^2 if all the subparts yield parallel measurements. Otherwise it is an estimate of a lower bound to ρ_{XT}^2.

WHY IS GENERALIZABILITY THEORY NECESSARY?

In the example introducing the propensity distribution, sources of variation included variables such as fatigue, guessing, and momentary fluctuations in attention, memory and state of motivation. These variables are all largely beyond the control of the test user and thus are bound to operate both within a particular testing situation and across testing situations. (Here and throughout this discussion the term control is used as it is used in experimental design.) While the test user will be interested in how these uncontrollable variables affect test-score reliability, the test user is also likely to be interested in how factors such as the following affect reliability: form-to-form content variation that is consistent with the test blueprint; variations in the occasion of testing; variation in the test administrator; and, in an essay test, variation in the graders. When a test user is interested in how a controllable factor affects reliability, is the classical reliability coefficient an appropriate coefficient?

To put the question in a different form, do the construction of a linear model and the formulation of a reliability coefficient appropriate in this situation result in a coefficient that is equivalent to the classical reliability coefficient? To answer this question, consider a concrete example. Suppose several forms of a test exist and the test user is interested in how reliable test scores are over the forms. Each examinee can be thought of as having a propensity distribution for each form. If the propensity distributions for a particular examinee are the same across forms, and if this situation obtains for every examinee in the population, then all forms of the test are parallel and the classical reliability coefficient provides the necessary information about test reliability. In this situation, all forms yield parallel measurements and the classical reliability coefficient has the same numeric value for each form. Further, the methods outlined in the preceding two sections can be used to estimate the coefficient.

Does the classical reliability coefficient provide the necessary information when the forms are not parallel? The answer is a qualified yes. It depends on the design for collecting the test-score data. When multiple test forms are available, but only a single form will be administered to each examinee, there are two basic designs for collecting the test-score data. In the first, every examinee is administered the same test, whereas in the second, the test form is randomly chosen for every examinee. The coefficient that is appropriate for the second design is equivalent to the classical reliability coefficient. (However, it should be estimated by the variance-component procedure described earlier or, equivalently, by the variance-component estimation procedure described subsequently for the i:p design.) One of two alternatives to the classical reliability coefficient is required for the first design, with the correct alternative depending, in part, on the test users' conceptualization of the design and, in part, on the number of available test forms. The formulation and estimation of the appropriate coefficients will be discussed in more depth in the section on generalizability theory. It can be shown that the classical reliability coefficient is not equivalent to either of the appropriate coefficients but rather is a special case of each coefficient.

Many test users will be interested in how two or more controllable factors affect test score reliability. For example, in standardized testing programs the reliability of test scores (a) over forms within an occasion; (b) over occasions for a single form; and (c) over both occasions and forms, is of interest. Similarly, in essay testing the individual and joint effects of topics and graders on score reliability is frequently of interest. In situations such as these, the classical reliability coefficient provides the appropriate information if all condition combinations result in parallel measurements. That failing, the classical reliability coefficient is appropriate for only one of the many designs that can be used to collect the test score data. Generalizability theory indicates the correct coefficient for a wide variety of designs. As importantly, generalizability theory leads to an error-variance decomposition that can be very valuable in planning a study with adequate test-score generalizability.

FORMULATION OF GENERALIZABILITY COEFFICIENTS

The section presents procedures for formulating generalizability coefficients and illustrates the procedures for a limited number of situations. There are actually two different kinds of generalizability coefficients: a coefficient for a specific measurement condition and a coefficient for a randomly chosen condition. The formulation of latter type of coefficient is of primary interest here. Before turning to this discussion, however, it is necessary to present some terminology.

Terminology

In generalizability theory, a distinction is made between a decision (D) study and a generalizability (G) study. A D-study is designed for the purposes of investigating a research question, evaluating a program, or making a decision about individuals. A G-study is designed to investigate the generalizability of a measurement procedure. Its purpose is to aid in the design of a D-study that will yield scores that have satisfactory generalizability. In principle, an investigator should establish the generalizability of the measurement procedure prior to using it in a D-study. For example, the designer of an investigation of correlates of children's behavior observed in classrooms (a D-study) should first conduct a G-study to insure that the observational design will yield scores with adequate generalizability. In practice test-score generalizability is frequently investigated by using the D-study data. However, this practice should be avoided when possible.

An investigator conducting a D-study will typically want to generalize the results to a wider set of measurement conditions than those used in the D-study. This wider set of conditions is called the universe of generalization. For example, when an achievement test is used as a criterion measure in the study of competing mathematics curricula, the researcher's universe of generalization might consist of all the mathematics achievement tests that could be constructed from the test plan for the test actually used in the study.

A set of measurement conditions is called a measurement facet. In the example of the investigation of competing curricula there is a single facet: mathematics achievement tests (consistent with the test plan for the test used in the study). In a study in which several raters will rate managers on several dimensions of manager-employee relationships there will be at least two facets: raters and dimensions of manager-employee relationships.

In the typical application of generalizability theory the purpose is to measure a sample from a population of people. However, as noted in the introduction some authors have applied generalizability theory in other contexts. Consequently, it may be more appropriate to speak of objects of measurement rather than of people. Also, although Cronbach et al. (1972) do not use the word facet to refer to persons or objects of measurement, here occasionally reference is made to the persons facet or to the objects of measurement facet.

An important step in fomulating a generalizability coefficient is to specify the structure of the universe of generalization. This involves specifying the crossing and nesting relationships among the measurement facets and whether each facet is crossed with or nested within the objects of measurement facet. Two facets are said to be crossed in the universe of generalization if every condition of the first facet can occur in combination with every condition of the second facet. In the example of the rating of managers on several dimensions of manager-employee relationships, the measurement facets would be crossed if every rater has the requisite background to rate each manager on every dimension. For a test in which the items are clustered into content categories, the universe of generalization would also have two facets: content categories and test items. However, in this case items are not crossed with content categories, rather items are nested within content categories. Facets can be either crossed with or nested within the objects of measurement, although usually facets are crossed with the objects of measurement facet.

A facet may have a finite or an infinite number of conditions. Further, a finite facet may be fixed or random. A facet is fixed if all conditions, comprising the facet, will be present in the D-study. Otherwise, the facet is random. We shall not consider random finite facets in this chapter. Random finite facets are discussed by Brennan (1980, chap. 5). An infinite facet, of course, can only be random. To illustrate, in the investigation of manager-employee relations the researcher may wish to generalize to all raters who might have been used in the study but only to the particular dimensions rated in the study. If so, raters would be considered random and dimensions would be considered fixed.

A researcher conducting a G-study must select particular conditions for the study. Typically the conditions appearing in the G-study will represent a more extensive set of conditions called the universe of admissable observations. When the universe of admissable observations is identical to or includes the universe of generalization, the results of the G-story may be useful for estimating generalizability coefficients for the D-study designs the investigator has in mind. However, if the universe of admissable observation excludes one or more facets that define the universe of generalization or has a facet defined more narrowly than it is defined in the universe of generalization, then the results of the G-study cannot be used to forecast the generalizability of the data that will be collected in the D-study.

Single-Facet Universes and D-Study Designs

Single-Facet Universes of Generalization

Formulating a generalizability coefficient first involves specifying the structure of the universe of generalization by completing the following steps:

1. Specify the facets in the universe of generalization.
2. For each facet, state whether it contains a finite or infinite number of conditions.
3. State the crossing and nesting relationships among the measurement facets and between the measurement facets and the objects of measurement facet.

To illustrate these steps, consider a psychologist who is constructing a fear of negative evaluation (FNE) scale that will consist of items describing evaluative situations. The response format will be true-false, with true indicating the examinee is concerned about negative evaluation in the situation. Suppose, for the sake of illustration, the psychologist believes FNE is a generalized trait. Thus, his universe of generalization has a single facet: evaluation situations. The psychologist also feels that the number of possible evaluation situations is unlimited. Consequently, the psychologist specifies an infinite number of conditions for the evaluation-situations facet. Moreover, because the psychologist views all evaluation situations in the universe as appropriate for all examinees, the evaluation situations facet is crossed with examinees, the object of measurement.

Once the structure of the universe of generalization is specified, the next step is to construct a linear model representing the universe of generalization and to decompose the total variance in the universe into its variance components. In the FNE example the linear model can be constructed as follows. First, for each potential item we postulate the classical true score model

$$X_{pi} = T_{pi} + E_{pi} \tag{3}$$

Here p is index for persons and i for conditions of the universe. Now the true-score variable, T_{pi}, is a random variable over both conditions and persons. Consequently we can take expected values over both conditions and persons. The expected value over conditions,

$$\mu_p = \epsilon_i T_{pi}$$

is called the universe score for examinee p. The expected value over persons,

$$\mu_i = \epsilon_p T_{pi}$$

is the mean for condition i. The expected value over both conditions and persons

$$\mu = \epsilon_i \epsilon_p T_{pi} = \epsilon_p \mu_p = \epsilon_i \mu_i$$

is called the grand mean. A linear model relating these three quantities to T_{pi} is

$$T_{pi} = \mu + (\mu_p - \mu) + (\mu_i - \mu) + \alpha_{pi} \tag{4}$$

The symbol α_{pi} is an interaction random variable and reflects the fact that the true scores for any two conditions are not assumed to be perfectly correlated. Substituting (4) into (3) we obtain

$$X_{pi} = \mu + (\mu_p - \mu) + (\mu_i - \mu) + \alpha_{pi} + E_{pi}$$

Because the last two terms are confounded we write $e_{pi} = \alpha_{pi} + E_{pi}$ to obtain

$$X_{pi} = \mu + (\mu_p - \mu) + (\mu_i - \mu) + e_{pi}$$

From the linear model for the universe of generalization, the variance components for the universe can be determined by taking the expected value of the squared deviation of the observed score random variable from the grand mean, $X_{pi} - \mu$ in the current example. The expected value is taken with respect to all facets in the universe and with respect to the object of measurement. In the current example we obtain

$$\begin{aligned} \epsilon_p\epsilon_i[X_{pi} - \mu]^2 &= \epsilon_p\epsilon_i[(\mu_p - \mu) + (\mu_i - \mu) + e_{pi}]^2 \\ &= \sigma_p{}^2 + \sigma_i{}^2 + \sigma_e{}^2 + \sigma_{pi} + \sigma_{pe} + \sigma_{ie} \end{aligned}$$

Because of the construction of the model, it can be shown that the covariance terms are zero (Lord & Novick, 1968, chap. 8). Consequently we obtain

$$\epsilon(X_{pi} - \mu)^2 = \sigma_p{}^2 + \sigma_i{}^2 + \sigma_e{}^2 \tag{5}$$

where $\sigma_p{}^2$ is the universe score variance, $\sigma_i{}^2$ is the variance of the condition means, and $\sigma_e{}^2$ is the residual variance.

The previous example had items as the conditions of single-facet universe of generalization. Consider a second example in which test forms comprise the conditions. A testing company has constructed one form of the ABC ethnocentrism test and views this form as a sample of one from an infinite number of forms that could be constructed. In this case the universe of generalization has a single facet, test forms, with an infinite number of conditions. Consequently the universe of generalization is formally the same as the universe in the FNE example, with test forms replacing evaluation-situation items.

Single-Facet D-Study Designs

Following the construction of the linear model for the universe of generalization and the decomposition of the total variance in the universe, the next step in formulating the generalizability coefficient is to specify the D-study designs the investigator is interested in and, for each design, to express the expected observed-score variance in terms of the variance components for the universe of generalization. Consider the example of the investigator constructing a FNE test. In this example, the universe of generalization had one infinite facet: evaluative-situation test items. Suppose the investigator is planning to study treatments designed to affect FNE. The planned investigation is a D-study. Most likely the study will require each examinee to respond to the same set of $n_i{}'$ items sampled from the universe of generalization. This design is an example of a design in which the measurement facet is crossed with the objects of measurement facet. The design is denoted as pxi which is read p (objects of measurement facet) crossed with i (measurement facet).

In the pxi design the observed score for examinee p is the mean over the n_i' conditions in the D-study:

$$X_{pI} = \sum_{i} X_{pi}/n_{i'} \tag{6}$$

In the FNE example X_{pI} is the proportion of items the examinee marked true. The sample mean of the X_{pI} is

$$X_{PI} = \sum_{p} X_{pI}/n_p$$

and the sample variance of X_{pI} is

$$S_p^2 = \sum_{p} (X_{pI} - X_{PI})^2/(n_{p'} - 1)$$

The expected observed-score variance is the expected value of S_p^2 with the expectation taken over all sets of n_i' items that can be assembled by random sampling from the universe of generalization. By expressing X_{pI} and X_{PI} in terms of μ, $\mu_p - \mu$, $\mu_i - \mu$, and e_{pi} it can be shown that the expected observed-score variance is

$$\sigma_p^2 + \sigma_e^2/n_i' \tag{7}$$

As a second example, suppose a study of correlates of ethnocentrism is to be conducted using the single available form of the ABC ethnocentrism test. With respect to the ethnocentrism test, the design is the pxi design with $n_1' = 1$ test forms. Using (6) and (7) with $n_i' = 1$ the observed score is simply X_{pi} and the expected observed-score variance is $\sigma_p^2 + \sigma_e^2$.

Generalizability Coefficients: Single-Facet Designs

One definition of a generalizability coefficient is the ratio of universe-score variance to expected observed-score variance. Thus, using (7) the generalizability coefficient for the pxi design is

$$\rho^2 = \frac{\sigma_p^2}{\sigma_p^2 + \sigma_e^2/n_{i'}} \tag{8}$$

a coefficient appropriate for the FNE example. When $n_{i'} = 1$, as in the ethnocentrism example, the generalizability coefficient given by (8) becomes

$$\rho^2 = \frac{\sigma_p^2}{\sigma_p^2 + \sigma_e^2}$$

Denote the squared correlation between X_{pi} and μ_p, as $\rho^2(x_{pi}, \mu_p)$. This is a generalizability coefficient for the specific condition used in the D-study. It can be shown that ρ^2 is a lower bound to the expected value of $\rho^2(x_{pi}, \mu_p)$ with the expectation taken over all conditions in the universe of generalization. Consequently ρ^2 can be thought of as a generalizability coefficient for a randomly selected condition, whereas $\rho^2(X_{pi}, \mu_p)$ is a generalizability coefficient for a specific condition.

It is possible, under certain conditions, to estimate $\rho^2(x_{pi}, \mu_p)$. Cronbach et al. (1963, p. 148) and Lord and Novick (1968, pp. 209–210) present the estimation procedure. Both Cronbach et al. and Lord and Novick agree that with regard to the generalizability of scores from a single test, $\rho^2(X_{pi}, \mu_p)$ is more informative than ρ^2. However, Cronbach et al. felt that $\rho^2(X_{pi}, \mu_p)$ would be impractical to estimate. In passing we note that when $n_i' > 1$ the generalizability coefficient for the specific set of n_i' conditions can be defined as $\rho^2(X_{pI}, \mu_p)$. This coefficient can be estimated by modifying the procedures presented by Cronbach et al. and Lord and Novick.

When the D-study design is changed the appropriate generalizability coefficient also changes. This is true even if the universe of generalization is not changed. Although the following is an unlikely example, suppose that in the FNE example every examinee will be administered a different sample of n_i' items. This is an example of a design in which conditions are nested within examinees. This design is denoted by i:p, read i nested within p. With this design, the observed score will again be X_{pI} and the sample observed-score variance will be

$$\sum_{p}(X_{pI} - X_{PI})^2/(n_{p'} - 1)$$

However the expected observed-score variance is

$$\sigma_p^2 + (\sigma_i^2 + \sigma_e^2)/n_i'$$

While this can be shown formally, intuitively the σ_i^2 component is included because each examinee takes a different set of n_i' items and consequently the variance among examinees is affected by the variance among the condition means. The generalizability coefficient for the i:p design is

$$\rho^2 = \frac{\sigma_p^2}{\sigma_p^2 + (\sigma_i^2 + \sigma_e^2)/n_{i'}}$$

In the section discussing why generalizability theory is necessary, a question was raised which can be rephrased as follows: "Does classical reliability theory lead to the correct reliability coefficient when the conditions of a single-faceted universe of generalization results in nonparallel measurements?" The answer is that the resulting coefficient is correct only if the i:p design is used.

The previous example indicated that the generalizability coefficient changes when the D-study design changes. It also changes when the universe of generalization changes. Reconsider the example of the ABC ethnocentrism test. Suppose the researcher argues that although an infinite number of forms can be conceptualized, he or she is only going to use a single form of the test and consequently his or her universe of generalization has a single finite facet, test forms, that has a single condition, the form the researcher will use in the experiment. Consequently, the linear model for the universe of generalization is the classical true-score model and the appropriate generalizability coefficient is the classical reliability coefficient, σ_T^2/σ_X^2.

Two-Facet Universes and D-Study Designs

The steps in formulating generalizability coefficients are the same for two-facet universes as they were for single-facet universes of generalization. Therefore, rather than restating these steps, it may be more helpful to describe several two-facet universes of generalization, several two-facet D-study designs, and the associated universe-score and expected observed-score variance. For universe 1, a universe with two infinite facets, the linear model and the variance decomposition are discussed. For the subsequent universes only the universe-score variance is discussed. Each of these subsequent universes has a finite facet, and only the case in which the finite facet is fixed in the D-study will be considered. In this case, the universe-score variance can be expressed in terms of the variance components for the universe with infinite facets. This convention is justified in the discussion of universe 2 and adopted throughout the remainder of the chapter.

Two-Facet Universes of Generalization

Universe 1. Perhaps the most common two-facet universe of generalization has two infinite facets that are crossed with one another and with the objects of measurement. This universe is denoted by pxixj. As an example consider a situation in which the award of a history scholarship is based on an essay exam consisting of five essays, each graded by two graders. In the universe of generalization, there are two facets, essay questions and raters. Each facet is considered infinite. Assuming that all graders have the background required to grade all essay questions, graders are crossed with essay questions. Because all questions are considered appropriate for all scholarship applicants, essay questions are crossed with examinees. Finally, graders are crossed with examinees if there are no logistical problems that prevent any grader from grading any applicant's paper.

The linear model for universe 1 is

$$\begin{aligned} X_{pij} = \mu &+ (\mu_p - \mu) + (\mu_i - \mu) + (\mu_j - \mu) \\ &+ (\mu_{pi} - \mu_p - \mu_i + \mu) + (\mu_{pj} - \mu_p - \mu_j + \mu) \\ &+ (\mu_{ij} - \mu_i - \mu_j + \mu) + e_{pij} \end{aligned}$$

Here, μ is the grand mean, the first three parenthetical terms are the effects due to objects of measurement, conditions of facet i, and the conditions of facet j, respectively. The last three parenthetical terms are the pi, pj, and ij interactions, respectively, and e_{pij} is a residual. Each mean is obtained by taking the expected value of X_{pij} over the indices not appearing in the mean's subscript. For example, $\mu_p = \epsilon_i \epsilon_j X_{pij}$. The total variance in the universe is resolved into the following sum of variance components:

$$\sigma_p^2 + \sigma_i^2 + \sigma_j^2 + \sigma_{pi}^2 + \sigma_{pj}^2 + \sigma_{ij}^2 + \sigma_e^2$$

The universe-score variance is σ_p^2.

Universe 2. Another universe of generalization has one infinite facet (j) and one finite facet (i) crossed with each other and with the objects of measurement. This universe is also denoted by pxixj and has the same linear model and variance decomposition as the first universe. The example from universe 1 serves here if the scholarship committee does not want to generalize beyond the five questions that appear on the test.

When a facet is finite in the universe of generalization, it may be fixed or random in the D-study. In the remainder of the chapter the former situation is assumed. To indicate that the facet will be fixed in the D-study the variance components for universe 2 are denoted as σ_p^{2*}, σ_{pi}^{2*} and so forth. The most common method of estimating variance components is the ANOVA method discussed in greater detail in the next section. When this method is used with a two-facet G-study design, it can be shown that

$$\hat{\sigma}_p^{2*} = \hat{\sigma}_p^2 + \hat{\sigma}_{pi}^2/n_i'$$

where σ_p^{2*} is estimated assuming facet i is fixed and σ_p^2 and σ_{pi}^2 are estimated assuming facet i is random. As a result the universe-score variance for universe 2 is frequently written as $\sigma_p^2 + \sigma_{pi}^2/n_i'$, where these variance components are defined for universe 1. This kind of convention is adopted in defining the universe-score variance for the universes of 2 and 3 and in the discussion of formulating and estimating generalizability coefficients. An alternative justification for this substitution procedure was given by Gleser et al. (1965). They argued that in many cases the i-facet conditions appearing in a G-study may be different than those appearing in the D-study even when the facet is fixed in the D-study. They then defined an expected universe-score variance for this situation. For universe 2 the expected-universe score variance is $\sigma_p^2 + \sigma_{pi}^2/n_i'$.

Universe 3. In this universe one facet (j) is finite. The second facet (i) is infinite with conditions of i nested in j. Both facets are crossed with the objects of measurement. The universe is denoted by (i:j)xp. Assuming that the universe score is defined as

$$\mu_p = \frac{1}{n_{j'}} \sum_j \epsilon_i X_{pij}$$

the universe score variance is $\sigma_p^2 + \sigma_{pj}^2/n_{j'}$. This assumption is introduced explicitly because in some situations the universe score is defined as the $\sum_j w_i \epsilon_i X_{pij}$, where $\mu_{pj} = \epsilon_i X_{pij}$ is the subuniverse score for condition j of facet j. For example, when the conditions of facet j are content categories, μ_{pj} is the subuniverse score for category j and it may be sensible to weight certain subuniverse scores heavier for some categories than for others. This situation is discussed by Brennan (1980, section 6.5) and Rajaratnam et al. (1965).

Two-Facet D-Study Designs

There are several possible two-facet D-study designs. Here four such designs are described and reports of the expected observed-score variances are presented. Gleser et al. (1965) report on an additional four designs.

The pxixj design. This design mirrors universe 1 with facet i, facet j, and the objects of measurement all crossed. The number of conditions for facet i and facet; are n_i' and n_j', respectively. An example is a history test consisting of five essays, with each essay graded by two graders. The observed score for person p is

$$X_{pIJ} = \frac{1}{n_{i'} n_{j'}} \sum_i \sum_j X_{pij}$$

The expected observed-score variance is

$$\sigma_p^2 + \sigma_{pi}^2/n_i' + \sigma_{pj}^2/n_j' + \sigma_e^2/n_i'n_j' \tag{9}$$

The (i:j)xp design. In this design n_i' conditions of facet i are nested in conditions of facet j. There are a total of n_j' conditions in facet j. Every person responds to every combination of i and j, so both facets are crossed with the objects of measurement. The design is illustrated by a test which consists of n_i' items constructed for each of n_j' content categories. The observed score is again X_{pIJ} and the expected observed-score variance is

$$\sigma_p^2 + \sigma_{pj}^2/n_j' + (\sigma_{pi}^2 + \sigma_e^2)/n_i'n_j'$$

The (i,j)xp design. In this design there are a total of k joint conditions formed by pairing one condition of facet i and one condition of facet j. These joint conditions are crossed with the objects of measurement. An example is a test consisting of 10 essays with each essay graded by a different grader. The observed score is the average of the scores earned in the k joint conditions. The expected observed-score variance is

$$\sigma_p^2 + (\sigma_{pi}^2 + \sigma_{pj}^2 + \sigma_e^2)/k \quad (10)$$

The j:(pxi) design. In the fourth design, facet i is crossed with the objects of measurement. However, for each of the resulting $n_p'n_i'$ combinations a different set of conditions from facet j is selected. An example is a computer-generated test constructed from a large pool of items. The pool is structured by n_i' content categories and each examinee takes a set of n_j' items for each content category. Within each content category a different set of n_j' items is selected for each examinee. The observed score is again X_{pIJ} and the expected observed-score variance is

$$\sigma_p^2 + \sigma_{pi}^2/n_i' + (\sigma_{pj}^2 + \sigma_j^2 + \sigma_{ij}^2 + \sigma_e^2)/n_i'n_j'$$

Although the investigator designing a D-study will often have several D-study designs to choose from, the pool of candidate D-study designs is sometimes limited by the investigator's universe of generalization. Suppose in the universe of generalization one facet is nested in a second. Then the first facet must also be nested in the second facet in the candidate D-study designs. A similar situation occurs if a facet is nested in the objects of measurement. Perhaps more obviously, if a fixed finite facet is crossed with a second facet in the universe of generalization, then it must be crossed with the second facet in the candidate D-study designs. Again, the same principle holds for fixed facets that are crossed with the objects of measurement in the universe of generalization.

Generalizability Coefficients: Two Facets

Once the investigator has determined the universe-score variance for the universe of generalization and the expected observed-score variance for the candidate D-study designs, formulating the generalizability coefficient is straightforward. For each design the generalizability coefficient is the ratio of universe-score to expected-observed-score variance. Reconsider the example of the essay examination used as a criterion for awarding a history scholarship. The universe score variance was σ_p^2. Each of the four D-study designs is a potential design for collecting the essay data, but for the purposes of discussion the pxixj and (i,j)xp designs will be considered. If the pxixj design is used, each examinee will write an essay on the same n_i' topic and each essay will be graded by the same n_j'

graders. The expected observed score variance is given by (9), so the generalizability coefficient is

$$\rho^2 = \frac{\sigma_p^{\ 2}}{\sigma_p^{\ 2} + \sigma_{pi}^{\ 2}/n_{i'} + \sigma_{pj}^{\ 2}/n_{j'} + \sigma_e^{\ 2}/n_{i'}n_{j'}}$$

If the (i,j)xp design is used a total of k graders will grade essays. Each grader will grade one of k topics. The expected observed-score variance is given by (10) and the generalizability coefficient is

$$\rho^2 = \frac{\sigma_p^{\ 2}}{\sigma_p^{\ 2} + (\sigma_{pi}^{\ 2} + \sigma_{pi}^{\ 2} + \sigma_e^{\ 2})/k}$$

ESTIMATING THE GENERALIZABILITY COEFFICIENT

As noted in the introduction to the previous section, it is good practice to conduct a G-study prior to conducting the D-study data. In this section the use of G-study data to estimate variance components and forecast the generalizability coefficients for the candidate D-study designs is discussed. In the two major subsections the ANOVA method for estimating variance components using balanced data from single-facet and two-facet G-studies is presented. In the third subsection the application of ANOVA methods to unbalanced data is discussed. Throughout the first three subsections variance-component estimation is discussed when all the facets are random. In the fourth subsection variance-component estimation when some facets are fixed is discussed. In the next subsection computer programs that implement the ANOVA method are briefly reviewed. In the final subsection other estimation methods are briefly discussed.

In designing a G-study two issues must be confronted. First, the G-study design should be compatible with the investigator's universe of generalization. Rules for determining compatibility between a design and an universe of generalization were given in the section on two-facet D-study designs. Second, the G-study design must permit estimation of all the variance components in the universe-score variance and the expected observed-score variance. As the G-study designs are discussed in the subsequent subsections, the variance components that can be estimated using the data from the design will be indicated.

Single-Facet G-Study Designs

In the ANOVA method, the MSs computed in the analysis are used to calculate estimates of the variance components. Formulas for estimating the variance components can be derived by inspecting the formulas for the EMSs. To illustrate the process, consider a G-study in which each of $n_p = 100$ examinees took a

Table 4. Summary ANOVA Table for a pxi Design

SV	*df*	*SS*	*MS*	*EMS*
Examinees (p)	99	2041.380	20.620	$\sigma_e^2 + n_i\sigma_p^2$
Items (i)	19	4498.896	236.784	$\sigma_e^2 + n_p\sigma_i^2$
Residual (r)	1881	7847.532	4.172	σ_e^2

$n_i = 20$ item test. The design of the G-study can be viewed as the pxi design with items as the measurement facet. A summary of the ANOVA is presented in Table 4. Note that the EMSs are functions of the variance components for the single-facet universe with an infinite facet. Consequently they can be manipulated to yield expressions that isolate the variance components:

$$\begin{aligned}\sigma_p^2 &= (EMS_p - EMS_r)/n_i \\ \sigma_i^2 &= (EMS_i - EMS_r)/n_p \\ \sigma_e^2 &= EMS_r\end{aligned}$$

Estimates of the variance components are obtained by substituting the MSs for the corresponding EMSs:

$$\begin{aligned}\hat{\sigma}_p^2 &= (MS_p - MS_r)/n_i \\ \hat{\sigma}_i^2 &= (MS_i - MS_r)/n_p \\ \hat{\sigma}_e^2 &= MS_r\end{aligned}$$

Substituting in the equations we obtain

$$\begin{aligned}\hat{\sigma}_p^2 &= (20.620 - 4.172)/20 = .822 \\ \hat{\sigma}_i^2 &= (236.784 - 4.172)/100 = 2.326 \\ \hat{\sigma}_e^2 &= 4.172\end{aligned}$$

The variance component estimates can then be used to estimate the generalizability coefficients appropriate for the investigator's universe of generalization and candidate D-study designs. Assume the investigator's universe of generalization has a single infinite facet and that the investigator plans to conduct the D-study using the pxi design. Replacing variance components by estimated variance components in (8) we obtain

$$\hat{\rho}^2 = \frac{\hat{\sigma}_p^2}{\hat{\sigma}_p^2 + \hat{\sigma}_e^2/n_{i'}}$$

which can be used to estimate the appropriate generalizability coefficient. Assuming the D-study will be conducted using $n_i' = 10$ items we obtain

$$\hat{\rho}^2 = \frac{.822}{.822 + 4.172/10} = .66$$

Although it seems unlikely, suppose the researcher in the current example is considering using the i : p design. That is, each examinee will take a different set of $n_{i'}$ items. The formula for estimating the appropriate generalizability coefficient is

$$\hat{\rho}^2 = \frac{\hat{\sigma}_p^2}{\hat{\sigma}_p^2 + (\hat{\sigma}_i^2 + \hat{\sigma}_e^2)/n_{i'}}$$

If each examinee will take $n_{i'} = 10$ items we obtain

$$\hat{\rho}^2 = \frac{.822}{.822 + (2.326 + 4.172)/10} = .56$$

The important point to note is that the data collected in a G-study using a pxi design can be used to estimate a generalizability coefficient for a D-study conducted using either the pxi design or the i:p design (Rajaratnam, 1960). This illustrates the important point that a well-designed G-study can provide generalizability information about D-studies conducted using a range of designs.

By contrast, consider a G-study conducted using the i:p design. In this study each of $n_p = 30$ examinees has an essay graded by $n_i = 3$ graders, but different graders grade each examinee's essay. The summary of the ANOVA is reported in Table 5. Inspecting the EMSs we see that with an i:p G-study design, only $(\sigma_i^2 + \sigma_e^2)$ and σ_p^2 can be estimated:

$$\hat{\sigma}_p^2 = (MS_p - MS_r)/n_i$$
$$\hat{\sigma}_e^2 + \hat{\sigma}_i^2 = MS_r$$

Substituting in these equations we obtain

$$\hat{\sigma}_p^2 = (42.622 - 5.728)/3 = 12.311$$
$$\hat{\sigma}_i^2 + \hat{\sigma}_e^2 = 5.728$$

Table 5. Summary ANOVA Table for an i : p Design

SV	*df*	*SS*	*MS*	*EMS*
Examinees (p)	29	1237.20	42.662	$\sigma_e^2 + \sigma_i^2 + n_i\sigma_p^2$
Residual (f)	60	343.68	5.728	$\sigma_e^2 + \sigma_i^2$

With these results we can estimate the generalizability coefficient for a i:p D-study but not for a pxi D-study. If the D-study will have $n_i' = 2$ graders per examinee then the former generalizability coefficient is

$$\hat{\rho}^2 = \frac{\hat{\sigma}_p^2}{\sigma_p^2 + (\sigma_i^2 + \sigma_e^2)/n_{i'}}$$

$$= \frac{12.311}{12.311 + (5.728)/2}$$

$$= .81$$

Two-Facet G-Study Designs

The ANOVA method can also be used with two-facet designs, and again involves constructing weighted linear combinations of EMSs that isolate the variance components. These, in turn, are estimated by substituting MSs for EMSs. Estimation formulas are presented when required in the subsequent discussion.

Table 6 indicates the variance components that can be estimated from data collected using each of each two-facet design considered previously. Clearly the pxixj design permits estimation of more variance components than the other designs permit. Consequently, if the pxixj design is compatible with the investigator's universe of generalization, use of this design, rather than the (i:j)xp, (i,j)p, or j:(pxi) designs, will permit the investigator to forecast the generalizability of data for a wider array of candidate D-study designs.

To illustrate the procedures for formulating and estimating generalizability coefficients, consider a pxixj G-study in which 18 examinees wrote $n_i = 2$ essays. The essays were scored for syntatic complexity by $n_j = 2$ scorers. The

Table 6. Variance Components and Variance-Component Combinations Estimable Using Two-Facet Designs

	Variance Component						
Design	σ_p^2	σ_i^2	σ_j^2	σ_{pi}^2	σ_{pj}^2	σ_{ij}^2	σ_e^2
pxixj	*	*	*	*	*	*	*
(i : j)xp	*	#	*	$	*	#	$
(i,j)xp	*	#	#	$	$	#	$
(j : p)xi	*	*	#	*	#	$	$

Note: Within a row, variance components marked by # cannot be estimated independently. Similarly for components marked by $.

Table 7. Summary ANOVA Table for a pxixj Design G-Study

SV	*df*	*MS*	*EMS*
Examinees (p)	17	14.982	$\sigma_e^2 + n_i n_j \sigma_p^2 + n_i \sigma_{pj}^2 + n_j \sigma_{pi}^2$
Essays (i)	1	2.350	$\sigma_e^2 + n_j n_p \sigma_i^2 + n_j \sigma_{pi}^2 + n_p \sigma_{ij}^2$
Scorers (j)	1	.110	$\sigma_e^2 + n_i n_p \sigma_j^2 + n_i \sigma_{pj}^2 + n_p \sigma_{ij}^2$
p × i	17	6.229	$\sigma_e^2 + n_j \sigma_{pi}^2$
p × j	17	.443	$\sigma_e^2 + n_i \sigma_{pj}^2$
i × j	1	.642	$\sigma_e^2 + n_p \sigma_{ij}^2$
Residual	17	.294	σ_e^2

measure of syntatic complexity was t-unit length. The summary of the ANOVA is presented in Table 7.

Suppose the investigator is primarily interested in scorer reliability. Consequently the universe is universe 2 with examinees, scorers, and essay topics mutually crossed; scorers is an infinite facet and essay topics is a fixed finite facet. The universe score is $\sigma_p^2 + \sigma_{pi}^2/n_i'$. Also suppose the investigator is considering using either a pxixj D-study with $n_i' = 3$ essays and $n_j' = 3$ scorers, or a (i,j)xp D-study with $k = n_i' = n_j' = 3$ essays and scorers. The difference between the two designs is that in the pxixj design every scorer scores every essay for every examinee whereas in the (i,j)xp design each scorer scores only one essay topic, but scores the same topic for each examinee. The observed-score variance for the former design is

$$\sigma_p^2 + \sigma_{pi}^2/n_i' + \sigma_{pj}^2/n_j' + \sigma_e^2/n_i'n_j'$$

and for the latter design the variance is

$$\sigma_p^2 + (\sigma_{pi}^2 + \sigma_{pj}^2 + \sigma_e^2)/k$$

Using the EMSs in Table 7 the following equations can be derived:

$$\hat{\sigma}_p^2 = (MS_p - MS_{pi} - MS_{pj} + MS_e)/n_i n_j \quad (11a)$$

$$\hat{\sigma}_{pi}^2 = (MS_{pi} - MS_e)/n_j \quad (11b)$$

$$\hat{\sigma}_{pj}^2 = (MS_{pj} - MS_e)/n_i \quad (11c)$$

$$\hat{\sigma}_e^2 = MS_r \quad (11d)$$

Substituting in the equations we obtain

$$\hat{\sigma}_p^2 = (14.982 - .443 - 6.229 + .294)/2.2 = 2.151$$

$$\hat{\sigma}_{pi}^2 = (6.229 - .294)/2 = 2.967$$

$$\hat{\sigma}_{pj}^2 = (.443 - .294)/2 = .074$$

$$\hat{\sigma}_e^2 = .294$$

Substituting estimated variance components for variance components we obtain the following equation for estimating the generalizability of the data in the pxixj D-study:

$$\hat{\rho}^2 = \frac{\hat{\sigma}_p^2 + \hat{\sigma}_{pi}^2/n_{i'}}{\hat{\sigma}_p^2 + \hat{\sigma}_{pi}^2/n_{i'} + \hat{\sigma}_{pj}^2/n_{j'} + \hat{\sigma}_e^2/n_{i'}n_{j'}} \tag{12}$$

$$= \frac{2.151 + 2.967/3}{2.151 + 2.967/3 + .074/3 + 294/9}$$

$$= .98$$

The corresponding equation and results for the (i,j)xp design are

$$\hat{\rho}^2 = \frac{\hat{\sigma}_p^2 + \hat{\sigma}_{pi}^2/n_{i'}}{\hat{\sigma}_p^2 + (\hat{\sigma}_{pi}^2 + \hat{\sigma}_{pj}^2 + \hat{\sigma}_e^2)/k}$$

$$\hat{\rho}^2 = \frac{2.151 + 2.967/3}{2.151 + (2.967 + .074 + .294)/3}$$

$$= .96$$

Clearly the differences in generalizability are small so the investigator is well-advised to use the (i,j)xp design which requires less work per scorer. The generalizability coefficients are so similar because the σ_e^2 is relatively small and consequently the size of the divisor of σ_e^2 does not have a major impact on the generalizability coefficient.

Now suppose the investigator views both scorers and essay topics as infinite facets (universe 1). This changes the generalizability coefficient because the universe-score variance becomes σ_p^2. Making the appropriate adjustment to (12) and substituting we obtain

$$\hat{\rho}^2 = \frac{2.151}{2.151 + 2.967/3 + .074/3 + .294/9}$$

$$= .67$$

for the pxixj design. For the (i,j)xp design the estimated generalizability coefficient is

$$\hat{\rho}^2 = \frac{2.151}{2.151 + (2.967 + .074 + .294)/3}$$

$$= .66$$

Suppose the investigator is not satisfied with these levels of generalizability. Because the largest component of variance is $\hat{\sigma}_{pi}^2 = 2.967$ the investigator needs a design that reduces its influence. The only way this can be done, without introducing other variance components into the expected-observed score variance, is to increase the number of essays. One possibility is to use (i:j)xp increasing the number of essays to $n_i' = 6$ and having two essays nested in each of $n_j' = 3$ raters. With this design the formula for estimating the generalizability coefficient is

$$\hat{\rho}^2 = \frac{\hat{\sigma}_p^2}{\hat{\sigma}_p^2 + \hat{\sigma}_{pj}^2/n_{j'} + (\hat{\sigma}_{pi}^2 + \hat{\sigma}_e^2)/n_{i'}n_{j'}}$$

The ANOVA Method for Unbalanced Data

In the preceding two sections the ANOVA method of estimation for balanced single-facet and two-facet G-study were discussed. Data are balanced if the range of any one subscript on X is the same for every possible combination of the other subscripts. Here a brief discussion of the ANOVA method for unbalanced data is provided. Searle (1971) refers to the ANOVA method for unbalanced data as Henderson's Method 3 (after Henderson, 1953) and gives a very complete discussion of the method.

With balanced data, for each source of variance, the EMS is unique. Consequently, the estimated variance components can be expressed as unique weighted linear combinations of MSs. Further, although different computational formulas may exist for computing a particular mean square, each formula, properly applied, will yield the same numeric value for the mean square. Therefore, the MSs lead to unique estimates of the variance components.

The situation is quite different with unbalanced data. Then the EMS for a particular source of variance depends on the formula used to calculate MS for the source of variance. As a result different ways of calculating the MSs lead to different variance-component estimates. The central problem is that no criteria exist for choosing among the multiple estimates of a particular variance component. In principle this problem can be solved by using one of the alternative methods discussed subsequently. However, the available computer programs that implement these methods make assumptions that are incompatible with generalizability theory. These assumptions are discussed in more detail in the next subsection.

The ANOVA Method for Mixed Models

When all of the facets are assumed to be random in the G-study, the linear model underlying the variance-component estimation procedure is called a random model. By contrast, when some of the facets are fixed and some are random the model is called a mixed model. In the presentation of variance-component estimation by the ANOVA method, a random model was assumed. In calculating generalizability coefficients, fixed facets were accomodated by writing the universe-score variance as a weighted sum of variance components defined for the random model. (See the preceding discussion of universes 2 and 3.) An alternate procedure for dealing with fixed facets is to estimate the variance components assuming a mixed model.

A complication arises, however, in variance-component estimation for mixed models. The complication is due to the fact that different assumptions about the interactions between fixed and random facets lead to different EMSs and consequently to different variance-component estimates. For example, consider the pxixj design. The EMSs, when both i and j are random, are reported in Table 7. Suppose now that facet i is fixed. One assumption made in the mixed-model literature is that the pi interaction, $(\mu_{pi} - \mu_p - \mu_i + \mu)$, and the ij interaction, $(\mu_{ij} - \mu_i - \mu_j + \mu)$, sum to zero when summed over i. This assumption leads to the deletion of σ_{pi}^2 in the line for examinees and the deletion of σ_{ij}^2 in the line for scorers. Searle (1971, pp. 400–404) provides the justification for the deletion. The sum-to-zero assumption is consistent with the construction of the linear model that underlies generalizability theory for the pxixj design. Consequently the revised EMSs are the correct EMSs to use in generalizability theory when facet i is fixed in the pxixj design. The second assumption about the pi and ij interactions is that they do not necessarily sum to zero. Consequently, neither σ_{pi}^2 or σ_{ij}^2 would be deleted from Table 7 and the estimated variance components will be the same as those obtained with the mixed model. These EMSs should not be used in generalizability theory for the pxixj design with i fixed.

Because of the complication discussed in the preceding paragraph, the investigator who uses published EMSs or rules of thumb for deriving EMSs must make sure the results are consistent with the assumptions made in generalizability theory. Rules of thumb, consistent with the generalizability-theory assumptions, have been published by Millman and Glass (1967) and Myers (1979) among others. Alternatively Brennan (1983) has presented a variance-component estimation procedure that is consistent with the assumptions of generalizability theory and can be applied to any balanced data set.

Although the complication, caused by differing assumptions, is fairly easily solved with balanced data, it is not easily solved with unbalanced data. This is because the assumption customarily made in the literature on mixed models for unbalanced data is that fixed effect—random effect interactions do not sum to zero. Consequently, the variance-component estimation presented in the literature on mixed models for unbalanced data is not appropriate for generalizability theory. This is true for the ANOVA method and most presentations of the methods to be discussed subsequently. Because of the incompatibility, the researcher who has unbalanced data and a mixed model might fall back on using a procedure appropriate for a random model to estimate the variance components and then adjusting the estimated universe-score variance for the fixed effect. One problem with this fallback is that one cannot justify the procedures by the argument that it results in the same generalizability coefficient as would be obtained from a mixed-model analysis. One must rely on the argument given by Gleser et al. (1965) which, strictly speaking, is only appropriate when the G-study does not contain the same fixed-facet conditions as the D-study will.

For universes 2 and 3, the expressions presented for the universe-score variance are appropriate only if the variance-component estimation is conducted assuming a random model for the G-study. If a mixed model is assumed, the universe-score variances become σ_p^{2*}, where the star indicates that the variance component is defined for a mixed model. Similarly, for the two-facet D-study designs the expressions for expected-observed score variance are appropriate only when the G-study data are analyzed using a random model. When a mixed model analysis is used, the correct expected observed-score variance can be obtained by deleting all variance components for interaction between a fixed facet and a random facet, or a fixed facet and the objects of measurement facet. Each remaining variance component is replaced by the corresponding starred variance component. For example, with the pxixj design, if the i facet is fixed and the variance components are estimated assuming a mixed model, by deleting σ_{pi}^2/n_i' from (9) the expected observed score variance becomes

$$\sigma_p^{2*} + \sigma_{pj}^{2*}/n_j' + \sigma_e^{2*}/n_i'n_j'$$

Generalizability coefficients are then defined as the ratio of universe-score variance to expected observed-score variance.

Computer Programs for the ANOVA Method

To implement the ANOVA method using the data collected in the G-study, it is necessary, at a minimum, to have access to a computer package that can produce the ANOVA summary table for the G-study design. While there are many such packages available, two widely available packages will be discussed here. Except where noted, in this subsection only the analysis of balanced data will be addressed.

The first package is the SAS (1985) computing package. PROC ANOVA of the SAS package is a useful program for completely crossed designs such as the pxi and pxixj designs. Before the 1985 version of SAS was developed, PROC ANOVA could be quite expensive to use with such designs. However, the introduction of the REPEATED command in PROC ANOVA appears to have solved that problem. Unfortunately, PROC ANOVA is still quite expensive for designs that have both crossed and nested factors. For completely crossed designs another reasonably inexpensive program is the BMDP2V program of the BMDP statistical package (Dixon et al., 1981).

Even more useful than programs that produce the summary ANOVA tables are programs that calculate variance components. One such program is PROC NESTED which can analyze balanced and unbalanced data. However it can only be used with designs that do not have any crossed factors. PROV VARCOMP can be used with virtually any design. However, it can be extremely expensive. A much more inexpensive alternative is BMDP8V which can handle both crossed and nested facets. With mixed models BMDP8V incorporates the assumptions made in generalizability theory about interactions between fixed and random facets.

Perhaps the most useful program is one designed especially for generalizability theory. There are several available. However, the most useful package appears to be GENOVA (Crick & Brennan, 1982). Brennan (1983) reports that GENOVA can perform G-study analyses for balanced data collected in designs with up to six facets, including the objects of measurement facet. GENOVA calculates variance components but, in addition, can calculate generalizability coefficients and standard errors of measurement for candidate D-study designs selected by the user. Other standard and optional output provided by GENOVA is described by Brennan (1983).

Alternative Methods of Estimation

The ANOVA variance-component estimators are examples of a class of variance-component estimators called unbiased quadratic estimators. That is, estimators that are unbiased and are weighted linear combinations of squares and cross products of the raw data. Graybill and Hultquist (1961) demonstrated that for balanced random models ANOVA estimators have minimum variance in the class of quadratic unbiased estimator. Furthermore if the effects are normally distributed the ANOVA estimators have minimum variance among all unbiased estimators.

There are several reasons why alternatives to the ANOVA estimators are desirable. First the optimality properties cited above do not extent to mixed models, nor to unbalanced random models. In addition, there is the problem that the ANOVA method does not yield unique variance component estimates with unbalanced data. Second, sample variance components computed by the ANOVA method can be negative even though the population variances component must, by definition, be nonnegative. Thus, nonnegative estimators are desirable. No distributional assumptions are made in deriving ANOVA estimators. Therefore negative estimates do not reflect a failure to meet distributional assumptions. Negative estimates may reflect specification error. For example, in a study in which two forms of a test are each taken in each week in a three-week period, the tests taken within a week may be taken on different days. Suppose the design is considered to be the pxixj design with weeks and tests as the measurement facets. Strictly speaking, the data do not match the design because the design does not reflect the fact that scores on the two tests taken within a particular week may vary as a function of test content and the days on which the tests were taken. However, negative estimates are not necessarily due to specification error. The possibility of negative estimates is a property of the procedure and consequently negative estimates may occur in any generalizability analysis conducted using the ANOVA method.

In the sequel three alternative estimation schemes are briefly considered: maximum likelihood estimation, minimum variance quadratic unbiased estimation (MIVQUE), and minimum norm quadratic unbiased estimation (MINQUE). Khuri and Sahai (1985) gave a more extensive review of these and several other variance component estimation procedures.

Maximum Likelihood Estimations

Under the assumption that all random effects are normally distributed, constrained maximum likelihood estimation procedures have been developed. The constraints are such that estimated variance components must be positive. Maximum likelihood estimates can be obtained using the BMDP3V or PROC VARCOMP. Miliken and Johnson (1984) claim that the maximum likelihood procedure implemented in BMDP3V works satisfactorily. They criticized the maximum likelihood procedure implemented by the 1982 edition of SAS on two counts. First, it can produce negative estimates and second, it may not produce accurate results with unbalanced designs. The *SAS User's Guide: Statistics* (1985) does not indicate that the procedure has been modified.

One criticism of the maximum likelihood estimators is that it does not take into account the loss of degrees of freedom that results from estimating the parameters associated with the fixed effects. This criticism applies even to random models, because in these models the grand mean is a fixed parameter. The failure to take account of the degrees-of-freedom loss makes the maximum likelihood estimator negatively biased. The failure to take account of the degrees-of-freedom loss is eliminated by the restricted maximum likelihood (REML) approach (Harville, 1977). This approach computes variance-components estimates by maximizing a likelihood function that is independent of the fixed effects. As typically discussed and implemented, the REML procedure does not incorporate the sum-to-zero assumption and consequently is incompatible with generalizability theory. With balanced data the REML approach, without non-negativity constraints, yields the same results as the ANOVA method yields when applied without the sum-to-zero assumption.

A comparison of the two maximum likelihood approaches in terms of mean squared error of estimation depends on the specific design and the true value of the variance components (Harville, 1977). Corbeil and Searle (1976), Hocking and Kutner (1975), and Swallow and Monahan (1984) have compared the two likelihood approaches for a limited number of designs and for both fixed and random models. Both BMDP3V and PROC VARCOMP calculate restricted maximum likelihood estimates.

With mixed models the procedures implemented by both PROC VARCOMP and BMDP3V are based on the assumptions that are incompatible with generalizability theory. Consequently, with mixed models, these procedures do not provide a solution, appropriate for generalizability theory, to the problem of variance-component estimation with unbalanced data. With random models, they do provide an appropriate solution.

MIVQUE and MINQUE

Rao (1971b) proposed a general procedure for minimum variance quadratic unbiased estimation (MIVQUE) of variance components. The variance-component estimators, however, are functions of the unknown variance components. Consequently, to implement MIVQUE it is necessary to make an a priori assignment of values to the variance components. (Actually the necessary specifications are the ratios of the variance component for each random facet to the variance component for the residual term.) The resulting estimator is a locally minimum variance quadratic unbiased estimator that is minimum variance in the class of unbiased quadratic estimators that incorporate the same a prior values. The estimator is (globally) minimum variance in the class of unbiased quadratic estimators if the a priori values are equal to the true values.

An alternative is to treat the a priori values as starting values in an iterative estimation scheme. The resulting estimators are, however, no longer minimum variance estimators and may not be unbiased. Both iterative and noniterative MIVQUE procedures can yield negative estimators unless nonnegativity constraints are incorporated.

Rao (1971a) introduced minimum norm quadratic unbiased estimation (MINQUE) of variance components. The name derives from the derivation of the procedure by minimizing the norm of a certain matrix. Rao presented computational details for the Euclidean norm, the sum of the squared elements of the matrix. The MINQUE procedure may be implemented either with or without an a priori specification of the variance components. As with MIVQUE, if an a priori specification is made, the specified values can be treated as starting values in an interative procedure. Rao (1979) indicates that the iterated MINQUE (with the Euclidean norm) is equivalent to a restricted maximum likelihood procedure without nonnegativity constraints. If the random effects are assumed to be normally distributed, MINQUE with the Euclidean norm is equivalent to MIVQUE.

Brown (1976) investigated the asymptotic properties of the estimators obtained by MINQUE and iterated MINQUE. He studied the situation in which, in generalizability-theory terminology, the G-study is replicated by taking new random samples of conditions from the universe of admissable observations and a new random sample from the population of the objects of measurement. Brown showed that as the number of replicates goes to infinity the estimators obtained by MINQUE and iterated MINQUE converge to their true values and are normally distributed. Further the estimators obtained by iterated MINQUE are independent of the starting values.

PROC VARCOMP implements an estimator called MIVQUEO. In this procedure the a priori values are zero for all variance components except σ_e^2 which receives a value of one. Strictly speaking the procedure is a MIVQUE procedure only under normality. If the effects are non-normal the procedure is a MINQUE procedure. Milliken and Johnson (1984) criticized MIVQUEO because it can yield negative estimates, is noniterative and can be unsatisfactory for some unbalanced designs. Milliken and Johnson presented an example of a non-iterative MINQUE analysis of unbalanced data collected in the i:p design. In this example the variance-component estimates were not very sensitive to the choice of a priori values, but the standard errors were.

REFERENCES

Algina, J. (1978). Comment on Bartko's ''On various intraclass reliability coefficients.'' *Psychological Bulletin, 85,* 135–138.

Brennan, R. L. (1980). Applications of generalizability theory. In R. B. Berk (Ed.), *Criterion-referenced measurement: The state of the art.* Baltimore: The Johns Hopkins University Press.

Brennan, R. L. (1983). *Elements of generalizability theory.* Iowa City, IA: The American College Testing Program.

Brennan, R. L., & Kane, M. T. (1977a). An index of dependability for mastery tests. *Journal of Educational Measurement, 14,* 277–289.

Brennan, R. L., & Kane, M. T. (1977b). Signal/noise ratios for domain-referenced tests. *Psychometrika, 42,* 609–625.

Brennan, R. L., & Kane, M. T. (1979). Generalizability theory: A review. In R. F. Traub (Ed.) *New directions for testing and measurement: Methodological developments* (No. 4). San Francisco: Jossey-Bass.

Brown, K. G. (1976). Asymptotic behavior of MINQUE-type estimators of variance components. *Annals of Statistics, 4,* 746–754.

Burt, C. (1955). Test reliability estimated by analysis of variance. *British Journal of Mathematical and Statistical Psychology, 8,* 103–118.

Cardinet, J., Tourneur, Y., & Allal, L. (1976). The symmetry of generalizability theory: Applications to educational measurement. *Journal of Educational Measurement, 13,* 119–135.

Cardinet, J., Tourneur, Y., & Allal, L. (1981). Extension of generalizability theory and its applications in eductional measurement. *Journal of Educational Measurement, 18,* 183–204.

Corbeil, R. R., & Searle, S. R. (1976). A comparison of variance component estimators. *Biometrics, 32,* 779–781.

Crick, J. E., & Brennan, R. L. (1982). *GENOVA: A generalized analysis of variance system* (FORTRAN IV computer program and manual). Dorchester, MA: Computer Facilities, University of Massachusetts at Boston.

Crocker, L. M., & Algina, J. (1985). *Introduction to classical and modern test theory.* New York: Holt, Rinehart, and Winston.

Cronbach, L. J. (1951). Coefficient alpha and the internal structure of tests. *Psychometrika, 16,* 297–334.

Cronbach, L. J., Gleser, G. C., Nanda, H., & Rajaratnam, N. (1972). *The dependability of behavioral measurements: Theory of generalizability for scores and profiles.* New York: John Wiley and Sons, Inc.

Cronbach, L. J., Rajaratnam, N., & Gleser, G. C. (1963). Theory of generalizability: A liberalization of reliability theory. *British Journal of Mathematical and Statistical Psychology, 16,* 137–163.

Dixon, W. J., Brown, M. D., Engleman, L., Frane, J., Hill, M., Jennrich, R., & Toporek, J. (Eds.) (1981). *BMDP statistical software*. Berkeley: University of California Press.

Ebel, R. L. (1951). Estimation of reliability of ratings. *Psychometrika, 16,* 407–424.

Finlayson, D. S. (1951). The reliability of marking essays. *British Journal of Educational Psychology, 21,* 126–134.

Fryans, L. J. (Ed.) (1983). *Generalizability theory: Inferences and practical applications*. San Francisco: Jossey-Bass.

Glesser, G. C., Cronbach, L. J., & Rajaratnam, N. (1965). Generalizability of scores influenced by multiple sources of variance. *Psychometrika, 30,* 395–418.

Graybill, F. A., & Hultquist, D. A. (1961). Theorems concerning Eisenhart's Model II. *Annals of Mathematical Statistics, 32,* 261–269.

Harville, D. A. (1977). Maximum-likelihood approaches to variance component estimation and to related problems. *Journal of the American Statistical Association, 72,* 320–340.

Hocking, R. R., & Kutner, M. H. (1975). Some analytical and numerical comparisons of estimators for the mixed A. O. V. model. *Biometrics, 31,* 19–28.

Henderson, C. R. (1953). Estimation of variance and covariance components. *Biometrics, 9,* 226–212.

Hoyt, C. J. (1941). Test reliability estimated by analysis of variance. *Psychometrika, 6,* 153–160.

Kane, M. T. (1982). A sampling model for validity. *Applied Psychological Measurement, 6,* 125–160.

Kane, M. T., & Brennan, R. L. (1977). The generalizability of class means. *Review of Educational Research, 47,* 267–292.

Kane, M. T., Gillmore, G. M., & Crooks, T. J. (1976). Student evaluation of teaching: The generalizability of class means. *Journal of Educational Measurement, 13,* 171–184.

Khuri, A. I., & Sahai, H. (1985). Variance components analysis: A selective literature review. *International Statistical Review, 53,* 279–300.

Kuder, F. G., & Richardson, M. W. (1937). The theory of estimation of test reliability. *Psychometrika, 2,* 151–160.

Lindquist, E. F. (1953). *Design and analysis of experiments in psychology and education*. Boston: Houghton-Mifflin.

Lord, F. M. (1955a). Estimating test reliability. *Educational and Psychological Measurement, 15,* 324–336.

Lord, F. M. (1955b). Sampling fluctuations resulting from the sampling of test items. *Psychometrika, 20,* 1–22.

Lord, F. M., & Novick, M. R. (1968). *Statistical theories of mental test scores*. Reading, MA: Addison-Wesley.

Medley, D. M., & Mitzel, H. E. (1963). Measuring classroom behavior by systematic observation. In N. L. Gage (Ed.) *Handbook of research on teaching*. Chicago: Rand McNally.

Medley, D. M., Mitzel, H. E., & Doi, A. N. (1956). Analysis-of-variance models and their use in three way designs without replication. *Journal of Experimental Education, 24,* 221–229.

Milliken, G. A., & Johnson, D. E. (1984). *Analysis of messy data*. Belmont, CA: Lifetime Learning Publications.

Millman, J., & Glass, G. V. (1967). Rules of thumb for writing the ANOVA table. *Journal of Educational Measurement, 4,* 41–51.

Myers, J. L. (1979). *Fundamentals of experimental design* (3rd Ed.). Boston: Allyn and Bacon.

Novick, M. R. (1966). The axioms and principal results of classical test theory. *Journal of Mathematical Psychology 3,* 1–18.

Rajaratnam, N. (1960). Reliability for independent decisions data when reliability data are matched. *Psychometrika, 25,* 261–271.

Rajaratnam, N., Cronbach, L. J., & Gleser, G. C. (1965). Generalizability of stratified-parallel tests. *Psychometrika, 30,* 39–56.

Rao, C. R. (1971a). Estimation of variance and covariance components-MINQUE theory. *Journal of Multivariate Analysis, 1,* 257–275.

Rao, C. R. (1971b). Minimum variance quadratic unbiased estimation of variance components. *Journal of Multivariate Analysis, 1,* 445–456.

Rao, C. R. (1979). MINQUE theory and its relation to ML and MML estimation of variance components. *Sankhya B, 41,* 138–153.

SAS Institute, Inc. (1985). *SAS user's guide: Statistics* (Version 5 ed.).

Searle, S. R. (1971). *Linear models.* New York: Wiley.

Shavelson, R., & Webb, N. (1981). Generalizability theory: 1973–1980. *British Journal of Mathematical and Statistical Psychology, 34,* 133–166.

Shrout, D. E., & Fleiss, J. L. (1979). Interclass correlations: Uses in assessing rater reliability, *Psychological Bulletin, 86,* 420–428.

Swallow, W. H., & Monahan, J. F. (1984). Monte carlo comparison of ANOVA, MIVQUE, REML, and ML estimators of variance components. *Technometrics, 26,* 265–272.

Thorndike, R. L. (1982). *Applied psychometrics.* Boston: Houghton Mifflin.

van der Kamp, L. J. T. (1976). Generalizability and educational measurement. In D. N. M. de Gruijter & L. J. T. van der Kamp (Eds.), *Advances in psychological and educational measurement.* New York: Wiley.

COVARIANCE STRUCTURE ANALYSIS:

EXTENSIONS AND DEVELOPMENTS

Richard G. Lomax

The development of methodologies to test hypotheses regarding the structure underlying covariance matrices appears to be the single-most important contribution of statistics to the social and behavioral sciences during the past twenty years. The term "covariance structure analysis" can be traced back through Bock and Bargmann (1966) to earlier statistical work on the estimation of variance and covariance components and to work on factor analysis (e.g., Spearman, 1904; Henderson, 1953; Burt, 1947; Lawley, 1940, 1943, 1944). As defined by Bock and Bargmann, the purpose of the method is "for analyzing a sample covariance matrix in order to detect and assess the potency of latent sources of variation and covariation in multivariate normal data" (p. 507).

Today covariance structure analysis represents a general methodology which includes procedures such as path analysis (early work by Wright, 1921, 1934; later work by Duncan, 1966, 1975; Blalock, 1971) which is a special case of the econometric simultaneous equations model (cf. Johnston, 1972), factor analysis (early work by Lawley, 1940, 1943, 1944; Joreskog, 1967), structural equation modeling (early work by Joreskog, 1973; Keesling, 1972; Wiley, 1973; also see Joreskog, 1970; Goldberger & Duncan, 1973), latent structure analysis (early work by Lazarsfeld, 1950; Lazarsfeld & Henry, 1968), cross-lagged panel correlation (early work by Campbell, 1963; Kenny, 1975; but see Rogosa, 1979),

---

Advances in Social Science Methodology, Volume 1, pages 171–204.

ISBN: 0-89232-736-7

and soft modeling (early work by Wold, 1975). The latter three methods will not be considered here.

The objective of covariance structure models analysis is to provide empirical tests of theoretically-based models. As such, the researcher is forced into specifying precisely those parameters of interest for the model(s) to be evaluated. Thus, the importance of theory cannot be emphasized enough in the formulation and testing of covariance structure models (see Cooley, 1978). Frequently many of these models are referred to as causal models although for philosophical reasons this is not the preferred terminology (for a philosophical discussion of causality, see Popper, 1959; Simon, 1977; James, Mulaik, & Brett, 1982). The purpose of this chapter is to review (1) the "standard" theory underlying covariance structure models, and (2) recent extensions and developments of the general covariance structure model. The general linear structural relationship (LISREL) model developed by Joreskog (1978) will mainly be considered here although other covariance structure models will be discussed as well.

THEORY

This section discusses the theoretical foundation of the measurement (or confirmatory factor analysis) model, the structural equation model, and collectively, the LISREL model. Computer programs to implement various models are discussed.

The Confirmatory Factor Analysis or Measurement Model

The aim of common-factor analysis, in general, is to reproduce (or explain) the interrelationships among a set of observed variables through a fewer number of synthetic variables known as common factors. The common factors are linear combinations of the common parts of the variables (usually with substantive meaning). The factor analysis model may be expressed as

$$x = \Lambda_x \xi + \delta, \tag{1}$$

where x ($q \times 1$) is a vector of observed variables (or indicator variables), ξ ($n \times 1$) is a vector of unobserved common factors, δ ($q \times 1$) is a vector of unobserved unique factors (or measurement errors), and Λ_x ($q \times n$) is a matrix of the factor loadings (or a regression matrix) of x on ξ. The factor loadings indicate how a unit change in a common factor influences an observed variable (similar to regression weights).

Initially a distinction must be made between exploratory and confirmatory factor analysis models. In an exploratory model, the only specification of the model is usually in the number of observed variables and common factors (i.e., q and n). Typically, the assumptions are that (1) all observed variables are a function of all common factors, (2) the unique factors are uncorrelated, (3) each observed variable is a function of a unique factor, and (4) the common and unique factors are uncorrelated. Additionally, the common factors may or may not be correlated (i.e., the factors may be oblique or orthogonal). Exploratory factor analysis models are those typically found in main-frame and microcomputer statistical packages. For a comparison of factor analysis programs in the most commonly used main-frame packages, see MacCallum (1983).

In a confirmatory factor analysis model, the researcher imposes some substantive constraints on the model. The constraints may determine (1) which observed variables are a function of which common factors, (2) which observed variables are a function of a unique factor (e.g., there may not be a unique factor for each observed variable), (3) which common factors are correlated, and (4) which unique factors are correlated. The assumptions are that (1) x, ξ and δ are measured as deviations from their means (i.e., have an expected value of zero), (2) $q > n$, and (3) the common factors are uncorrelated with the unique factors (Long, 1983a). In both the exploratory and confirmatory models, one cannot examine the structural relationships among the common factors, only their intercorrelations. This would necessitate a structural equation model, which will be discussed in the next section.

The population covariance matrix of the observed variables is defined as the matrix Σ ($q \times q$). If the observed variables are standardized to have a variance of one, then Σ is a correlation matrix. The covariance equation may be written as

$$\Sigma = \Lambda_x \Phi \Lambda_x' + \Theta, \qquad (2)$$

where Φ ($n \times n$) is a covariance matrix of the common factors and Θ ($q \times q$) is a covariance matrix of the unique factors. One particular application of the confirmatory model is in assessing convergent and discriminant validity via the Campbell and Fiske (1959) multitrait-multimethod (MTMM) matrix (cf. Lomax & Algina, 1979).

Prior to estimation of the parameters of the model, the identification problem must be resolved. Identification involves whether the parameters of the model can be uniquely determined or estimated based on the amount of information contained in S, the sample covariance matrix. This is analogous to the situation in algebra where the number of equations is compared to the number of unknowns. If a model is not identified, then one cannot uniquely determine all of the parameters. For example, even if Σ is known, we may not be able to find unique estimates of the parameters in Λ_x, Φ and Θ. We could find numerous values for the parameters all of which are consistent with the covariance equation in (2). Estimation assumes that the model is identified; otherwise the estimates are arbitrary and meaningless (even though a computer program may go ahead and estimate the parameters anyway). By imposing constraints on the factor model, we hope to find a solution to the identification problem. Constraints typically involve fixing elements of Λ_x, Φ and Θ to values such as zero or unity (although parameters can also be constrained to equal other parameters). If we impose enough constraints on the model to eliminate all but one set of values of the parameters, then the model is said to be identified.

A confirmatory factor analysis model cannot be identified until the metric or scale of the common factors has been set. That is, there is an indeterminacy between the variance of the common factor and the loadings of the observed variable on that factor. The solution to the indeterminacy is to either fix the variances of the common factors to a value such as unity, or fix one loading of each common factor to a value such as unity. This will eliminate the scale indeterminacy, but not necessarily the identification problem (for additional information on identification, see Long, 1983a; Joreskog & Sorbom, 1984).

There are three levels of model identification, which depend on the amount of information in S necessary for uniquely estimating the parameters of the model. First, a model is said to be *under-identified* (or not identified) if one or more parameters may not be uniquely determined, due to not enough information in S. Second, a model is said to be *just-identified* if all of the parameters may be uniquely determined, due to just enough information in S. Third, a model is said to be *over-identified* when there is more than one way of estimating a parameter (or parameters), due to more than enough information in S. There are several conditions for establishing identification. A necessary, but insufficient, condition for identification is the order condition where the number of independent parameters to be estimated must be less than or equal to the number of distinct values in S. Sufficient conditions exist such as the rank condition (cf. Duncan, 1975; Johnston, 1972). The best method for evaluating identification is to solve the identification problem algebraically.

Once the identification problem has been solved, then estimation of the parameters may proceed. It is desired to find estimates of Λ_x, Φ and Θ that produce a matrix Σ that is as close as possible to S. Estimation then involves the use of a particular fitting function to minimize this difference. There are three fitting functions in common use today, although other newer estimation procedures will be discussed later. These functions are the methods of unweighed (or ordinary) least squares (ULS), generalized (or weighted) least squares (GLS), and maximum likelihood (ML). In ULS, estimation involves minimization of the fitting function

$$F(ULS) = tr(S - \Sigma)^2. \tag{3}$$

ULS estimators are consistent, have no distributional assumptions or associated statistical tests, and are scale dependent (i.e., changes in variable scale yield different solutions).

The GLS and ML methods are scale-free and involve more complex fitting functions. The GLS fitting function is

$$F(GLS) = tr((S - \Sigma)\ W)^2, \tag{4}$$

where W is a weight matrix (such as S^{-1}), and the ML fitting function is

$$F(ML) = tr(S\,\Sigma^{-1}) + (\log|\Sigma| - \log|S|) - q. \quad (5)$$

Both methods have desirable asymptotic properties (i.e., large sample properties) such as minimum variance and unbiasedness. Also, both methods assume multivariate normality of the observed variables, although the GLS assumptions are not quite as stringent (see Joreskog & Goldberger, 1972; Browne, 1974, 1984). Until recently little was known about the robustness of these methods to assumption violations and to use of small sample sizes. This recent research will be discussed in later sections of the chapter. In addition, if standardization of the common factors is desired, one may obtain a standardized solution (and thereby standardized estimates) when the variances of the common factors are fixed at unity.

Once estimation has been completed, testing of the model for goodness of fit follows. That is, the sample data set is examined to determine its consistency with the theoretically specified model. Only one fit index was originally applied to assess the goodness of fit of covariance structure models. Others have subsequently been developed and will be discussed later. A large sample likelihood ratio test, the chi-square statistic, may be computed for a specified model. The likelihood ratio is distributed in large samples as chi-square with degrees of freedom equal to the number of distinct variances and covariances in S minus the number of unique parameters to be estimated. If the chi-square value is large relative to degrees of freedom, then the fit of the model to the data generation process is not optimal. If the chi-square value is small relative to degrees of freedom, then the fit of the model to the data generation process is plausible. In considering a single model, this statistic is not particularly informative as it is a direct function of sample size. In large samples, a "good fit" as defined by the chi-square statistic may be difficult to find. In small samples, many competing models may yield a "good fit."

The chi-square statistic is somewhat more useful in considering the improvement in fit of nested or hierarchical models where one model is less restrictive (i.e., having more free parameters and fewer degrees of freedom) than another. The difference between the chi-square fit statistics of the two models is also distributed as chi-square with degrees of freedom equal to the difference in the two models' degrees of freedom. If the chi-square difference is large relative to the degrees of freedom difference, then the additional free parameters in the less restricted model have led to a better fit than the more restricted model. If the chi-square difference is small relative to the degrees of freedom difference, then the additional free parameters in the less restricted model have not led to a better fit as compared to the more restricted model. The reconstructed matrix Σ based on the specified theoretical model may be compared to S. The difference between S and Σ is shown in a matrix of residuals, and indicates those relationships among the observed variables which are not explained by the model. However, it has been shown by Costner and Schoenberg (1973) that the residual matrix may be misleading in certain cases.

Theory underlying the confirmatory factor model was developed by Joreskog (1967, 1969) for the single sample case. The multiple sample analog was developed by Joreskog (1971a) (further refined by Sorbom, 1974; Rock, Werts, & Flaugher, 1978) where parameters may be estimated for G independent samples. Constraints may be imposed across samples for the factor loadings, common factor variances, and/or unique factor variances (Long, 1983a). Some examples of applications of the confirmatory factor analysis model are Kroonenberg and Lewis (1982) for the single sample case, Tanaka and Bentler (1983) for the multiple sample case, and Cole and Maxwell (1985) for MTMM matrices. These are all examples of first-order factor models where the only structure imposed on the common factors is whether they are orthogonal or oblique. Higher-order factor models are used when, for example, there are several first-order intelligence factors such as verbal and quantitative ability, and a second-order factor of general intelligence is of substantive interest. Examples of second-order factor models are shown in Weeks (1980) for the single sample case, and Marsh (1985) for the multiple sample case.

The Structural Equation Model and the LISREL Model

If one is interested in the structural relationships between common factors, then a model which represents these relationships, that is, the structural equation model, must be implemented. A distinction is made between two types of common factors, hereafter referred to as latent independent variables (or latent exogenous variables) and latent dependent variables (or latent endogenous variables). If we let η ($m \times 1$) and ξ ($n \times 1$) be vectors of the latent endogenous and exogenous variables, respectively, then a system of linear structural equations is

$$\eta = B\,\eta + \Gamma\,\xi + \zeta, \tag{6}$$

where B ($m \times m$) and Γ ($m \times n$) are matrices of structure coefficients relating the endogenous variables to one another and the exogenous variables to the endogenous variables, respectively, and ζ ($m \times 1$) is a vector of residuals due to errors in equations (or disturbances). The assumptions are that (1) η, ξ, and ζ are measured as deviations from their respective means (i.e., with expected values of zero), (2) ζ is uncorrelated with ξ, and (3) $I - B$ is singular.

The path analysis model is a special case of the structural equation model, as defined here, where all of the variables are observed; that is, there are no latent variables and thus no need for a measurement model. Originally devised by Wright (1921, 1934), the path model is simply a system of multiple linear regression equations. A major problem with the path analytic approach is in assuming that each of the observed variables is measured without error, in a construct validity and reliability sense. Considerable measurement error can be introduced into path models which may have an unpredictable effect on the structure coefficients (Mason, Hauser, Kerckhoff, Poss, & Manton, 1976; Bielby, Hauser, & Featherman, 1977; Patterson & Wolfle, 1981; Won, 1982; Gallini & Mandeville, 1984). The amount of measurement error can be quite large when we consider the types of variables typically dealt with in the social and behavioral sciences. One solution, of course, is to obtain multiple indicators through factor analysis models. Further discussion of path models is contained in Anderson and Evans (1974), Anderson (1978), Wolfle (1980), and Asher (1983). A recent example of a path model is shown in Keith and Page (1985).

When there are both latent independent and dependent variables, a factor analysis or measurement model needs to be specified for each type of common factor (i.e., exogenous and endogenous). In the measurement model, since η and ξ are unobservable, let y $(p \times 1)$ and x $(q \times 1)$ be vectors of observable indicator variables, such that

$$y = \Lambda_y \eta + \epsilon, \tag{7}$$

and

$$x = \Lambda_x \xi + \delta, \tag{8}$$

where ϵ $(p \times 1)$ and δ $(q \times 1)$ are vectors of unique factors (or measurement errors) in y and x, respectively. The vectors y and x are assumed to be measured as deviations from their respective means. Let Λ_y $(p \times m)$ and Λ_x $(q \times n)$ be matrices of common factor loadings (or regression matrices) of y on η and of x on ξ, respectively. The errors of measurement ϵ are assumed to be uncorrelated with the errors of measurement δ, and ϵ and δ are assumed to be uncorrelated with η, ξ and ζ.

Next we combine aspects of the structural equation and measurement models. Let Φ $(n \times n)$ and Ψ $(m \times m)$ be covariance matrices of ξ and ζ, respectively, and let Θ_ϵ $(p \times p)$ and Θ_δ $(q \times q)$ be covariance matrices of ϵ and δ, respectively. A population covariance matrix Σ is constructed from the eight matrices Λ_y, Λ_x, B, Γ, Φ, Ψ, Θ_ϵ and Θ_δ as shown in Joreskog and Sorbom (1984). Elements of these eight matrices may consist of parameters which are fixed (to values such as zero or unity), free (to be estimated), or constrained (to equal other parameters). In summary, the LISREL model consists of the structural equation model which describes the relationships among the latent variables via a set of general linear equations, and the measurement model which describes the measurement of the latent variables by a combination of the observable indicator variables, and allows for better measurement of the latent variables.

The identification problem for the structural equation model is similar to that for the measurement model as previously described (although technically more complex). In addition to the level of identification issue (i.e., an under-, just-, or over-identified model), is the notion of the type of structural model specified (i.e., a recursive or nonrecursive model). A structural model is said to be recursive when all of the structural relationships are uni-directional such that no two latent variables are reciprocally related. That is, no feedback loops may exist where a latent variable feeds back upon itself. Nonrecursive structural models include a reciprocal or bi-directional relationship, such that there is feedback. Fisher (1966) describes the identification problem for structural equation models.

Let us consider the estimation problem for the structural equation model. If a model is under-identified, it is impossible to estimate all of the parameters with any estimation procedure without additional constraints. If a model is just-identified and recursive, either the ULS or the indirect least squares (ILS) (or reduced form method in econometrics) method is appropriate. If a model is just-identified and nonrecursive, the ILS method is appropriate. More complex methods of estimation may be used for the latter two cases, but the estimates will yield the exact same values. If a model is overidentified, one of the following methods is appropriate: the two-stage least squares (2SLS), three-stage least squares (3SLS), or maximum-likelihood methods (ML) (limited or full information ML methods). While the ULS, ILS and 2SLS methods are applied to one structural equation at a time, the 3SLS and ML methods are applied to all of the equations of the model at the same time, and thus yield estimates for all of the parameters simultaneously. For further discussion of estimation procedures, see Johnston (1972) or Duncan (1975). Testing of the structural equation model is the same as with the confirmatory factor analysis model.

If standardization of the latent variables is desired, then standardized estimates of the parameters may be obtained by fixing the latent variable variances to unity; this is known as the standardized solution. A separate but related issue is standardization of the observed variables. When the unit of measurement for the indicator variables is of no particular interest to the researcher (i.e., arbitrary or irrelevant), then only an analysis of the correlation matrix is typically of interest (although current standard errors and goodness-of-fit indices may not be appropriate). Since the correlation matrix involves a rescaling of the observed variables, the parameters estimated for the measurement model (in particular, the factor loadings) will be of the same order of magnitude (i.e., on the same scale). When the same indicator variables are measured either over time (i.e., longitudinal analysis) or for multiple samples, or when equality constraints are imposed on two or more parameters, an analysis of the covariance matrix is appropriate so as to capitalize upon the metric similarities of the variables (Lomax, 1982). For further discussion of standardization issues, see Kim and Ferree (1981), Gerbing and Hunter (1982), and Long (1983b).

Theory underlying the structural equation and LISREL models was developed by Joreskog (1970, 1973, 1977, 1978) and Joreskog and Goldberger (1975). For further discussion of these models, see Goldberger and Duncan (1973), Duncan (1975), Heise (1975), Bielby and Hauser (1977), Kenny (1979), and Long (1983b). Other general introductory references to the LISREL model are Bentler (1980), Maruyama and McGarvey (1980), Lomax (1982), and Wolfle (1982).

Unfortunately, few advanced statistics texts for the social and behavioral sciences provide much of a discussion of covariance structure models (although see Pedhazur, 1982). An application of the complete LISREL model is Gallini and Bell (1983).

It is also possible to apply the general covariance structure model to the multiple sample situation in the analysis of experimental, quasi-experimental, cross-sectional, and/or longitudinal data. In the multiple sample case, one may (1) estimate separately the parameters for each of G independent samples, (2) test whether specified parameters are equivalent across groups (i.e., for any of the parameter matrices in the measurement and/or structural equation models), (3) test whether there are group differences on the latent exogenous variables, and (4) test whether there are differential effects for one or more of the structural equations. Specifically, in the multiple sample case the measurement model becomes

$$y = \upsilon_y^{(g)} + \Lambda_y^{(g)} \eta + \epsilon, \tag{9}$$

and

$$x = \upsilon_x^{(g)} + \Lambda_x^{(g)} \xi + \delta, \tag{10}$$

where $g = 1, \ldots, G$ identifies the sample, and υ_y and υ_x are vectors of constant intercept terms for the indicator variables (previously constrained to be zero in (7) and (8)). The structural model becomes

$$\eta = \alpha^{(g)} + B^{(g)} \eta + \Gamma^{(g)} \xi + \zeta, \tag{11}$$

where α is a vector of effects for the structural equations of η [previously constrained to be zero in (6)]. The expected values of ξ are no longer constrained to zero so that these values are the effects due to ξ. Theoretical references on the multiple sample case include Joreskog (1971b), Sorbom (1982), Lee and Tsui (1982), and Lomax (1983). An example of the multiple sample LISREL case is Lomax (1985).

Other Covariance Structure Models

There are several formulations of the general covariance structure model other than the Joreskog (1978) LISREL model. Bentler and Weeks (1979, 1980) have reformulated the LISREL model where no distinction is made between latent variables and observed (or manifest) variables. The structural equation model becomes

$$\eta^* = B^* \eta^* + \Gamma^* \xi^*, \tag{12}$$

where η^* is a vector of dependent variables (latent or manifest), ξ^* is a vector of independent variables (latent or manifest), B^* is a matrix representing relationships between dependent variables, and Γ^* is a matrix representing relationships between independent and dependent variables. Since (12) includes manifest and latent variables, it is desirable to provide a representation for the relationships between the variables in (12) and the measured variables. The representation (known as the selection model) is specified as

$$y = \mu_y + G_y \eta^*, \tag{13}$$

and

$$x = \mu_x + G_x \xi^*, \tag{14}$$

where G_y and G_x are known matrices with zero entries except for a single unit in each row to select y from η and x from ξ. The vectors μ_y and μ_x are vectors of means [as in (9) and (10)]. Thus η^* consists of η and y, B^* consists of B and Λ_y, Γ^* consists of Γ and Λ_x, and ξ^* consists of ξ, x, ζ, ϵ and δ. The covariance equation is shown in Bentler and Weeks (1979, 1980).

The Bentler-Weeks formulation is simpler (e.g., less matrices), and more general than the Joreskog formulation. For example, the Bentler-Weeks model explicitly allows for higher-order factors, while the Joreskog model requires special procedures involving the redefinition of certain matrices. The Bentler-Weeks approach can also handle a wider range of linear parametric constraints than the Joreskog approach. A variation on the Bentler-Weeks model is the Reticular Action Model (RAM) developed by McArdle (1978) and described in McArdle and McDonald (1984) and McDonald (1985).

The Covariance Structure Analysis (COSAN) model developed by McDonald (1978, 1980, 1985) is a block-recursive model obtained by repeating a simplified version of LISREL in a block-recursive sequence. The COSAN model, also more general than the LISREL model, makes no distinction between independent and dependent variables. The COSAN model is much more complex than the LISREL and Bentler-Weeks models, and due to space limitations, the reader is referred to McDonald (1978, 1980, 1985).

Computer Programs

The Joreskog model (1978) is currently implemented in LISREL VI (Joreskog & Sorbom, 1984) and is written in mainframe computer (stand-alone or through SPSS-X) and microcomputer (IBM-PC) versions (available from Scientific Software, Inc., P. O. Box 536, Mooresville, IN 46158). As input, the program can handle raw data, and correlation, covariance and moment matrices. Parameter estimates may be obtained for any of the following estimation methods: ULS, instrumental variables, 2SLS, GLS, or ML. Output may include the following: parameter estimates, standard errors (ML only), and t values (ML only) for each parameter estimated; goodness of fit indices (although not for ULS); first-order derivatives of F for the fixed parameters; the residual matrix of $S - \Sigma$; correlations among the parameters estimated (ML only); and factor score regressions (i.e., regressions among the latent variables).

The Bentler-Weeks model (1979, 1980) is implemented in the EQS computer program (Bentler, 1984) distributed by BMDP Statistical Software (1964 Westwood Blvd., Suite 202, Los Angeles, CA 90025) and is currently available in mainframe computer and microcomputer (IBM-PC) versions. The EQS computer program does not use matrix algebra in formulating equations, but uses the rather convenient convention of regression-like equations. The program can estimate parameters using ULS, GLS, and ML methods and also may utilize non-normal theory to generate parameter estimates for observed non-normal variables having similar marginal kurtoses. Parameters may be constrained to equal other parameters, constrained to linear combinations of other parameters, or constrained between an upper and lower bound.

The McDonald model (1978, 1980, 1985) can be utilized with the COSAN computer program written for mainframe computers (available from Colin Fraser, The Centre for Behavioural Studies in Education, University of New England, Armidale, N.S.W. Australia 2351). The estimation procedures available are the ULS, GLS, and ML methods. Input data can be raw scores, correlation or covariance matrices. The statistical portion of the output may consist of results of the minimization procedure, parameter estimates and their standard errors, and residuals.

Muthen (1984) has developed a LISREL Companion computer program (known as LISCOMP) to perform covariance structure analysis of dichotomous, ordered categorical, and continuous indicator variables (also available from Scientific Software, Inc.). LISCOMP generates ULS and GLS estimators and can also compute univariate and bivariate probit regression by the ML method. The program allows for both simple and multiple sample analyses.

EXTENSIONS AND DEVELOPMENTS

In this section, recent extensions and developments of the general covariance structure model are described. Herein are contained discussions of (1) goodness of fit indices, (2) estimation methods, (3) discrete and non-normally distributed variables, (4) sample size, (5) misspecification, (6) measurement error, (7) missing data, (8) direct and indirect effects, (9) constraints, and (10) nonlinear and interactive effects.

Goodness of Fit

Following the development of the chi-square likelihood ratio test for the assessment of goodness of fit, other goodness of model fit indices have been developed. Tucker and Lewis (1973) derived a goodness of fit index for ML exploratory factor analysis models. The index ρ, which Tucker and Lewis termed a reliability coefficient, was originally devised to determine how well a factor model with k common factors represents the observed covariance matrix S as compared to a factor model with zero common factors. The Tucker-Lewis index is

$$\rho = (Q_0 - Q_k)/(Q_0 - 1), \tag{15}$$

where Q = (chi-square/df), 0 represents a model with no factors and k represents a model with k factors. Thus the index compares a model with no factors (a null model indicating independence) to a model with k factors. However, the Tucker-Lewis index is not normed and does not necessarily fall between zero and one. This index has also been applied to more general types of covariance structure models.

Bentler and Bonett (1980) have extended the Tucker-Lewis coefficient to include a null model (M_0), a more restricted model (M_k) and a less restricted model (M_1). One may compare the restricted models M_k and M_1 where the null model M_0 serves as a baseline as follows

$$\rho_{k1} = (Q_k - Q_1)/(Q_0 - 1). \tag{16}$$

Bentler and Bonett refer to ρ_{k1} as the nonnormed fit index. They also devised a normed fit index which is given as

$$\Delta_{k1} = (F_k - F_1)/F_0, \tag{17}$$

where F (F = chi-square/N − 1) is any fit function (e.g., ULS, GLS, ML) and Δ_{k1} is theoretically scaled from zero to one. The denominator of Δ_{k1} (and ρ_{k1}) is in general the most restricted model tested and may be a general null model [e.g., independence of observed variables where $\Sigma = D\ (\Phi)$], a null measurement model or a null structural model. In addition to their utility in comparing nested and non-nested models within a sample, the normed and nonnormed fit indices may be used to compare a particular model across multiple samples, regardless of sample size, since the indices are independent of N.

Recently, Sobel and Bohrnstedt (1985) have extended the work of Bentler and Bonett (1980). Sobel & Bohrnstedt argue that the null model as defined by Bentler and Bonett is too restrictive and that a less restrictive, more general version of the null model, termed the baseline model, may be more useful. Several baseline models are proposed for covariance structure analysis which take into account the exploratory-confirmatory continuum in terms of an empirical basis for model-testing. Sobel and Bohrnstedt believe that only in the purely exploratory situation is the null model appropriate and show for other less-exploratory situations that the null model may lead to inappropriate conclusions. Since previous empirical results are usually taken into account in the construction of covariance structure models, it would seem reasonable from a Bayesian point of view that such prior knowledge be utilized in a baseline model. This model could be compared to a less restricted model where some of the parameters to be estimated have little or no known empirical basis.

Another method for comparing alternative covariance structure models is proposed by Cudeck and Browne (1983). Since models in the social and behavioral sciences are typically only approximations to reality, stringent goodness of fit procedures leading to a statistical decision may not always be appropriate. Consider the situation where one is interested in evaluating several alternative models, from a baseline to a least restrictive or saturated model. Cudeck and Browne propose a cross-validation procedure where the sample is randomly split in half, one sub-sample to be used as a calibration sample and the other sub-sample to be used as a validation sample. From the calibration sample, the usual fitting function F is obtained. The validation sample is used to obtain the "cross-validation index" which is a measure of the difference between the validation sample covariance matrix S and the calibration sample reproduced covariance matrix Σ. This procedure is conducted for each model to be considered, and the model with the best "predictive validity" is the model with the smallest cross-validation index. A double cross-validation is also recommended where the samples are reversed in the process. However, the Cudeck-Browne procedure tends to select the saturated model when sample size is large. When sample size is small, the cross-validation procedure may not be practical, although Cudeck and Browne suggest two indices which may be appropriate for this situation.

An informal index of goodness of fit which has often been used (particularly prior to Bentler & Bonett, 1980) is a ratio of the chi-square statistic to degrees of freedom. However, this index is also nonnormed and researchers disagree as to a "rule of thumb" of what the ratio should be for a model to be deemed plausible. Therefore this index is not recommended.

In the latest version of the LISREL program (LISREL VI, Joreskog & Sorbom, 1984), several new goodness of fit indices have been included. The goodness-of-fit index (GFI) is a measure of the relative amount of the sample covariance matrix S that is accounted for by the theoretically specified model. In contrast to the chi-square test, the GFI is independent of sample size and is said to be rather robust with respect to violations of the normality assumption. These are important considerations. The adjusted GFI (AGFI) adjusts for the number of degrees of freedom in the model. Both of these indices are theoretically scaled from zero to one (one indicative of a perfect fit). The root mean square residual is a measure of the average residual covariance.

In conclusion, there are numerous procedures for assessing the goodness of fit of a covariance structure model. Of course, one reason why a model may yield an unacceptable fit is model misspecification, an issue to be discussed in a subsequent section. For additional discussion of goodness of fit in covariance structure models, see Bentler and Bonett (1980), Hoelter (1983) (critical N procedure), Joreskog and Sorbom (1984), and Sobel and Bohrnstedt (1985). Recently Satorra and Saris (1985) have proposed a procedure for approximating the power of the chi-square likelihood ratio test using statistics from the output of available computer programs.

Estimation Methods

Three estimation methods were previously described in detail: unweighted least squares (ULS), weighted or generalized least squares (GLS), and maximum-likelihood (ML). Recently, several new estimation procedures have been devised for the analysis of covariance structure models. In the latest version of the LISREL computer program (LISREL VI, Joreskog & Sorbom, 1984), starting values are automatically estimated for each parameter. Prior to LISREL V, the user had to specify starting values for each of the parameters to be estimated, and this frequently led to difficulties. The automatic starting values are referred to as initial estimates and involve a fast, non-iterative procedure (as is the 2SLS method while the other methods in LISREL involve iterative procedures). The initial estimates involve the instrumental variables and least squares (ULS and 2SLS) methods developed by Hagglund (1982). Often the user may wish to obtain only the initial estimates (due to cost efficiency), or use them as starting values in subsequent analyses. The initial estimates are consistent and rather efficient relative to the ML estimator.

If one can assume multivariate normality of the observable variables, then moments beyond the second (e.g., skewness and kurtosis) can be ignored. As shown in the next section of this chapter, for violations of the normality assumption, parameter estimates, standard errors, and chi-square goodness of fit tests may be suspect. One alternative is the previously mentioned method of GLS developed by Browne (1974) which assumes multivariate normality, but only stipulates that the fourth-order moments (i.e., kurtosis) are zero. Browne (1982, 1984) later recognized that the weight matrix of GLS may be modified to yield asymptotically distribution-free (ADF) estimates, standard errors, and test statistics. Here the distribution of variables is assumed to be elliptical, that is, the marginal distributions have equal kurtoses. Another general class of ADF estimators was derived by Shapiro (1983) based on the min- and max-functions. Bentler (1983) developed a more general elliptical GLS estimation procedure for covariance structure models. All of these methods are based on the GLS method by specifying the weight matrix to be of a certain form, which include for Bentler both distribution-specific and distribution-free estimates, although none of these methods take multivariate kurtosis into account. In fact, Bentler (1983) sees "little reason to continue to use normal theory statistics . . . since the more general elliptical alternative is available" (p. 510). It must be pointed out that computational complexity of the ADF estimators is such that large samples (and large computers) are needed to provide stable estimates. A maximum number of variables for ADF estimation would appear to be 20 to 25 at present. See Bentler (1983) for a more thorough discussion of these estimators.

Huba and Harlow (1983) compared ML, GLS, ULS, and ADF estimators for two real LISREL-type models, and concluded that in general the methods yielded the same results. Several of the variables in the models had rather high kurtoses. Similar conclusions were reached by Huba and Bentler (1983), although much simulation research must be conducted before conclusive statements may be made (see next section). Browne's (1984) asymptotic theory, however, suggests that goodness of fit indices and standard errors of parameter estimates derived under the assumption of multivariate normality should not be employed if the distribution of observations has a non-zero value of kurtosis. Thus, either elliptical theory should be utilized, or a correction for kurtosis should be made (Browne, 1984).

Two other estimation methods have been proposed. In 1977, Dempster, Laird and Rubin introduced the EM algorithm for ML estimation. More recently, Rubin and Thayer (1982) derived algebraically the EM algorithm for ML factor analysis (confirmatory and exploratory models) where the common factors are treated as missing data. Since that time there has been some discussion as to whether the EM algorithm will converge to a single local maximum if the algorithm converges (see Bentler & Tanaka, 1983; Rubin & Thayer, 1983). Bock and Aitkin (1981) have applied the EM algorithm to ML exploratory factor analysis models with categorical response variables. Lee (1981) has developed a Bayesian approach to confirmatory factor analysis. Certainly more research is needed to determine the utility, statistical and practical, of the newer estimation methods in covariance structure analysis.

Discrete and Non-normally Distributed Variables

An implicit assumption of ML estimators is that information contained in the first- and second-order moments (i.e., location and dispersion, respectively) of the observed variables is sufficient so that information contained in higher-order moments (e.g., skewness and kurtosis) can be ignored. If the observed variables are intervally scaled and multivariate normal, then the ML estimates, standard errors and chi-square test are appropriate. However, if the observed variables are ordinally scaled and/or extremely skewed or peaked (and thus non-normally distributed), then the ML estimates, standard errors and chi-square test may not be appropriate.

Theoretical research on the prediction of a categorical response variable by latent variables with single indicators (using standard regression-type procedures) is well-known and is reviewed by Amemiya (1981). Most notable are the probit and logit regression models, for both the univariate and multivariate cases (cf. Maddala & Lee, 1976; Amemiya, 1978; Heckman, 1978; Muthen, 1979). If we consider next the categorical factor analysis model, seminal work was conducted by Christoffersson (1975) and Muthen (1978) for the single sample case, and by Muthen and Christoffersson (1981) for the multiple sample case (see application by Muthen, 1981). Research on path analysis models with categorical data is also fairly well-known and is described in Goodman (1972, 1973, 1979), Bishop, Fienberg, and Holland (1975), and Fienberg (1980) utilizing loglinear analysis of contingency tables.

The extension to LISREL-type structural equation models was made by Muthen (1982, 1984). Muthen proposed a three-stage limited information GLS estimator which provides a large sample chi-square test of the model and large sample standard errors. The Muthen CVM (categorical variable methodology) approach is believed to produce more suitable coefficients of association than the ordinary Pearson product-moment correlations and covariances applied to ordered categorical variables (Muthen, 1983). This is so particularly with markedly skewed categorical variables where correlations must be "stretched" to assume values throughout the −1, +1 range, as is done in the LISREL computer program. A limitation of the Muthen method at present is that the creation of the weight matrix limits practical use to about 20 to 25 observed variables; further research on an appropriate weight matrix is needed.

The LISREL VI program handles ordinal variables by computing a polychoric correlation for two ordinal variables (Olsson, 1979a), and a polyserial correlation for an ordinal and an interval variable (Olsson, Drasgow, & Dorans, 1981), where the ordinal variables are assumed to have an underlying bivariate normal distribution (which is not necessary with the Muthen approach). All correlations (i.e., the Pearson product-moment, polychoric, and polyserial) are then placed into a correlation matrix for LISREL to analyze (although Joreskog and Sorbom caution the user about using ML estimation for such mixed correlation matrices).

Various simulation studies shed light on these considerations, and the factor analytic case will be discussed first. Muthen (1983) and Olsson (1979b) found that the use of the Pearson product-moment coefficient results in underestimates of the ML factor loadings of ordered categorical variables and inflated values of the chi-square statistic. In the case studies of Joreskog and Goldberger (1972), Browne (1982), Huba and Bentler (1983), Huba and Tanaka (1983), and Huba and Harlow (1983, 1984), comparisons were made of the ML, GLS, and ADF (limited information of second order; however, see Mooijaart, 1985, for a model where the estimators take advantage of higher-order information) estimators in the factor analysis of categorical variables. In general, no large differences were found among the estimated factor loadings for these procedures, although (1) the ADF measurement error variances tended to be lowest, (2) the ADF chi-square index tended to have the lowest value, and (3) the standard errors of the ML and GLS estimators tended to be lowest.

Muthen and Kaplan (1985) considered non-normal categorical (Likert) variables in factor analysis. In general, the ADF and CVM estimators were found to outperform the ML and GLS methods. When skewnesses and kurtoses are small (in the range of −1 to +1), the methods showed no marked differences. When skewnesses and kurtoses exceed 2.0 in absolute value, distortions of ML and GLS chi-square tests and standard errors may occur, although the estimates themselves do not differ much. Muthen, Kaplan, and Chan (1985) obtained similar results for the multiple sample case. However, somewhat different results were reported by Tanaka (1984) and Browne (1984) when the data were generated from distributions of non-skewed continuous variables with high kurtoses and of highly skewed continuous variables with high kurtoses. Tanaka found the ML chi-square values to be overestimated and that the ADF chi-square behaved more appropriately. Factor loadings and measurement error variances were underestimated by both methods, more so for error variances. The ML estimated standard errors were downwardly biased while the bias was much less for ADF. Brown obtained similar results except that the ML parameter estimates were not biased. Thus, the simulation results appear to be specific to the type of data considered.

Wolfle and Ethington (1985a) conducted a simulation study of four ordered dichotomous independent variables in a path model, and found that the tetrachoric and polyserial correlations yielded more accurate estimates of the structure coefficients based on the underlying continuous data than did the product-moment correlations.

Ethington (1985) conducted a simulation study on the robustness of structural and measurement model parameters to the dichotomizing of four continuous variables with varying degrees of skewness. A comparison was made of correlation matrices consisting of Pearson product-moment correlations only and of tetrachoric, polyserial, and Pearson product-moment correlations as appropriate. The Pearson product-moment correlation matrices resulted in biased structural parameter estimates when skewed dichotomous variables were present, for both ML and ULS estimators. While parameter estimates were underestimated, the standard errors were inflated resulting in unreliable significance tests, particularly in cases of extreme skewness. In general, the analysis of correlation matrices based on the appropriate coefficients yielded estimates close to the parameter values, although the estimates were more variable than expected and the chi-square goodness of fit statistic was inflated. Ethington's data were generated from continuous distributions and the variables were then dichotomized.

In contrast, Boomsma (1983) conducted a similar study where the observed variables were categorical. He then analyzed the multinomial correlation matrix. Parameter estimates and standard errors were found to be relatively unbiased for less-skewed cases when sample size was large (N = 400). For more-skewed cases, particularly with medium- and large-size correlations, the variation of the estimates was larger than would be expected. An application of a multiple sample structural model using tetrachoric and polyserial measures of association is presented by Ethington and Wolfle (1984). Much work remains to be done to determine those situations where not having intervally scaled, normally-distributed variables results in a serious problem.

Sample Size

Since much of the estimation process is based upon large sample properties, there is concern over the robustness of covariance structure analysis when small sample sizes are employed. Thus far, the definitive study of sample size in covariance structure analysis is the work of Boomsma (1982, 1983, 1985). Boomsma examined two LISREL models with both structural and measurement components (referred to as models "a" and "b"), and numerous variations on a two factor model. Among other things, Boomsma was interested in the effect of sample size (N = 25, 50, 100, 200, 400, each with 300 replications) on nonconvergence problems (i.e., when a final or convergent ML solution was not reached after 250 iterations), improper solutions (i.e., where a variance term was estimated to be negative), bias of parameter estimates and standard errors, and the sampling distribution of the chi-square statistic. The LISREL models (presented in Boomsma, 1983, 1985) will be considered first. Non-convergence was generally not a problem if sample size was at least 100. For model "a" improper solutions only occurred if sample size was less than 400, while for model "b" improper solutions occurred if sample size was less than 200. In model "a" almost no bias was evident for estimates of the parameters and standard errors when sample size was at least 200, while for model "b" the same may be said for samples of at least 100. The sampling distribution of the chi-square statistic seemed to be appropriate for samples of size 100.

For the factor analysis models tested by Boomsma (1982, 1983, 1985), two factor models were considered with 3 or 4 indicator variables each, with correlated (.3) or uncorrelated factors, and with factor loadings of three sizes (thus 12 different models were tested). With small factor loadings and sample sizes less than 100, nonconvergence problems were serious. No improper solutions occurred if sample size was at least 100. Estimates of the parameters and standard errors were relatively unbiased for samples of at least 200. The sampling distribution of the chi-square statistic was appropriate for samples of size 50 with small factor loadings, and for size 200 with medium and large factor loadings. Results were slightly better for 4 than for 3 indicator models. All of these analyses were conducted using the covariance matrix; results using the correlation matrix were not as good, and in particular the variance of the parameter estimates was imprecise. In summary, Boomsma (1985) suggests that in a confirmatory situation one needs a sample size of at least 100, and in an exploratory situation, where numerous models are tested and cross-validation should be done, one needs a sample size of at least 200.

Anderson and Gerbing (1984) also examined sample size (N = 50, 75, 100, 150, 300, each with 100 replications) in factor analysis models. The number of indicators per latent variable was 2, 3, and 4, while factor loadings of moderate, large and mixed sizes were included. The number of factors in the model was 2, 3, or 4, while the correlations among the factors were either .3 or .5. The proportion of convergent solutions increased as sample size increased, the number of indicators per factor increased, factor loading size increased, and factor correlations increased. Similar findings were obtained for the proportion of proper solutions although the effects were not as dramatic (particularly for the factor correlation). These results are similar to those of Boomsma (1982, 1983, 1985). Anderson and Gerbing suggest that with at least three indicators per factor, a sample of size 100 will generally result in a convergent solution, while with only two indicators per factor, a sample of size 150 is generally required for convergence. Gerbing and Anderson (1985) extended their research to consider the effects of sample size on estimates of parameters and standard errors. Sample size had a minimal effect on parameter estimates and estimates of standard errors even when samples were as small as 50. Anderson and Gerbing and Geweke and Singleton (1980) have studied the behavior of various goodness of fit indices for varying sample sizes.

In summary, based on the limited available research it seems advisable to have a minimum of three indicators per latent variable, a sample size of at least 100 (if not 200), and reasonably high factor loadings to obtain optimal results in covariance structure analysis.

Misspecification

Misspecification will occur when the true model, that which generated the data, differs from the model tested. These differences may be due to errors of omission and/or inclusion of any variable or parameter. A misspecified model may result in biased parameter estimates, and this bias is known as specification error. In the presence of specification error, it is likely that one's particular model may not be deemed statistically acceptable. One would like to have available procedures for the detection of specification errors so that subsequently more properly specified models may be evaluated. In general, these procedures are used for performing what is termed a specification search (cf. Leamer, 1978; Long, 1983a). The purpose of a specification search is to alter the original model specification in the search of a more parsimonious, theoretically relevant model which is "best fitting" in some sense. Such procedures are designed to detect and correct for specification errors. Typically applications of covariance structure analysis include some sort of a specification search, informal or otherwise, although the search process may not always be explicated.

An intuitive method of examining misspecification is an examination of the residual matrix (i.e., the differences between the observed covariance matrix and the reconstructed covariance matrix). Costner and Schoenberg (1973) have shown that a simple examination of the residual matrix for a particular model may be misleading unless the specification is extremely simple (possibly then as well). They discuss a procedure of considering sub-models, where for example, all two indicator submodels (i.e., each latent variable is measured by only two indicator variables) are tested to investigate the existence of correlated measurement errors. All three indicator submodels may suggest the existence of other relationships between latent and manifest variables. While the procedure is time-consuming, it does provide the researcher with a reasonable method for the detection of certain types of misspecification, particularly those involving the manifest variables.

Sorbom (1975) considered misspecification of correlated measurement error terms in the analysis of longitudinal data. Like the Costner-Schoenberg procedure, Sorbom's method is ad hoc. Sorbom proposes considering the derivatives of the fitting function F (since F is minimized, free parameters have values of zero and fixed parameters have non-zero values). The largest derivative (in absolute terms) identifies that fixed parameter likely to improve model fit the most. A second model is then estimated and goodness of fit is assessed. The derivatives of the second model are examined and the process continues until an acceptable fit is achieved. Sorbom defines an acceptable fit as occurring when the difference between successive model's chi-square values is not significant. However, Sorbom's procedure is restricted to the derivatives of the observed variables, and only provides indications of misspecification in terms of correlated measurement error.

Saris, de Pijper, and Zegwaart (1979) propose a procedure where the derivatives of all parameter matrices are computed so that other types of misspecification can be considered. Saris et al. compared their procedure with that of Sorbom and found that (1) the Saris et al. method tended to yield more parsimonious models, and (2) the optimal criteria for stopping the procedure is when the probability of the chi-square statistic exceeds the critical value at some specified alpha level.

James (1980) considered the unmeasured variables problem in path analysis, which involves another kind of specification error. In a review by Billings and Wroten (1978), the authors note that one reason for biased structure coefficients is the omission of relevant variables from the model. An underlying assumption of structural equation models is that all relevant variables are included; otherwise the disturbance for a particular endogenous variable will be correlated with the exogenous variables in the equation. However, it may not be possible to measure all such variables, and all such variables may not even be known. Therefore, in many applications there may indeed be unmeasured variables. The question then is the extent to which the unmeasured variables result in biased structure coefficients. Estimates will not be seriously biased for an unmeasured exogenous variable which is highly correlated with a measured exogenous variable. Also, the unmeasured variable problem is less likely to have a serious impact as the number of measured variables increases. James describes a series of decision steps to assess the severity of the unmeasured variables problem for each endogenous variable.

Four types of model misspecification in path analysis were considered by Gallini (1983). First Gallini examined specification error where the disturbances and exogenous variables were correlated, and found biases similar to James (1980). Two other types of specification error considered are only treated as error in an OLS path model, where it is assumed that the disturbances are uncorrelated and that the model contains no reciprocal relationships among the latent variables. In covariance structure models no such assumptions need be made unless OLS estimation is performed on a path model. Other types of estimation will result in unbiased estimates for these situations. The final kind of specification error discussed is that of measurement error in the variables. An implicit assumption of path models is that the variables are perfectly measured in terms of construct validity and reliability. As described by Lomax (1986), several procedures are available to correct for measurement error, such as disattenuation and the use of multiple indicators (the LISREL measurement model). With single indicator models, measurement error can introduce significant bias into parameter estimates as Gallini and previously mentioned other researchers have found.

Gallini and Mandeville (1984) have considered specification errors in LISREL-type structural equation models. The three types of misspecification examined were omission and/or inclusion of structural relationships, correlated measurement error and/or correlated disturbances, and measurement error in the observed variables. Three levels of sample size (N = 50, 100, 500) were included in the simulation study. The results, when the true model was compared to a misspecified model, indicated that (a) a structural model closest to the true model was least likely to be rejected (i.e., best fitting), even with small samples, (b) models with correlated measurement error and/or correlated disturbances were not likely to be rejected, especially for larger samples, and (c) models with single indicators for exogenous and for both exogenous and endogenous variables were almost always rejected, while for the endogenous-only case no models were rejected, regardless of sample size.

MacCallum (1986) conducted a simulation study where a properly specified model was constructed from artificial data, misspecified models were fit to the data, and a determination was made as to whether the specification search led to the correct model. Misspecification was allowed for the structural relationships only and included errors of omission and inclusion. MacCallum considered the number of specification errors made, sample size, and type of search (unrestricted vs. restricted, where theoretical restrictions are made on the modifications that could be made). The unrestricted search results (N = 300) indicated that (1) when only a single specification error of omission or an error of omission and inclusion was made, usually the search was successful after one modification, and (2) when two errors of omission and one error of inclusion or two errors of each were made, usually the search was unsuccessful after one modification. Restricted search results (N = 300) were somewhat better for more serious misspecification. For samples of size 100, searches were always unsuccessful even for minor misspecification. It is recommended that (1) specification searches do not stop when a nonsignificant chi-square difference is obtained as further modifications may still improve model fit, (2) restricted searches be conducted, and (3) specification searches require larger samples to be successful.

Several procedures are available in the LISREL VI program for diagnosing a lack of fit. Normalized residuals are reported for each element of the sample covariance matrix S. These may be thought of as z scores, such that residuals larger than say 2 should be examined for possible misspecification of the model. A plot of these residuals (Q-plot) provides a useful graphic summary. Modification indices are also reported for each nonfree parameter and are based on the derivatives of the fitting function. A modification index for a particular nonfree parameter indicates that if this parameter were allowed to become free in a subsequent model, the chi-square value would decrease by at least the value of the index. Thus, large modification indices would suggest ways in which the LISREL model might be relaxed by allowing the corresponding parameters to become free, and thus arrive at a better-fitting model. If the automatic model modification option is invoked, the fixed parameter with the largest modification index will automatically become free in a second model. While the user may specify that certain parameters remain fixed for theoretical reasons, extreme caution must be taken to maintain a theoretical approach to model testing (and perhaps not even using this option!).

Squared multiple correlations are computed for each observed variable separately and coefficients of determination for all of the observed variables jointly. These values indicate how well the observed variables serve as measures of the latent variables, and are scaled between zero and one. Squared multiple correlations are also given for each structural equation separately and coefficients of determination for the structural equations jointly. These values serve as an indication of the strength of the structural relationships and are also scaled from zero to one.

MacCallum (1986) points out that current specification searches typically utilize several types of information to determine possible model modifications (e.g., t-values of each parameter estimated, modification indices, residuals). MacCallum recommends correcting specification errors in the measurement model first, and making only one modification at a time (both also suggested by Lomax, 1982). Saris and Stronkhorst (1984) recommend that new parameters be added to a model prior to the deletion of parameters. In general, it is recommended that when a procedure is used for the detection of specification errors, the procedure be tempered with theoretical considerations. That is, parameters should not be allowed to become free as recommended by these procedures when they are inconsistent with the empirical base. If such changes are consistent with the theory or if no theory exists, then these model modification procedures are likely to be informative.

Measurement Error

Since the notion of measurement error is so crucial to many applications of the covariance structure model, it seems useful to consider the general concept of measurement error. Lomax (1986) considered the measurement or common-factor model and expanded it following the suggestion of Alwin and Jackson (1979). In the common-factor model, the total observed variance may be decomposed into common variance (i.e., due to the common factors) and unique variance (i.e., due to the measurement errors or unique factors). In the expanded factor analysis model, unique variance is subdivided into specific and error variance. Error variance is random, unsystematic and due to unreliability (i.e., due to the differences in observed scores for repeated parallel measures). The error variance is equal to one minus the parallel-measures reliability coefficient, when it is assumed that the total variance is unity. Specific variance is non-random, systematic, reliable and due to the particular selection of variables by the researcher (e.g., due to a method or occasion factor).

Specifically, the expanded factor model is

$$x = \Lambda_x \xi + s + e, \tag{18}$$

where s ($q \times 1$) represents a vector of specific factors and e ($q \times 1$) represents a vector of error factors. The covariance equation then becomes

$$\Sigma = \Lambda_x \Phi \Lambda_x' + \Theta_s + \Theta_e, \tag{19}$$

where Θ_s ($q \times q$) represents a diagonal matrix of specific variances and Θ_e ($q \times q$) represents a diagonal matrix of error variances.

Lomax (1986) conducted a simulation study where a covariance structure model consisted of three exogenous variables influencing a single endogenous variable. The results indicated that when the level of specific variance (due to reliability) was systematically reduced for a single exogenous variable (but not for the other two), (1) error variance for that variable increased systematically since specific and error variance are analytically, inversely related, (2) the ML estimate and standard error for the relevant structure coefficient (i.e., relating the reduced exogenous variable to the endogenous variable) increased at the same rate, (3) the ML estimate of the disturbance variance also increased, and (4) the remaining parameters of the structural and measurement models were not affected. Thus, in those situations where indicator variable reliability differs substantially from unity, say 0.8 or less, consideration needs to be given to taking the unreliability into account in the analysis; otherwise, certain important parameter estimates may be biased leading to possible model misinterpretation.

Missing Data

Frequently researchers using covariance structure analysis are faced with missing data. The literature on this issue is primarily devoted to ML estimation in analysis of variance (e.g., Anderson, 1957; Afifi & Elashoff, 1966; Orchard & Woodbury, 1970). Several methodologies have been developed to handle missing data for covariance structure and other models. These methodologies include

(1) the complete data method where cases with any missing data are not included (i.e., listwise deletion), (2) the mean replacement method where means replace missing values (due to Afifi & Elashoff, 1966), (3) the complete pair only method (i.e., pairwise deletion due to Wilks, 1932), (4) the regression replacement and principal component methods (due to Gleason & Staelin, 1975), (5) ML estimation (due to Wilks, 1932; Rubin, 1976), and (6) the EM method for ML estimation (due to Dempster, Laird, & Rubin, 1977; Rubin & Thayer, 1982). Underlying these methods are assumptions about the mechanisms which result in the missingness, which include concepts such as data missing completely at random, data missing at random, listwise present approach, or ignoring the missing data if certain conditions hold. Preliminary results are presented by Finkbeiner (1979) for factor analysis, and by Muthen, Kaplan, and Hollis (1985) for LISREL-type models and indicate that the ML method shows some advantages. Clearly research on the missing data problem is necessary before its effects will be understood and appropriate methods utilized.

Direct and Indirect Effects

In the path analysis literature, the zero-order correlations among observed variables can be decomposed into direct effects, indirect effects, and non-causal effects (often further divided into spurious effects and joint associations) (see Finney, 1972; Wolfle, 1980). In recursive models, direct effects are estimated by the structure coefficients, while indirect effects are estimated by the sum of the products of direct effects through intervening variables. Previously a tedious process, Alwin and Hauser (1975) derived a method for calculating indirect effects for just-identified recursive models. Fox (1980) then developed a more general technique for estimating indirect effects for all structural models. Later Joreskog and Sorbom (1981) derived an even more general procedure for models with latent and manifest variables, which was first integrated into the LISREL V computer program.

Until recently, the probability distribution of the indirect effect was unknown, such that standard errors could not be estimated. Bobko and Rieck (1980) and Sobel (1982) independently addressed this issue by deriving an asymptotic distribution of indirect effects for large samples. These methods however were based on rather tedious computations of partial derivatives by hand. Wolfle and Ethington (1985b) designed a computer program to compute standard errors of indirect effects for recursive models, which was then integrated into a total computer program for the analysis of recursive models (Wolfle & Ethington, 1985c). Stone (1985) introduced a computer program for the calculation of standard errors of indirect effects for the general covariance structure model, with latent and manifest variables. A general model for the decomposition of effects in LISREL-type structural models is shown in Graff and Schmidt (1982).

Constraints

In the current version of the LISREL computer program (LISREL VI), two types of constraints may be imposed on parameters; parameters may be fixed to a specific value, or parameters may be constrained to be equal to other parameters. Recently procedures have been developed to handle other types of constraints such as inequality and polynomial constraints. Rindskopf (1983, 1984) has shown that the LISREL program can be forced into dealing with other types of constraints through an alternative representation of the LISREL model using phantom or imaginary latent variables.

Rindskopf (1983) has considered three situations involving inequality constraints. First Heywood cases, where negative variance estimates are obtained, can be prevented by fixing the variance in question to unity. Second, if the reliabilities of some of the indicator variables are known and the correlation matrix is analyzed, one may choose to constrain the values of the relevant error variances to be greater than a specified constant by taking reliability into account. This involves a model with general inequalities for each measurement error having a known reliability. Third, inequality constraints may be imposed so that the relative sizes of measurement error variances are in a specified order. Unfortunately in each of these situations the constrained model will have the same number of degrees of freedom as the unconstrained model so that the validities of the constraints are not testable.

Rindskopf (1984) has considered other types of inequality constraints which may be used in LISREL. A structure coefficient may be constrained to be nonnegative, greater than or equal to a constant, less than or equal to a constant, or larger than another structure coefficient, either generally or by a constant. Similar constraints may be imposed on the factor loadings. If models are expressed as products of parameter matrices, much the same as the reparameterized versions of the LISREL model discussed by Bentler and Weeks (1979, 1980) and by McDonald (1978, 1980, 1985), one may evaluate other types of constraints. These include constraining error variances to take reliability into account in the analysis of a covariance matrix, polynomial equality constraints on the structure coefficients, and constraining factor variances to unity in analyzing the correlational structure of a covariance matrix. All of these types of constraints may also be imposed in a multiple group situation.

Both the Bentler-Weeks and the McDonald models can handle linear equality constraints directly, although the techniques developed by Rindskopf can also be applied. In the McDonald model one can also restrict a parameter to lie in a specified range. Lee (1980) has developed an algorithm based on the penalty function method for use in situations where equality and inequality constraints are necessary. Lee and Jennrich (1984) have shown that the PAR program of the BMDP series (Dixon, 1981) can be used to analyze covariance structure models having linear equality and inequality constraints and provides ULS, GLS, and

ML estimates. PAR is a general derivative-free nonlinear regression program. Bentler and Lee (1983) derived a method for evaluating models with polynomial constraints, which include virtually all constraints that might be used in covariance structure analysis, including nonlinear constraints such as quadratic. It is expected that eventually commonly used programs for covariance structure analysis will be able to handle all of these types of constraints.

Nonlinear and Interactive Effects

While nonlinear and interactive effects have been quite popular with standard regression-type models, testing of such effects in covariance structure models has been virtually nonexistent. In 1967, McDonald developed a nonlinear factor analysis model (see Etezadi-Amoli & McDonald, 1983 for a second generation model). Since that time, little work has been done in this area until recently. As discussed in Busemeyer and Jones (1983), one problem had been that there was no procedure available for estimating such effects in models with latent variables. Kenny and Judd (1984) describe a procedure for estimating nonlinear and interactive effects, where for estimation purposes the usual normality assumption cannot be made. Instead, a GLS estimation procedure is utilized where the weighting matrix is the inverse of S, following McDonald's COSAN computer program. However, a procedure for estimating the standard errors of nonlinear and interactive effects is not yet known.

SUMMARY

Undoubtedly the methodology of covariance structure analysis has developed in many ways, particularly in terms of its accepted application in the social and behavioral sciences and in terms of the new technical developments. Many problems have been resolved and many procedures have been proposed. It is also clear that much theoretical and applied work remains to be done. At present the theoretical work has advanced beyond the implementation of these procedures in widely available computer programs. That is, newer technical developments in such areas as non-normality, discrete variables, missing data and constraints are not generally available to the research community, although the methods will be with time.

Finally, some cautions must be noted regarding the use of covariance structure models. Cliff (1983) discusses four principles underlying the scientific method that should not be forgotten. These principles are the following: (1) data do not confirm a model, they only fail to disconfirm it, and many models may not be disconfirmed; (2) if two variables x and y are related and x precedes y in time, then x may not have caused y; (3) the well-known nominalistic fallacy that because a latent variable can be named does not necessarily imply an understanding of the latent variable; and (4) ex post facto explanations are not really confirmatory when numerous models are considered. The use of covariance structure analysis (and thus their computer programs) does not (1) magically provide the researcher with the most plausible theoretical model, (2) provide definitive proof of causality, (3) allow latent factors to become manifest, or (4) lead to true tests of models in a confirmatory sense (here, cross-validation is suggested; see Cudeck & Browne, 1983). The existence of the present volume as one in a series shows that there is no panacea among currently available research methods, only tools which must be appropriately utilized.

REFERENCES

Afifi, A. A., & Elashoff, R. M. (1966). Missing observations in multivariate statistics I. Review of the literature. *Journal of the American Statistical Association, 61*, 595–604.

Alwin, D. F., & Hauser, R. M. (1975). The decomposition of effects in path analysis. *American Sociological Review, 40*, 37–47.

Alwin, D. F., & Jackson, D. J. (1979). Measurement models for response errors in surveys: Issues and applications. In K. F. Schuessler (Ed.), *Sociological methodology, 1980*, San Francisco: Jossey-Bass.

Amemiya, T. (1978). The estimation of a simultaneous equation generalized probit model. *Econometrika, 46*, 1193–1206.

Amemiya, T. (1981). Qualitative response models: A survey. *Journal of Economic Literature, 19*, 1483–1536.

Anderson, J. G. (1978). Causal models in educational research: Nonrecursive models. *American Educational Research Journal, 15*, 81–97.

Anderson, J. G., & Evans, F. B. (1974). Causal models in educational research: Recursive models. *American Educational Research Journal, 11*, 29–39.

Anderson, J. C., & Gerbing, D. W. (1984). The effect of sampling error on convergence, improper solutions, and goodness-of-fit indices for maximum likelihood confirmatory factor analysis. *Psychometrika, 49*, 155–173.

Anderson, T. W. (1957). Maximum likelihood estimates for multivariate normal distributions when some observations are missing. *Journal of the American Statistical Association, 52*, 202–203.

Asher, H. B. (1983). *Causal modeling* (2nd ed.). Beverly Hills: Sage.

Bentler, P. M. (1980). Multivariate analysis with latent variables: Causal modeling. *Annual Review of Psychology, 31*, 419–456.

Bentler, P. M. (1983). Some contributions to efficient statistics in structural models: Specification and estimation of moment structures. *Psychometrika, 48*, 493–517.

Bentler, P. M. (1984). *Theory and implementation of EQS: A structural equation program*. Los Angeles: BMDP Statistical Software.

Bentler, P. M., & Bonett, D. G. (1980). Significance tests and goodness of fit in the analysis of covariance structures. *Psychological Bulletin, 88*, 588–606.

Bentler, P. M., & Lee, S.-Y. (1983). Covariance structures under polynomial constraints: Applications to correlation and alpha-type structural models. *Journal of Educational Statistics, 8*, 207–222.

Bentler, P. M., & Tanaka, J. S. (1983). Problems with EM algorithms for ML factor analysis. *Psychometrika, 48*, 247–251.

Bentler, P. M., & Weeks, D. G. (1979). Interrelations among models for the analysis of moment structures. *Multivariate Behavioral Research, 14*, 169–186.

Bentler, P. M., & Weeks, D. G. (1980). Linear structural equations with latent variables. *Psychometrika, 45,* 289–308.

Bielby, W. T., & Hauser, R. M. (1977). Structural equation models. *Annual Review of Sociology, 3,* 137–161.

Bielby, W. T., Hauser, R. M., & Featherman, D. L. (1977). Response errors of black and nonblack males in models of intergenerational transmission of socioeconomic status. *American Journal of Sociology, 82,* 1242–1288.

Billings, R. S., & Wroten, S. P. (1978). Use of path analysis in industrial/organizational psychology: Criticisms and suggestions. *Journal of Applied Psychology, 63,* 677–688.

Bishop, Y. M. M., Fienberg, S. E., & Holland, P. W. (1975). *Discrete multivariate analysis: Theory and practice.* Cambridge, MA: MIT Press.

Blalock, H. M., Jr. (Ed.). (1971). *Causal models in the social sciences.* Chicago: Aldine.

Bobko, P., & Rieck, A. (1980). Large sample estimators for standard errors of functions of correlation coefficients. *Applied Psychological Measurement, 4,* 385–398.

Bock, R. D., & Aiken, M. (1981). Marginal maximum likelihood estimation of item parameters: Application of an EM algorithm. *Psychometrika, 46,* 443–459.

Bock, R. D., & Bargmann, R. E. (1966). Analysis of covariance structures. *Psychometrika, 31,* 507–534.

Boomsma, A. (1982). The robustness of LISREL against small sample sizes in factor analysis models. In K. G. Joreskog & H. Wold (Eds.), *Systems under indirect observation: Causality, structure, prediction.* Amsterdam: North-Holland.

Boomsma, A. (1983). *On the robustness of LISREL (maximum likelihood estimation) against small sample size and nonnormality.* Unpublished dissertation, University of Groningen, Groningen.

Boomsma, A. (1985). Nonconvergence, improper solutions, and starting values in LISREL maximum likelihood estimation. *Psychometrika, 50,* 229–242.

Browne, M. W. (1974). Generalized least-squares estimators in the analysis of covariance structures. *South African Statistical Journal, 8,* 1–24.

Browne, M. W. (1982). Covariance structures. In D. M. Hawkins (Ed.), *Topics in applied multivariate analysis.* Cambridge: Cambridge University Press.

Browne, M. W. (1984). Asymptotically distribution-free methods for the analysis of covariance structures. *British Journal of Mathematical and Statistical Psychology, 37,* 62–83.

Burt, C. (1947). Factor analysis and analysis of variance. *British Journal of Psychology, 1,* 3–26.

Busemeyer, J. R., & Jones, L. E. (1983). Analysis of multiplicative combination rules when the causal variables are measured with error. *Psychological Bulletin, 93,* 549–562.

Campbell, D. T. (1963). From description to experimentation: Interpreting trends as quasi-experiments. In C. W. Harris (Ed.), *Problems in measuring change.* Madison: University of Wisconsin Press.

Campbell, D. T., & Fiske, D. W. (1959). Convergent and discriminant validation by the multitrait-multimethod matrix. *Psychological Bulletin, 56,* 81–105.

Christoffersson, A. (1975). Factor analysis of dichotomized variables. *Psychometrika, 40,* 5–32.

Cliff, N. (1983). Some cautions concerning the application of causal modeling methods. *Multivariate Behavioral Research, 18,* 115–126.

Cole, D. A., & Maxell, S. E. (1985). Multitrait-multimethod comparisons across populations: A confirmatory factor analysis. *Multivariate Behavioral Research, 20,* 389–417.

Cooley, W. W. (1978). Explanatory observational studies. *Educational Researcher, 7*(9), 9–15.

Costner, H. L., & Schoenberg, R. (1973). Diagnosing indicator ills in multiple indicator models. In A. S. Goldberger & O. D. Duncan (Eds.), *Structural equation models in the social sciences.* New York: Seminar Press.

Cudeck, R., & Browne, M. W. (1983). Cross-validation of covariance structures. *Multivariate Behavioral Research, 18,* 147–167.

Dempster, A. P., Laird, N. M., & Rubin, D. B. (1977). Maximum likelihood from incomplete data via the EM algorithm. *Journal of the Royal Statistical Society, Series B, 39,* 1–38 (with discussion).

Dixon, W. J. (Ed.). (1981). *BMDP: Biomedical Computer Programs-P series.* Los Angeles: University of California Press.

Duncan, O. D. (1966). Path analysis: Sociological examples. *American Journal of Sociology, 72,* 1–16.

Duncan, O. D. (1975). *Introduction to structural equation models.* New York: Academic Press.

Etezadi-Amoli, J., & McDonald, R. P. (1983). A second generation nonlinear factor analysis. *Psychometrika, 48,* 315–342.

Ethington, C. A. (1985). *The robustness of LISREL estimates in structural equation models with categorical data.* Unpublished dissertation, Blacksburg: Virginia Polytechnic Institute and State University.

Ethington, C. A., & Wolfle, L. M. (1984). *A structural model of sex differences in mathematics achievement using tetrachoric and polyserial measures of association.* Paper presented at the annual meeting of the American Educational Research Association, New Orleans.

Fienberg, S. E. (1980). *The analysis of cross-classified categorical data* (2nd ed.). Cambridge, MA: MIT Press.

Finkbeiner, C. (1979). Estimation for the multiple factor model when data are missing. *Psychometrika, 44,* 409–420.

Finney, J. M. (1972). Indirect effects in path analysis. *Sociological Methods & Research, 1,* 175–186.

Fisher, F. M. (1966). *The identification problem in econometrics.* New York: McGraw-Hill.

Fox, J. (1980). Effect analysis in structural equation models: Extensions and simplified methods of computation. *Sociological Methods & Research, 9,* 3–28.

Gallini, J. K. (1983). Misspecifications that can result in path analysis structures. *Applied Psychological Measurement, 7,* 125–137.

Gallini, J. K., & Bell, M. E. (1983). Formulation of a structural equation model for the evaluation of curriculum. *Educational Evaluation and Policy Analysis, 5,* 319–326.

Gallini, J. K., & Mandeville, G. K. (1984). An investigation of the effect of sample size and specification error on the fit of structural equation models. *Journal of Experimental Education, 53,* 9–19.

Gerbing, D. W., & Anderson, J. C. (1985). The effects of sampling error and model characteristics on parameter estimation for maximum likelihood confirmatory factor analysis. *Multivariate Behavioral Research, 20,* 255–271.

Gerbing, D. W., & Hunter, J. E. (1982). The metric of the latent variables in a LISREL-IV analysis. *Educational and Psychological Measurement, 42,* 423–427.

Geweke, J. F., & Singleton, K. J. (1980). Interpreting the likelihood ratio statistic in factor models when sample size is small. *Journal of the American Statistical Association, 75,* 133–137.

Gleason, T. C., & Staelin, R. (1975). A proposal for handling missing data. *Psychometrika, 40,* 229–252.

Goldberger, A. S., & Duncan, O. D. (Eds.). (1973). *Structural equation models in the social sciences.* New York: Seminar Press.

Goodman, L. A. (1972). A general model for the analysis of surveys. *American Journal of Sociology, 77,* 1035–1086.

Goodman, L. A. (1973). Causal analysis of data from panel studies and other kinds of surveys. *American Journal of Sociology, 78,* 1135–1191.

Goodman, L. A. (1979). A brief guide to the causal analysis of data from surveys. *American Journal of Sociology, 84,* 1078–1095.

Graff, J., & Schmidt, P. (1982). A general model for decomposition of effects. In K. G. Joreskog & H. Wold (Eds.), *Systems under indirect observation: Causality, structure, prediction.* Amsterdam: North-Holland.

Hagglund, G. (1982). Factor analysis by instrumental variables methods. *Psychometrika, 47,* 209–222.

Heckman, J. J. (1978). Dummy endogenous variables in a simultaneous equation system. *Econometrika, 46,* 931–959.

Heise, D. R. (1975). *Causal analysis.* New York: Wiley.

Henderson, C. R. (1953). Estimation of variance and covariance components. *Biometrics, 9,* 226–252.

Hoelter, J. W. (1983). The analysis of covariance structures: Goodness of fit indices. *Sociological Methods and Research, 11,* 325–344.

Huba, G. J., & Bentler, P. M. (1983). Test of a drug use causal model using asymptotically distribution free methods. *Journal of Drug Education, 13,* 3–17.

Huba, G. J., & Harlow, L. L. (1983). Comparison of maximum likelihood, generalized least squares, ordinary least squares and asymptotically distribution free parameter estimates in drug abuse latent variable causal models. *Journal of Drug Education, 13,* 387–404.

Huba, G. J., & Harlow, L. L. (1984). Robust estimation for causal models: A comparison of methods in some developmental data sets. In R. M. Lerner & D. L. Featherman (Eds.), *Life-span development and behavior* (Vol. 6). New York: Academic Press.

Huba, G. J., & Tanaka, J. S. (1983). Confirmatory evidence for three daydreaming factors in the short imaginal processes inventory. *Imagination, Cognition and Personality, 3,* 139–147.

James, L. R. (1980). The unmeasured variables problem in path analysis. *Journal of Applied Psychology, 65,* 415–421.

James, L. R., Mulaik, S. A., & Brett, J. M. (1982). *Causal analysis: Assumptions, models, and data.* Beverly Hills: Sage.

Johnston, J. J. (1972). *Econometric methods* (2nd ed.). New York: McGraw-Hill.

Joreskog, K. G. (1967). Some contributions to maximum likelihood factor analysis. *Psychometrika, 32,* 443–482.

Joreskog, K. G. (1969). A general approach to confirmatory maximum likelihood factor analysis. *Psychometrika, 34,* 183–220.

Joreskog, K. G. (1970). A general method for analysis of covariance structures. *Biometrika, 57,* 239–251.

Joreskog, K. G. (1971a). Simultaneous factor analysis in several populations. *Psychometrika, 36,* 409–426.

Joreskog, K. G. (1971b). Statistical analysis of sets of congeneric tests. *Psychometrika, 36,* 109–133.

Joreskog, K. G. (1973). A general method for estimating a linear structural equation system. In A. S. Goldberger & O. D. Duncan (Eds.), *Structural equation models in the social sciences.* New York: Seminar Press.

Joreskog, K. G. (1977). Structural equation models in the social sciences: Specification, estimation and testing. In P. R. Krishnaiah (Ed.), *Applications of statistics.* Amsterdam: North-Holland.

Joreskog, K. G. (1978). Structural analysis of covariance and correlation matrices. *Psychometrika, 43,* 443–477.

Joreskog, K. G., & Goldberger, A. S. (1972). Factor analysis by generalized least squares. *Psychometrika, 37,* 243–260.

Joreskog, K. G., & Goldberger, A. S. (1975). Estimation of a model with multiple indicators and multiple causes of a single latent variable. *Journal of the American Statistical Association, 70,* 631–639.

Joreskog, K. G., & Sorbom, D. (1981). *LISREL V: Analysis of linear structural relationships by the method of maximum likelihood.* Chicago: National Educational Resources.

Joreskog, K. G., & Sorbom, D. (1984). *LISREL VI: Analysis of linear structural relationships by maximum likelihood, instrumental variables, and least squares methods.* Mooresville, IN: Scientific Software, Inc.

Keesling, J. W. (1972). *Maximum likelihood approaches to causal flow analysis*. Unpublished dissertation. University of Chicago, Department of Education.

Keith, T. Z., & Page, L. B. (1985). Do Catholic high schools improve minority student achievement? *American Educational Research Journal, 22,* 337–349.

Kenny, D. A. (1975). Cross-lagged panel correlation: A test for spuriousness. *Psychological Bulletin, 82,* 887–903.

Kenny, D. A. (1979). *Correlation and causality*. New York: Wiley.

Kenny, D. A., & Judd, C. M. (1984). Estimating the nonlinear and interactive effects of latent variables. *Psychological Bulletin, 96,* 201–210.

Kim, J.-O., & Ferree, G. D., Jr. (1981). Standardization in causal analysis. *Sociological Methods & Research, 10,* 187–210.

Kroonenberg, P. M., & Lewis, C. (1982). Methodological issues in the search for a factor model: Exploration through confirmation. *Journal of Educational Statistics, 7,* 69–89.

Lawley, D. N. (1940). The estimation of factor loadings by the method of maximum likelihood. *Proceedings of the Royal Society of Edinburgh, 60,* 64–82.

Lawley, D. N. (1943). The application of the maximum likelihood method to factor analysis. *British Journal of Psychology, 33,* 172–175.

Lawley, D. N. (1944). The factorial analysis of multiple test items. *Proceedings of the Royal Society of Edinburgh, 61,* 273–287.

Lazarsfeld, P. F. (1950). The logical and mathematical function of latent structure analysis. In S. A. Stouffer et al. (Eds.), *Measurement and prediction*. Princeton, NJ: Princeton University Press.

Lazarsfeld, P. F., & Henry, N. W. (1968). *Latent structure analysis*. Boston: Houghton Mifflin.

Leamer, E. E. (1978). *Specification searches*. New York: Wiley.

Lee, S.-Y. (1980). Estimation of covariance structure models with parameters subject to functional restraints. *Psychometrika, 45,* 309–324.

Lee, S.-Y. (1981). A Bayesian approach to confirmatory factor analysis. *Psychometrika, 46,* 153–160.

Lee, S.-Y., & Jennrich, R. I. (1984). The analysis of structural equation models by means of derivative free nonlinear least squares. *Psychometrika, 49,* 521–528.

Lee, S.-Y., & Tsui, K.-L. (1982). Covariance structure analysis in several populations. *Psychometrika, 47,* 297–308.

Lomax, R. G. (1982). A guide to LISREL-type structural equation modeling. *Behavior Research Methods & Instrumentation, 14,* 1–8.

Lomax, R. G. (1983). A guide to multiple-sample structural equation modeling. *Behavior Research Methods & Instrumentation, 15,* 580–584.

Lomax, R. G. (1985). A structural model of public and private schools. *Journal of Experimental Education, 53,* 216–226.

Lomax, R. G. (1986). The effect of measurement error in structural equation modeling. *Journal of Experimental Education, 54,* 157–162.

Lomax, R. G., & Algina, J. (1979). Comparison of two procedures for analyzing multitrait multimethod matrices. *Journal of Educational Measurement, 16,* 177–186.

Long, J. S. (1983a). *Confirmatory factor analysis*. Beverly Hills, Sage.

Long, J. S. (1983b). *Covariance structure models: An introduction to LISREL*. Beverly Hills, CA: Sage.

MacCallum, R. (1983). A comparison of factor analysis programs in SPSS, BMDP, and SAS. *Psychometrika, 48,* 223–231.

MacCallum, R. (1986). Specification searches in covariance structure modeling. *Psychological Bulletin, 100,* 107–120.

Maddala, G. S., & Lee, L. F. (1976). Recursive models with qualitative endogenous variables. *Annals of Economic and Social Measurement, 5,* 525–545.

Marsh, H. W. (1985). The structure of masculinity/femininity: An application of confirmatory factor analysis to higher-order factor structures and factorial invariance. *Multivariate Behavioral Research, 20,* 427–449.

Maruyama, G., & McGarvey, B. (1980). Evaluating causal models: An application of maximum-likelihood analysis of structural equations. *Psychological Bulletin, 87,* 502–512.

Mason, W. M., Hauser, R. M., Kerckhoff, A. C., Poss, S. S., & Manton, K. (1976). Models of response error in students report of parental socioeconomic characteristics. In W. H. Sewell, R. M. Hauser, & D. L. Featherman (Eds.), *Schooling and achievement in American society.* New York: Academic.

McArdle, J. J. (1978). *A structural view of structural models.* Paper presented at Winter Workshop on Latent Structure Models Applied to Developmental Data, University of Denver.

McArdle, J. J., & McDonald, R. P. (1984). Some algebraic properties of the reticular action model for moment structures. *British Journal of Mathematical and Statistical Psychology, 37,* 234–254.

McDonald, R. P. (1967). Nonlinear factor analysis. *Psychometric Monograph, No. 15.*

McDonald, R. P. (1978). A simple comprehensive model for the analysis of covariance structures. *British Journal of Mathematical and Statistical Psychology, 31,* 59–72.

McDonald, R. P. (1980). A simple comprehensive model for the analysis of covariance structures: Some remarks on applications. *British Journal of Mathematical and Statistical Psychology, 33,* 161–183.

McDonald, R. P. (1985). *Factor analysis and related methods.* Hillsdale, NJ: Lawrence Erlbaum Associates.

Mooijaart, A. (1985). Factor analysis for non-normal variables. *Psychometrika, 50,* 323–342.

Muthen, B. (1978). Contributions to factor analysis of dichotomous variables. *Psychometrika, 43,* 551–560.

Muthen, B. (1979). A structural probit model with latent variables. *Journal of the American Statistical Association, 74,* 807–811.

Muthen, B. (1981). Factor analysis of dichotomous variables: American attitudes toward abortion. In D. J. Jackson & E. F. Borgatta (Eds.), *Factor analysis and measurement in sociological research.* Beverly Hills, CA: Sage.

Muthen, B. (1982). Some categorical response models with continuous latent variables. In K. G. Joreskog & H. Wold (Eds.), *Systems under indirect observation: Causality, structure, prediction.* Amsterdam: North-Holland.

Muthen, B. (1983). Latent variable structural equation modeling with categorical data. *Journal of Econometrics, 22,* 43–65.

Muthen, B. (1984). A general structural equation model with dichotomous, ordered categorical, and continuous latent variable indicators. *Psychometrika, 49,* 115–132.

Muthen, B., & Christofferson, A. (1981). Simultaneous factor analysis of dichotomous variables in several groups. *Psychometrika, 46,* 407–419.

Muthen, B., & Kaplan, D. (1985). A comparison of some methodologies for the factor analysis of non-normal Likert variables. *British Journal of Mathematical and Statistical Psychology, 38,* 171–189.

Muthen, B., Kaplan, D., & Chan, C.-R. (1985). *A study of the robustness to non-normality of multiple group factor analysis.* Paper presented at the annual meeting of the American Educational Research Association, Chicago.

Muthen, B., Kaplan, D., & Hollis, M. (1985). *Latent variable modeling with missing data: Attrition in longitudinal studies.* Paper presented at the annual meeting of the American Educational Research Association, Chicago.

Olsson, U. (1979a). Maximum likelihood estimation of the polychoric correlation coefficient. *Psychometrika, 44,* 443–460.

Olsson, U. (1979b). On the robustness of factor analysis against crude classification of the observations. *Multivariate Behavioral Research, 14,* 485–500.

Olsson, U., Drasgow, F., & Dorans, N. J. (1982). The polyserial correlation coefficient. *Psychometrika, 47,* 337–347.

Orchard, T., & Woodbury, M. A. (1970). A missing information principle: Theory and applications. *Proceedings of the Sixth Berkeley Symposium on Mathematical Statistics and Probability, 1,* 697–715.

Patteson, B. J., & Wolfle, L. M. (1981). Specification bias in causal models with fallible indicators. *Multiple Linear Regression Viewpoints, 11,* 75–89.

Pedhazur, E. J. (1982). *Multiple regression in behavioral research* (2nd ed.). New York: Holt, Rinehart and Winston.

Popper, K. R. (1959). *The logic of scientific discovery.* London: Hutchinson.

Rindskopf, D. (1983). Parameterizing inequality constraints on unique variances in linear structural models. *Psychometrika, 48,* 73–83.

Rindskopf, D. (1984). Using phantom and imaginary latent variables to parameterize constraints in linear structural models. *Psychometrika, 49,* 37–47.

Rock, D. A., Werts, C. E., & Flaugher, R. L. (1978). The use of analysis of covariance structures for comparing the psychometric properties of multiple variables across populations. *Multivariate Behavioral Research, 13,* 403–418.

Rogosa, D. (1979). Causal models in longitudinal research: Rationale, formulation, and interpretation. In J. R. Nesselroade & P. R. Baltes (Eds.), *Longitudinal research in the study of behavior and development.* New York: Academic.

Rubin, D. A. (1976). Inference and missing data. *Biometrika, 63,* 581–592.

Rubin, D. B., & Thayer, D. T. (1982). EM algorithms for ML factor analysis. *Psychometrika, 47,* 69–76.

Rubin, D. B., & Thayer, D. T. (1983). More on EM for ML factor analysis. *Psychometrika, 48,* 253–257.

Saris, W. E., de Pijper, W. M., & Zegwaart, P. (1979). Detection of specification errors in linear structural equation models. In K. F. Schuessler (Ed.), *Sociological methodology, 1979.* San Francisco: Jossey-Bass.

Saris, W. E., & Stronkhorst, L. H. (1984). *Causal modeling in nonexperimental research: An introduction to the LISREL approach.* Amsterdam: Sociometric Research Foundation.

Satorra, A., & Saris, W. E. (1985). Power of the likelihood ratio test in covariance structure analysis. *Psychometrika, 50,* 83–90.

Shapiro, A. (1983). Asymptotic distribution theory in the analysis of covariance structures (a unified approach). *South African Statistical Journal, 17,* 33–81.

Simon, H. A. (1977). *Models of discovery.* Dordrecht, Holland: R. Reidel.

Sobel, M. E. (1982). Asymptotic confidence intervals for indirect effects in structural equation models. In S. Leinhardt (Ed.), *Sociological methodology, 1982.* San Francisco: Jossey-Bass.

Sobel, M. E., & Bohrnstedt, G. W. (1985). Use of null models in evaluating the fit of covariance structure models. In N. B. Tuma (Ed.), *Sociological methodology, 1985.* San Francisco: Jossey-Bass.

Sorbom, D. (1974). A general method for studying differences in factor means and factor structure between groups. *British Journal of Mathematical and Statistical Psychology, 27,* 229–239.

Sorbom, D. (1975). Detection of correlated errors in longitudinal data. *British Journal of Mathematical and Statistical Psychology, 28,* 138–151.

Sorbom, D. (1982). Structural equation models with structured means. In K. G. Joreskog & H. Wold (Eds.), *Systems under indirect observation: Causality, structure, prediction.* Amsterdam: North-Holland.

Spearman, C. (1904). The proof and measurement of association between two things. *American Journal of Psychology, 15,* 72–101.

Stone, C. A. (1985). *A computer program for obtaining standard errors of total indirect effects in the*

Joreskog covariance structure model. Paper presented at the annual meeting of the American Educational Research Association, Chicago.

Tanaka, J. S. (1984). *Some results on the estimation of covariance structure models.* Unpublished dissertation, University of California, Los Angeles.

Tanaka, J. S., & Bentler, P. M. (1983). Factor invariance of premorbid social competence across multiple populations of schizophrenics. *Multivariate Behavioral Research, 18,* 135–146.

Tucker, L. R., & Lewis, C. (1973). A reliability coefficient for maximum likelihood factor analysis. *Psychometrika, 38,* 1–10.

Weeks, D. G. (1980). A second-order longitudinal model of ability structure. *Multivariate Behavioral Research, 15,* 353–365.

Wiley, D. E. (1973). The identification problem for structural equation models with unmeasured variables. In A. S. Goldberger & O. D. Duncan (Eds.), *Structural equation models in the social sciences.* New York: Seminar Press.

Wilks, S. S. (1932). Moments and distributions of estimates of population parameters from fragmented samples. *Annals of Mathematical Statistics, 3,* 163–195.

Wold, H. (1975). Path models with latent variables: The NIPALS approach. In H. M. Blalock, A. Aganbegian, F. N. Borodkin, R. Boudon, & V. Capecchi (Eds.), *Quantitative sociology: International perspectives on mathematical and statistical modeling.* New York: Academic.

Wolfle, L. M. (1980). Strategies of path analysis. *American Educational Research Journal, 17,* 183–209.

Wolfle, L. M. (1982). Causal models with unmeasured variables: An introduction to LISREL. *Multiple Linear Regression Viewpoints, 11,* 9–54.

Wolfle, L. M., & Ethington, C. A. (1985a). *Robustness of regression estimates for ordered dichotomous variables.* Paper presented at the annual meeting of the American Educational Research Association, Los Angeles.

Wolfle, L. M., & Ethington, C. A. (1985b). SEINE: Standard errors of indirect effects. *Educational & Psychological Measurement, 45,* 161–166.

Wolfle, L. M., & Ethington, C. A. (1985c). GEMINI: Program for analysis of structural equations with standard errors of indirect effects. *Behavior Research Methods, Instruments, & Computers, 17,* 581–584.

Won, E. Y. T. (1982). Incomplete corrections for regressor reliabilities: Effects on the correlation estimates. *Sociological Methods and Research, 10,* 271–284.

Wright, S. (1921). Correlation and causality. *Journal of Agricultural Research, 20,* 557–585.

Wright, S. (1934). The method of path coefficients. *Annals of Mathematical Statistics, 5,* 161–215.

INTERPRETING THE RESULTS OF MULTIVARIATE ANALYSIS OF VARIANCE

H. Swaminathan

INTRODUCTION

Univariate analysis of variance procedures (ANOVA), stemming from the work of R. A. Fisher in the 1920s, have been the mainstay of experimental researchers in the social and natural sciences for several decades. The multivariate extensions of the univariate procedures were given by Hotelling (1931) for the comparison of two vectors of means and by Wilks (1932) for the comparison of k vectors of means. Despite the fact that multivariate analysis of variance (MANOVA) procedures were developed relatively soon after ANOVA procedures, they were not as immediately popular. Surprisingly enough, discriminant analysis, a closely related procedure developed by Fisher (1936), received much more recognition and has enjoyed more widespread usage. It may have been that the MANOVA procedures were perceived as too mathematically and computationally complex in experimental research, where the more tractable univariate repeated measures approach was seen as adequate for the analysis of multiresponse data. Nonexperimental researchers, on the other hand, were primarily interested in classification and the prediction of group membership, and used discriminant analysis solely for this purpose, without extending the investigation

Advances in Social Science Methodology, Volume 1, pages 205–232.

ISBN: 0-89232-736-7

to a detailed examination of the group differences. These reasons may have at least partially contributed to the lack of widespread use of MANOVA procedures in both experimental and nonexperimental research.

The generality and versatility of the multivariate linear model, and its applications to MANOVA, were not appreciated until a more modern formulation was given by Roy and Gnanadesikan (1959). This formulation not only provided the basis for the analysis of any experimental design model, but also gave solutions based on matrix operations. Bock (1963) extended this formulation to provide a solution ideally suited for computer programming. With this solution, user-oriented computer programs were developed and are now widely available. As a result, multivariate analysis of variance procedures have become an accepted tool for data analysis in experimental research.

With the introduction of multiple response variables, the analysis of data and the interpretation of results becomes complex. While for the univariate case there is a unique statistic for testing hypotheses of interest, there is generally no uniformly most powerful test statistic for the multivariate case. The effects of the response variables can be assessed in a variety of ways, none of which may be appropriate to the purposes of the study. Furthermore, as in the univariate case, suitable multiple comparison procedures must be chosen.

The purpose of this paper is to provide a discussion of:

1. The general linear model and hypothesis.
2. Commonly used test statistics and their interpretations.
3. Multiple comparison procedures: procedures for analyzing group differences and contributions of response variables.

THE GENERAL LINEAR MODEL

The linear model appropriate for analyzing a single response variable y is:

$$y = \beta_0 + \beta_1 x_1 + \beta_2 x_2 + \ldots + \beta_{q-1} x_{q-1} + e. \tag{1}$$

Here $\beta' = [\beta_0\ \beta_1\ \ldots\ \beta_{q-1}]$ is the $(1 \times q)$ vector of "regression" coefficients, and e is a random variable with mean zero and variance σ^2. Writing the model in terms of the observations on the variable y, we have

$$y = X\beta + e \tag{2}$$

where $y' = [y_1\ y_2\ \ldots\ y_N]$, $X = [1\ x_1\ x_2\ \ldots\ x_{q-1}]$ is the $(N \times q)$ matrix of observations on the $q - 1$ independent variables (with $1' = [1\ 1\ 1\ \ldots\ 1]$), and $e' = [e_1\ e_2\ \ldots\ e_N]$ is the vector of errors that are independently and identically distributed. The matrix X is a full rank matrix with rank q.

The most general hypothesis in the above case is

$$H_0: C\beta = 0 \tag{3}$$

against the alternative

$$H_1: C\beta \neq 0$$

Here C is a $(r \times q)$ constant matrix of rank r whose elements are specified according to the hypothesis being tested. The statistic for testing this hypothesis can be derived using the union-intersection procedure developed by Roy (1953, 1957). Since certain multiple comparison procedures can be explained within this framework, we shall derive the test statistic here. According to the union-intersection procedure, the null hypothesis given in (3) is accepted if for any non-null vector u, the hypothesis

$$H_0(u): u'C\beta = 0 \tag{4}$$

is accepted against the alternative

$$H_1(u): u'C\beta \neq 0.$$

The estimate of $u'C\beta$ is given by $u'Cb$ where $b = (X'X)^{-1}X'y$. Under the assumption that $e \sim \mathcal{N}(0, \sigma^2 I)$,

$$u'Cb \sim \mathcal{N}(u'C\beta, \sigma^2 [u'C(X'X)^{-1}C'u]). \tag{5}$$

The estimate s^2 of σ^2 is $y'(I - X(X'X)^{-1}X')y/(N - q)$. Since $(N - q)s^2/\sigma^2 \sim \chi^2_{N-q}$, the statistic for testing the hypothesis in (4) is

$$t(u) = u'Cb/\surd\{s^2u'C(X'X)^{-1}C'u\}. \tag{6}$$

The acceptance region for $Ho(u)$ is $t^2(u) \leqslant t^2(\alpha/2, N - q)$.

Since the original hypothesis given in (3) is accepted if and only if (4) is accepted for all non-null u, the acceptance region for H_0: $C\beta = 0$ is the intersection

$$\cap \{t^2(u) \leqslant t^2(\alpha/2, N-q)\}.$$

This is true if and only if

$$\max t^2(u) \leqslant t^2(\alpha/2, N-q).$$

It can be shown that the maximum value of

$$t^2(u) = u'Cbb'C'u/\{s^2u'C(X'X)^{-1})C'u\}$$

is the largest eigenvalue of the matrix

$$Cbb'C'[s^2C(X'X)^{-1}C']^{-1}. \tag{7}$$

The rank of the matrix $Cbb'C'$ is one; hence the matrix given in (7) has only one nonzero eigenvalue. Since the sum of the eigenvalues is equal to the trace of the matrix, the nonzero eigenvalue λ is given by

$$\begin{aligned}\lambda &= \text{Trace}\,\{Cbb'C'[s^2C(X'X)^{-1}C']^{-1}\}\\ &= \text{Trace}\,\{b'C'[s^2C(X'X)^{-1}C']^{-1}Cb\}\\ &= b'C'[C(X'X)^{-1}C']^{-1}Cb/s^2. \end{aligned} \tag{8}$$

(The above follows from the well known result that Trace (AB) = Trace (BA), and the fact that the final product is a scalar.) When the null hypothesis (3) is true,

$$\lambda/r = b'C'[C(X'X)^{-1}C']^{-1}Cb/rs^2 \sim F_{r,N-q}. \tag{9}$$

Thus, the acceptance region for the hypothesis given in (3) is

$$\lambda/r \leqslant F_{\alpha,r,N-1}. \tag{10}$$

When the null hypothesis is rejected, the vector u that yielded the maximum value can be determined from the relationship

$$u \propto [C(X'X)^{-1}C']^{-1}Cb. \tag{11}$$

Swaminathan and Defriesse (1979) have demonstrated that when the null hypothesis (3) is rejected, the linear contrast $u'\beta$, where u is given above, may be the only contrast that is significantly different from zero.

The development given above is valid when the matrix X has full rank. This is not the case in ANOVA models. As an illustration, consider the regression model

$$y = \mu + \tau_1 d_1 + \tau_2 d_2 + \ldots\ldots + \tau_k d_k + e \tag{12}$$

where

$$d_g = \begin{cases} 1 & \text{if the observation belongs to Group g} \\ 0 & \text{otherwise.} \end{cases}$$

This model can be written in the traditional form in terms of y_{gh}, the observation on the hth unit in the gth group, as

$$y_{gh} = \mu + \tau_g + e_{gh}. \tag{13}$$

In matrix terms, the above model can be written as

$$y = A\,\tau + e \tag{14}$$

where $\tau' = [\mu\ \tau_1\ \tau_2\ \ldots\ \tau_k]$ is the $(k + 1 \times 1)$ vector of parameters, and A is the $(N \times k+1)$ matrix defined as

$$A = \begin{bmatrix} \underline{1} & \underline{1} & \underline{0} & . & . & . & \underline{0} \\ \underline{1} & \underline{0} & \underline{1} & . & . & . & \underline{0} \\ . & . & . & . & . & . & . \\ . & . & . & . & . & . & . \\ \underline{1} & \underline{0} & \underline{0} & . & . & . & \underline{1} \end{bmatrix} \tag{15}$$

The rank of the matrix A is clearly k and not k+1. Only k linear combinations of the k+1 parameters can be estimated.

The reparametrization of the model in (14) can be accomplished using the procedure given by Roy and Gnanadesikan (1959) or that given by Bock (1963). The matrix A can be decomposed as

$$A = XL \tag{16}$$

where X and L are full rank matrices of dimension (N×k) and (k × k+1) respectively. The model given in (14) can, therefore, be written as

$$y = X\,L\tau + e \tag{17}$$

$$= X\,\beta + e \tag{18}$$

where $\beta = L\tau$. The matrix L can be thought of as the contrast matrix that determines the k linear combinations of the parameters. Since in this formulation the matrix X is a full rank matrix, the procedures outlined above for testing the general hypothesis can be readily carried out.

A convenient choice of parameters is $\mu + \tau.$, $\tau_1 - \tau.$, $\tau_2 - \tau.$, . . . , $\tau_k - \tau.$, where $\tau.$ is $\Sigma\tau_g/k$. With this,

$$L = \begin{bmatrix} 1 & 1/k & 1/k & \cdot\ \cdot & 1/k \\ 0 & (1-1/k) & -1/k & \cdot\ \cdot & -1/k \\ 0 & -1/k & (1-1/k) & \cdot\ \cdot & -1/k \\ \cdot & \cdot & \cdot & \cdot\ \cdot & \cdot \\ \cdot & \cdot & \cdot & \cdot\ \cdot & \cdot \\ 0 & -1/k & -1/k & \cdot\ \cdot & (1-1/k) \end{bmatrix}. \tag{19}$$

Solving for X in the equation XL = A, we obtain

$$X = AL'(LL')^{-1}. \tag{20}$$

In this case X is the well known matrix

$$X = \begin{bmatrix} \underline{1} & \underline{1} & \underline{0} & \cdot\ \cdot\ \cdot & \underline{0} \\ \underline{1} & \underline{0} & \underline{1} & \cdot\ \cdot\ \cdot & \underline{0} \\ \cdot & \cdot & \cdot & \cdot\ \cdot\ \cdot & \cdot \\ \cdot & \cdot & \cdot & \cdot\ \cdot\ \cdot & \cdot \\ \underline{1} & \underline{0} & \underline{0} & \cdot\ \cdot\ \cdot & \underline{1} \\ \underline{1} & -\underline{1} & -\underline{1} & \cdot\ \cdot\ \cdot & -\underline{1} \end{bmatrix}. \tag{21}$$

The advantage of this formulation is that for multifactor designs, the full rank design matrices for each factor can be written down, the interaction terms can be obtained as the product of the appropriate columns, and the design matrix for the entire factorial design can be constructed. A complete discussion of this procedure is given in Bock (1975).

The univariate model is readily extended to the multivariate case where there are p response variables. The general linear model appropriate for multivariate regression analysis is:

$$y_i = X\,\beta_i + e_i \qquad i = 1, 2, \ldots, p$$

Defining $Y = [y_1\, y_2 \ldots y_p]$, and $B = [\beta_1\, \beta_2 \ldots \beta_p]$, we obtain the multivariate model

$$Y = X\,B + E \tag{22}$$

where Y is the $(N \times p)$ matrix of N independent observations on p response variables, X is the $(N \times q)$ matrix of scores of rank q, B is the $(q \times p)$ matrix of regression coefficients, and E is the $(N \times p)$ matrix of errors such that the rows of E are independently and identically distributed with zero mean vector and nonsingular dispersion matrix Σ.

In the multivariate analysis of variance situation, the model is

$$Y = A\,T + E.$$

In the one factor design, the A matrix has the form given in (15) and the columns of the matrix of parameters T are

$$\tau_i' = [\mu\; \tau_1\; \tau_2 \ldots \tau_k] \qquad i = 1, 2, \ldots, p.$$

As the matrix A is of deficient rank, the matrix T must be reparametrized as shown previously. Factoring A into factors X and L as before, we obtain the reparametrized model

$$Y = XB + E \tag{23}$$

where $B = LT$.

Here, B is the $(q \times p)$ matrix of effects. As with the univariate model, the best linear unbiased estimate of B is

$$\hat{B} = (X'X)^{-1}\,X'Y. \tag{24}$$

The estimate S of the dispersion matrix Σ is obtained by replacing the vector y in the univariate expression for s^2 by the matrix Y. This yields the expression

$$S = Y'[I - X(X'X)^{-1}X']Y \;/\; (N-q). \tag{25}$$

The rank of Y is p, and the rank of $[I - X(X'X)^{-1}X']$ is $(N-q)$. Thus for S to be of full rank, $N-q \geqslant p$.

EXAMPLE

The computations described above are illustrated through the following example in which subjects, measured on six dependent variables, are randomly assigned to four treatment conditions. The model appropriate for the ith dependent variable of this one-way MANOVA design is

$$y_{ghi} = \mu_i + \tau_{gi} + e_{ghi} \quad (g = 1, \ldots, 4; i = 1, \ldots, 6)$$

where y_{ghi} is the observation on the ith dependent variable for the hth subject in the gth treatment condition, μ_i is the mean of variable i, τ_{gi} is the effect of treatment g on variable i, and e_{ghi} is the error. With 8 subjects in each treatment condition, the design matrix A of dimension (32 × 5) is:

$$A = \begin{bmatrix} \underline{1} & \underline{1} & \underline{0} & \underline{0} & \underline{0} \\ \underline{1} & \underline{0} & \underline{1} & \underline{0} & \underline{0} \\ \underline{1} & \underline{0} & \underline{0} & \underline{1} & \underline{0} \\ \underline{1} & \underline{0} & \underline{0} & \underline{0} & \underline{1} \end{bmatrix},$$

where $\underline{1}$ is a (8 × 1) vector of ones, and $\underline{0}$ is a (8 × 1) vector of zeros. The corresponding matrix of parameters is:

$$T = \begin{bmatrix} \mu_1 & \mu_2 & \mu_3 & \mu_4 & \mu_5 & \mu_6 \\ \tau_{11} & \tau_{12} & \tau_{13} & \tau_{14} & \tau_{15} & \tau_{16} \\ \tau_{21} & \tau_{22} & \tau_{23} & \tau_{24} & \tau_{25} & \tau_{26} \\ \tau_{31} & \tau_{32} & \tau_{33} & \tau_{34} & \tau_{35} & \tau_{36} \\ \tau_{41} & \tau_{42} & \tau_{43} & \tau_{44} & \tau_{45} & \tau_{46} \end{bmatrix}.$$

The columns of T correspond to the dependent variables, while the rows of T correspond to the independent variables. Clearly, the rank of A is 4 and hence only four of the five rows of T are estimable. If the parameters of interest are $\mu_i + \tau_{.i}$, $\tau_{1i} - \tau_{4i}$, $\tau_{2i} - \tau_{4i}$, and $\tau_{3i} - \tau_{4i}$ for i = 1, . . . , 6, where $\tau_{.i} = \Sigma\tau_{gi}/4$, then the matrix L for transforming the matrix to yield the parameters of interest is:

$$L = \begin{bmatrix} 1 & .25 & .25 & .25 & .25 \\ 0 & 1 & 0 & 0 & -1 \\ 0 & 0 & 1 & 0 & -1 \\ 0 & 0 & 0 & 1 & -1 \end{bmatrix}.$$

With this choice of L, the (4×6) matrix of parameters B and the reparametrized design matrix X, a basis matrix of A, are:

$$B = LT = \begin{bmatrix} \mu_1 + \tau_{.1} & \mu_2 + \tau_{.2} & \mu_3 + \tau_{.3} & \mu_4 + \tau_{.4} & \mu_5 + \tau_{.5} & \mu_6 + \tau_{.6} \\ \tau_{11} - \tau_{41} & \tau_{12} - \tau_{42} & \tau_{13} - \tau_{43} & \tau_{14} - \tau_{44} & \tau_{15} - \tau_{45} & \tau_{16} - \tau_{46} \\ \tau_{21} - \tau_{41} & \tau_{22} - \tau_{42} & \tau_{23} - \tau_{43} & \tau_{24} - \tau_{44} & \tau_{25} - \tau_{45} & \tau_{26} - \tau_{46} \\ \tau_{31} - \tau_{41} & \tau_{32} - \tau_{42} & \tau_{33} - \tau_{43} & \tau_{34} - \tau_{44} & \tau_{35} - \tau_{45} & \tau_{36} - \tau_{46} \end{bmatrix},$$

and,

$$X = AL'(LL')^{-1} = \begin{bmatrix} \underline{1} & .75\underline{1} & -.25\underline{1} & -.25\underline{1} \\ \underline{1} & -.25\underline{1} & .75\underline{1} & -.25\underline{1} \\ \underline{1} & -.25\underline{1} & -.25\underline{1} & .75\underline{1} \\ \underline{1} & -.25\underline{1} & -.25\underline{1} & -.25\underline{1} \end{bmatrix}.$$

Table 1. Estimates of MANOVA Model Parameters

Independent Variable	*Dependent Variable* 1	2	3	4	5	6
$\mu + \tau.$	8.35	7.97	6.67	7.89	8.43	7.77
$\tau_1 - \tau_4$	−1.61	1.34	1.61	2.73	0.93	2.74
$\tau_2 - \tau_4$	−1.65	5.20	6.31	3.16	3.15	3.98
$\tau_3 - \tau_4$	2.53	3.40	2.29	−0.49	−1.26	2.15

In order to obtain the estimates of the parameters, the matrices $(X'X)^{-1}$ and $X'Y$, where Y is the (32×6) data matrix, are needed. Since there are eight subjects in each treatment group, the first eight rows of Y contain the data for subjects in Treatment 1, the next eight rows contain the data for subjects in Treatment 2, and so on. Now,

$$(X'X)^{-1} = \begin{bmatrix} .03125 & 0 & 0 & 0 \\ 0 & .250 & .125 & .125 \\ 0 & .125 & .250 & .125 \\ 0 & .125 & .125 & .250 \end{bmatrix},$$

and

$$X'Y = \begin{bmatrix} 267.20 & 255.10 & 213.30 & 252.40 & 269.70 & 248.50 \\ -11.42 & -9.60 & -7.54 & 11.04 & 1.80 & 4.18 \\ -11.74 & 21.72 & 30.06 & 14.48 & 19.56 & 14.10 \\ 21.70 & 7.30 & -2.10 & -14.72 & -15.72 & -0.54 \end{bmatrix}.$$

The estimate $\hat{B}$ of B given in Table 1 is the product of $(X'X)^{-1}$ and $X'Y$.

It should be noted that the estimates of the parameters above can be obtained directly from the cell means of the dependent variables given in Table 2.

The elements of the variance-covariance matrix of errors S, or the pooled

Table 2. Cell Means

Group	*Dependent Variable* 1	2	3	4	5	6
1	6.93	6.83	5.73	9.26	8.65	8.29
2	6.89	10.69	10.43	9.70	10.88	9.53
3	11.06	8.89	6.40	6.05	6.46	7.70
4	8.54	5.49	4.11	6.54	7.73	5.55
Grand Mean	8.35	7.97	6.67	7.89	8.43	7.77

Table 3. Pooled within Cell Error Variance-Covariance Matrix

Variable	*Dependent Variable*					
	1	*2*	*3*	*4*	*5*	*6*
1	12.76					
2	6.11	16.42				
3	4.49	7.49	14.42			
4	5.34	3.52	6.72	10.19		
5	2.57	3.80	3.70	5.83	10.42	
6	−.25	.37	3.38	−.73	1.25	8.21

within cell error variance-covariance matrix, [Eq. (25)] are given in Table 3.

To calculate the standard errors of the estimates of the parameters, it is necessary to multiply the elements of the error variance-covariance matrix S by the appropriate elements of the matrix $(X'X)^{-1}$. The matrix $(X'X)^{-1}$ is known as the matrix of variance-covariance factors. For completeness the elements of this matrix are given in Table 4.

For example, suppose that it is of interest to determine the estimate and the standard error of the parameter $(\tau_{14} - \tau_{24}) - (\tau_{15} - \tau_{25})$. The estimate of $\tau_{14} - \tau_{24}$ is the estimate of $(\tau_{14} - \tau_{44}) - (\tau_{24} - \tau_{44})$. From Table 1 the estimate of this parameter is $2.73 - 3.16 = -.43$. Similarly, the estimate of $(\tau_{15} - \tau_{25}) = (\tau_{15} - \tau_{45}) - (\tau_{25} - \tau_{45})$ is -2.22. Hence, the required estimate is $-.43 - (-2.22) = 1.79$.

Since the parameter of interest is the difference between the dependent variables 4 and 5 for the independent variable $(\tau_{1i} - \tau_{4i}) - (\tau_{2i} - \tau_{4i})$, the variance-covariance factor is $.250 + .250 - 2(.125) = .250$. The variance of the difference between variables 4 and 5, obtained from Table 3, is $10.19 + 10.42 - 2(5.83) = 9.95$. The variance of the estimate of the parameter is $.250(9.95) = 2.4875$. The standard error is, therefore, 1.577. The parameter of interest in this case can be expressed as $u'Bv$ where $u' = [0\ 1\ -1\ 0]$ and $v' = [0\ 0\ 0\ 1\ -1\ 0]$. The variance of this linear combination is $[u'(X'X)^{-1}u][v'Sv]$.

Table 4. Variance-Covariance Factors

Parameter	*Parameter**			
	$\mu_i + \tau_{\cdot i}$	$\tau_{1i} - \tau_{4i}$	$\tau_{2i} - \tau_{4i}$	$\tau_{3i} - \tau_{4i}$
$\mu_i + \tau_{\cdot i}$	.03125			
$\tau_{1i} - \tau_{4i}$	0	.250		
$\tau_{2i} - \tau_{4i}$	0	.125	.250	
$\tau_{3i} - \tau_{4i}$	0	.125	.125	.250

Note: *The variance-covariance factors are the same for all dependent variables (i=1, . . . ,6).

THE GENERAL LINEAR HYPOTHESIS

The most general linear hypothesis on B is

$$H_0: CBM = 0 \tag{26}$$

where C and M are known full rank matrices of dimensions $(r \times q)$ and $(p \times u)$ respectively. The necessary and sufficient condition for the testability of this hypothesis is that

$$\text{Rank } [A' \; C'] = \text{Rank } [A'].$$

For the one-way analysis of variance model with k groups, the matrix C may be taken as:

$$C = [\mathit{0} \; I_{k-1}] \tag{27}$$

where I_{k-1} is the $(k-1 \times k-1)$ identity matrix and $\mathit{0}$ is a $(k-1 \times 1)$ column vector of zeros. This results in the hypothesis

$$H_{0i}: \tau_{1i} = \tau_{2i} = \ldots = \tau_{ki} \qquad i = 1, 2, \ldots, p,$$

against the alternative

$$H_{1i}: \text{not } H_{0i}$$

The matrix M is determined according to the hypotheses of interest concerning the response variables. If M is specified as the $(p \times 1)$ column vector

$$M = \mathit{1}/p, \tag{28}$$

then with C specified in (27), the hypothesis tested is that there are no group differences on the *average* of the p response variables (i.e., group main effect). With $C = [\mathit{0} \; I_{k-1}]$ and

$$M_n = \begin{bmatrix} 1 & 0 & . & . & . & 0 \\ 0 & 1 & . & . & . & 0 \\ . & . & . & . & . & . \\ . & . & . & . & . & . \\ 0 & 0 & . & . & . & 1 \\ -1 & -1 & . & . & . & -1 \end{bmatrix}, \tag{29}$$

the hypothesis H_0: CBM = 0 is equivalent to the hypothesis of no Group × Response variable interaction. With M specified above, but with $C = [1 \; 0 \; 0 \ldots 0]$, the hypothesis tested is that there are no differences among the p response variables. These hypotheses are appropriate when comparisons among the response variables are meaningful, as in repeated measures designs. When the response variables are not commensurate, comparisons among the response variables are meaningless, and in this case M may be chosen as the $(p \times p)$ identity matrix. Thus suitable specifications of C and M yield the hypotheses of interest in MANOVA.

TEST STATISTICS

There are currently four statistics available for testing the hypothesis H_0: CBM = 0 against the alternative H_1: CBM $\neq$ 0. We shall derive one test statistic using the union-intersection procedure of Roy (1957), since this procedure provides an understanding of the nature of the hypothesis being tested.

According to the union-intersection principle, the hypothesis H_0: CBM = 0 is accepted if for all non-null v, the hypothesis $H_0(v)$: CBMv = *0* is accepted. To determine the acceptance region for the hypothesis $H_0(v)$ we reformulate the model Y = XB + E to reflect the hypothesis being tested. Multiplying both sides of (23) by Mv, we obtain

$$YMv = XBMv + EMv. \tag{30}$$

Writing $y = YMv$, $\beta = BMv$, and $e = EMv$, we now have the familiar univariate model

$$y = X\beta + e.$$

Since the rows of the matrix E are independently and identically multivariate normally distributed, the ith row of E has the distribution

$$e_i \sim \mathcal{N}(0,\Sigma) \qquad i = 1,2, \ldots, N$$

$$\text{and} \quad \epsilon(e_i,e_j') = 0.$$

Thus

$$e_iMv \sim \mathcal{N}(0,v'M'\Sigma Mv)$$

and hence,

$$y = YMv \sim \mathcal{N}(XBMv,(v'M'\Sigma Mv)I). \tag{31}$$

The region of acceptance for $H_0(v)$: CBMv = *0*, or equivalently, for $H_0(v)$: $C\beta = 0$ is

$$F(v) = \frac{(N-q)}{r} \frac{b'C'[C(X'X)^{-1}C']^{-1}Cb}{y'[I - X(X'X)^{-1}X']y} \leqslant F_{\alpha,r,N-q}. \tag{32}$$

The accepıance region for the multivariate hypothesis H_0: CBM = 0 is the intersection of the univariate regions, i.e.,

$$\cap \{F(v) \leqslant F_{\alpha,r,N-q}\} \tag{33}$$

This is equivalent to the acceptance region defined by

$$\max F(v) \leqslant F_{\alpha,r,N-q}.$$

Let

$$Q_H = b'C'[C(X'X)^{-1}]Cb$$
$$= M'Y'X(X'X)^{-1}C'[C(X'X)^{-1}C']^{-1}C(X'X)^{-1}X'YM,$$

and

$$Q_E = M'Y'[I - X(X'X)^{-1}X']YM.$$

The region of acceptance for H_0: CBM = 0 is

$$\max \{[(N-q)/r]\ v'Q_Hv/v'Q_Ev\} \leqslant F_{\alpha,r,N-q}.$$

The maximum value of $(v'Q_Hv)/(v'Q_Ev)$ is the largest eigenvalue, λ_{max}, of the matrix $Q_HQ_E{}^{-1}$. Thus the multivariate hypothesis H_0: CBM = 0 is accepted if

$$\lambda_{max} \leqslant \lambda_{\alpha,s,m,n}$$

wher $\lambda_{\alpha,s,m,n}$ is the 100α percentage point of the largest eigenvalue distribution when the hypothesis is true.

The test statistic based on the union-intersection principle given by Roy is one of four available for testing the general linear hypothesis. The other three are Wilks', Lawley-Hotelling's, and Pillai's test statistics. The distributions of all of these test statistics depend upon the following parameters:

$$\begin{aligned}
\lambda_1 &= \text{the ith eigenvalue of } Q_HQ_E{}^{-1};\\
\Theta_i &= \lambda_i/(1 + \lambda_i);\\
\nu_H &= r;\\
\nu_E &= N - q;\\
s &= \min(\nu_H, u) \text{ where u is the rank of M};\\
m &= \{|u - \nu_H| - 1\}/2;\\
n &= \{\nu_E - u - 1\}/2.
\end{aligned}$$

These test statistics are summarized in Table 5.

For the example given earlier (p = 6, q = 4, N = 32), the hypothesis given in (27) can be specialized by setting k = 4. The matrix C of dimension (3 × 4) is:

$$C = \begin{bmatrix} 0 & 1 & 0 & 0 \\ 0 & 0 & 1 & 0 \\ 0 & 0 & 0 & 1 \end{bmatrix}.$$

Assuming that all possible comparisons among the dependent variables may be of interest, the matrix M is most easily specified as the (6 × 6) identity matrix, I_6. Thus, r = 3 and u = 6. The values of s, m, and n are:

Table 5. Test Statistics for Testing H_o: CBM = 0

Name	*Statistic*	*Parameters*	*Criterion*
Wilks	$\Pi_i(1-\theta_i)$	u, ν_H, ν_E	$U(\alpha;u,\nu_H,\nu_E)$
Roy	θ_{max}	s, m, n	$\theta_o(\alpha;s,m,n)$
Lawley-Hotelling	$\Sigma_i\theta_i/(1-\theta_i)$	s, m, n	$U_o(\alpha;s,m,n)$
Pillai	$\Sigma_i\ \theta_i$	s, m, n	$V(\alpha;s,m,n)$

$$s = \min(3,6) = 3;$$
$$m = \{|r-u| - 1\}/2 = 1;$$
$$n = \{\nu_E - u - 1\}/2 = \{28\text{-}6\text{-}1\}/2 = 10.5.$$

Since s = 3, there are three non-zero eigenvalues of $Q_H Q_E^{-1}$. These are: λ_1 = 1.294, λ_2 = .446, λ_3 = .218. The corresponding values of $\Theta = \lambda/(1 + \lambda)$ are: Θ_1 = .564; Θ_2 = .308; Θ_3 = .179.

The four test statistics and their significance levels are given in Table 6.

The hypothesis H_0: CBM = 0 is rejected at the .01 level of significance using the Wilks', Lawley-Hotelling's, and Pillai's criteria. With the Roy's criterion, the hypothesis is rejected at a much higher level of significance.

The four criteria generally yield different results. However, when s = 1, the four test statistics are identical. In this case there is only one non-zero eigenvalue and it can be shown that

$$F = \lambda\ (n+1)/(m+1) \sim F_{2m+2,2n+2}$$

(Morrison, 1976, p. 178). Unfortuntely, when s > 1, there is no uniformly most powerful test of H_0. However, when the largest eigenvalue is the dominant eigenvalue, Roy's criterion yields the most powerful test. When the eigenvalues are of roughly equal importance, Pillai's criterion yields the best results. When the eigenvalues do not show the patterns described above, Lawley-Hotelling's and Wilks' criterion are the most powerful (Olson, 1976; Anderson, 1984, pp. 332–333). This is the case in the example given above. The eigenvalues are distinct and hence the Lawley-Hotelling's and the Wilks' test statistics are the most powerful while Roy's is the least powerful.

Table 6. Test Statistics for the Example

Test Statistic	*Value*	*Significance*
Wilks	.248	.007
Roy	.564	.023
Lawley-Hotelling	1.958	.006
Pillai	1.051	.008

The above-mentioned test statistics are appropriate for testing the hypothesis given in (26). In reality, as demonstrated earlier in this section and in the first section, the hypothesis tested is the intersection of an infinite number of more primitive composite hypotheses with the alternate being the union of the corresponding alternatives, that is,

$$H_o : \bigcap_i \bigcap_j H_{oij} \tag{34a}$$

with

$$H_1 : \bigcup_i \bigcup_j H_{1ij}. \tag{34b}$$

For Roy's procedure, these primitive hypotheses are

$$H_{oij} : u_i'\mathrm{CBMv}_j = 0 \tag{35a}$$

$$H_{1ij} : u_i'\mathrm{CBMv}_j = 0 \tag{35b}$$

and u_i and v_j are non-null vectors. These are not necessarily the primitive and alternate hypotheses for other test procedures (Roy, Gnanadesikan, & Srivastava, 1971).

The bilinear forms given above are doubly infinite, "response-wise" and "contrast-wise." As a result of this, the overall tests are generally powerful. However, as noted earlier, the hypothesis H_0: CBM = 0 may be rejected as the result of a hypothesis of the type H_0: u'CBMv = 0 being rejected. Since the vectors u and v responsible for the rejection of the hypothesis may not represent comparisons of interest, it is important to follow up with multiple comparison procedures when the hypothesis is rejected. Alternatively, the overall test may be bypassed and other procedures for answering questions of interest may be explored. Follow-up multiple comparison procedures and alternatives to the overall test procedures are discussed below.

MULTIPLE COMPARISONS

The multiple comparison procedures and alternatives to the overall test procedures can be conveniently classified as follows:

a. Response-wise infinite and contrast-wise infinite
b. Response-wise finite and contrast-wise infinite
c. Response-wise infinite and contrast-wise finite
d. Response-wise finite and contrast-wise finite
e. Graphical

This classification follows that given by Roy, Gnanadesikan, and Srivastava (1971).

Response-wise Infinite and Contrast-wise Infinite Procedures

When the hypothesis H_0: CBM = 0 is rejected, confidence intervals may be established for bilinear forms of the type

$$\psi = u'\text{CBMv} \tag{36}$$

where u and v are given vectors. By choosing the elements of these vectors any linear combination of the parameters in CBM may be obtained. The BLUE estimate $\hat{\psi}$ of ψ is obtained by replacing B by its estimate, given by (24).

The $(1-\alpha)$% confidence interval for ψ is given by

$$\psi \pm \sqrt{\{k_0\ [v'M'Q_E Mv]\ [u'C(A'A)^{-1}C'u]\}} \tag{37}$$

where k_0 depends on the test statistic employed to reject H_0. The values of k_0 for the four test procedures, given by Gabriel (1968), are summarized in Table 7.

The critical values for these test criteria can be found in Anderson (1984), Bock (1976), Morrison (1976) and Roy, et al. (1971). In our example, the critical value for the Roy-Bose 95% confidence interval is $\sqrt{(\nu_E \lambda_{.05;3,1,10.5})}$ = 5.68 and the confidence limits for the contrast $(\tau_{14} - \tau_{24}) - (\tau_{15} - \tau_{25})$ are 1.79 ± (1.58)(5.68), yielding the interval [−7.18, 10.76].

The confidence intervals given above are simultaneous confidence intervals and have an experiment-wise error rate of α. Because the experiment-wise error rate is controlled for all possible contrasts, these confidence intervals are extremely conservative. Although the Roy procedure yields the shortest interval (Gabriel, 1968), even this may be too conservative to be of much use. This implies that, in practice, *it may be found that there is no significant meaningful contrast after a rejection of the null hypothesis*. This dilemma indicates an inherent weakness in the overall test procedure. The rejection of the overall

Table 7. Critical Values for Confidence Intervals Based on Four Multivariate Test Procedures

Test Procedure	k_o
Wilks	$(1-U_\alpha)/U_\alpha$
Roy-Bose[1]	$\theta_\alpha/(1-\theta_\alpha)$
Lawley-Hotelling	$U_{o\alpha}$
Pillai	$V_\alpha/(1-V_\alpha)$

Note: [1]Although the test procedure was developed by Roy, the confidence bounds were given by Roy and Bose (1953).

hypothesis guarantees that for some u and v, a contrast of the type u'CBMv is different from zero (Swaminathan & DeFriesse, 1979) and not that some element of CBM is different from zero. While this is strictly true for the test based on Roy's procedure, we can expect this to hold for the other procedures as well. Thus, testing the overall hypothesis may not be meaningful if only the particular elements of CBM are of interest.

The multiple comparison procedures based on the criteria given in Table 7 are appropriate even if the overall hypothesis is not tested. The overall test merely indicates that some contrasts may be different from zero. Thus, in an exploratory situation where the researcher does not have any particular contrast in mind, an overall test followed by the logical simultaneous confidence intervals procedure is appropriate. By "logical" it is meant that the overall test must be followed by its own counterpart. This raises a problem, given the fact that while there is no uniformly most powerful test procedure, the Roy-Bose (Roy & Bose, 1953) procedure yields the shortest confidence bounds. Consequently, some researchers have suggested that, since the Roy's procedure is the least powerful for a diffuse dispersion structure, the other test procedures should be used to test the overall hypothesis and the Roy-Bose procedure be used as the follow-up procedure (Bird & Hadzi-Pavlovic, 1983). The recommendation of this protected procedure raises at least two problems, the first one being that the experiment-wise error rate is not necessarily α.

The second problem concerns the point made earlier that the overall multivariate procedures, being infinite intersection procedures, are generally powerful and the rejection of the overall hypothesis does not guarantee that comparisons of interest will be significant. Given this apparent paradox, there is no point in choosing a test statistic that has great power if the follow-up procedure used is not directly related to it. When particular comparisons are of interest and are to be tested using the procedure which yields the shortest confidence bounds, then the overall test can be by-passed and the Roy-Bose procedure can be used to explore the comparisons. This approach will result in the experiment-wise error rate being maintained at α no matter how many contrasts are examined.

The above approach can be used to determine which, if any, of the response variables should be studied further. The union-intersection principle assures that for any linear combination $v'y$ of the dependent variables,

$$P[\max(v'Q_H v / v'Q_E v) \leq \lambda_{\alpha:s,m,n}] = 1-\alpha.$$

If the vector v' has 1 in the ith column and zeros elsewhere, then $v'Q_H v/v'Q_e v = (r/\nu_E)F_i$ where F_i is the univariate F statistic for testing the hypothesis H_0: $C\beta_i = 0$ for the ith dependent variable. Thus

$$P[F_i \leq (\nu_E/r)\ \lambda_{\alpha:s,m,n}] = 1-\alpha, \tag{38}$$

and those response variables whose univariate F values exceed the Roy-Bose critical value may be identified as the appropriate variables to be studied further.

The above confidence region for the ith dependent variable was obtained by specifying M = I, $u = 1$ (a scalar), and v a column vector with a 1 in the ith row and zeros elsewhere. Similarly, to obtain a confidence region for a group contrast, u is specified with a one in the appropriate location and zeros elsewhere with M = I and v a scalar.

For the example introduced earlier, we may wish to determine which, if any, of the dependent variables was responsible for the rejection of the null hypothesis. The univariate F statistics for the dependent variables are reported in Table 8.

From the tables of the largest root criterion (Roy et al., 1971), $\lambda_{.05:3,1,10.5} = 1.15$; $(\nu_E/r)\lambda = 10.73$. Since no univariate F statistic exceeds this value, we conclude that there are no group differences on any of the dependent variables.

Although group contrasts and response variables can be studied in this manner, the procedure is contrast-wise and response-wise infinite and thus is usually too conservative.

Response-wise Finite and Contrast-wise Infinite Procedures

In the strict sense, response-wise finite procedures should only involve a finite number of contrasts of the response variables. The overall hypothesis is

$$H_o : \bigcap_i \{H_{oi} : u_i'CBM = \underline{0}\}. \tag{39}$$

Since all linear combinations of the response variables are not tested, the parameter space is not doubly infinite as in the situation given in (34a, 34b). The hypothesis in (39) indicates that only linear combinations of the response variables specified by the matrix M are of interest. In this sense, then, comparisons among the response variables are "planned." The most direct approach to testing these response-wise finite and contrast-wise infinite comparisons is to employ procedures based on the Bonferroni inequality. The simultaneous confi-

Table 8. Univariate Test Statistics for the Example

Dependent Variable	*Mean Sum of Squares*			
	Between	*Within*	F^1	*Significance*
1	30.83	12.76	2.72	.063
2	41.87	16.42	2.54	.076
3	57.62	14.42	3.99	.017
4	27.67	10.19	2.72	.063
5	27.72	10.42	2.66	.067
6	22.08	8.21	2.69	.065

Note: [1]Based on F value with $r=3$ and $\nu_E=28$ degrees of freedom.

dence intervals/regions procedures described in the previous section are clearly appropriate but these are not response-wise finite procedures.

The Bonferroni procedure is based on the well known inequality

$$P[\cup_i A_i] \leq \Sigma_i P(A_i)$$

where A_i is the event that the ith statement is true. If $P(A_i) = 1-\alpha_i$, $i=1,2,\ldots,k$, then the probability $(1-\gamma)$ that all k statements are simultaneously true is given as

$$\begin{aligned} 1-\gamma = P[\cap_i A_i] &= 1 - P[\overline{\cap_i A_i}] \\ &= 1 - P[\cup_i \bar{A}_i] \\ &\geq 1 - \Sigma_i P(\bar{A}_i) = 1 - \Sigma_i \alpha_i. \end{aligned}$$

When $\alpha_i = \alpha$,

$$1-\gamma = P[\cap_i A_i] \geq 1 - k\alpha.$$

when k comparisons are made, each at the $1-\alpha$ confidence level, the true experiment-wise error rate γ is given as

$$\gamma \leq k\alpha. \tag{40}$$

The above inequalities, known as Bonferroni inequalities, provide the basis for controlling the experiment-wise error rate for k comparisons by adjusting the comparison-wise error rate to be $\alpha^* = \alpha/k$. Since the true experiment-wise error rate γ may be considerably less than α, the procedure may be more conservative than necessary. Sidak (1967) showed that

$$1-\gamma \geq (1-\alpha)^k$$

and hence that

$$\gamma \leq 1 - (1-\alpha)^k. \tag{41}$$

With the Sidak procedure, the value of α^* needed to yield an overall experiment-wise error rate α can be computed more accurately than with the Bonferroni procedure, using the expression

$$\alpha^* = 1 - (1-\alpha)^{1/k}.$$

Sidak (1967) showed that positive or negative correlations among the comparisons will increase the overall confidence level $1-\gamma$ and thus decrease the true experiment-wise error rate γ.

To apply the Bonferroni procedure in making response-wise finite and contrast-wise infinite comparisons, univariate F statistics are computed for each of the k combinations of the response variables and compared with F_{α^*}.

For example, for the data given in Table 8, we are interested in determining which of the six dependent variables were responsible for the rejection of the overall hypothesis. Setting $\alpha = .05$ yields $\alpha^* = .05/6 = .0083$. The Bonferroni critical value, $F_{.0083:3,28}$, is 4.76. Since none of the F values for the dependent variables exceeded this value, we conclude as with the Roy-Bose procedure, that there are no group differences on any of the variables. The critical value obtained with the Bonferroni procedure is much smaller than that obtained with the Roy-Bose procedure. The same conclusion can be arrived at simply by comparing the significance levels given in Table 8 with the value of α^*.

In general, when k is not too large, $F_{\alpha^*} \leqslant \lambda_\alpha$, the critical value for the Roy-Bose confidence bounds. Thus the Bonferroni procedure will result in shorter confidence intervals than the Roy-Bose procedure.

Comparisons of the Bonferroni and the Roy-Bose confidence intervals are presented in Tables 9 and 10. Table 9 gives comparisons for a two group design with several response variables (s = 1). When p = 2, the number of Bonferroni comparisons which can be performed without exceeding the experiment-wise error rate of .05 is four. As p increases, the number of permissible Bonferroni contrasts for the given experiment-wise error rate rapidly increases. For example, when p = 5 and $\nu_E = 30$, 90 Bonferroni comparisons can be performed, considerably more than are likely to be of interest. Table 10 contains comparisons between the Roy-Bose and Bonferroni procedures for s = 2, 3, 5, and m = −1/2. The case m = −1/2 is chosen because it yields the narrowest Roy-Bose confidence intervals and thus shows the procedure to the best advantage. Except in the case of s = 2, the Bonferroni procedure permits a large number of contrasts (>150) before the experiment-wise error rate is exceeded. Thus, in

Table 9. Comparison of Bonferroni and Roy-Bose Multiple Comparison Procedures

N	*r*	*p*	*(s,m,n)*	ν_E	*Roy-Bose* $\sqrt{\nu_E \lambda}$	*Bonferroni*[1] *Comparisons*
20	1	2	(1,0,7.5)	18	2.76	4
30			(1,0,12.5)	28	2.64	4
50			(1,0,22.5)	48	2.55	4
100			(1,0,47.5)	98	2.50	4
20	1	3	(1,0.5,7.0)	18	3.31	13
30			(1,0.5,12.0)	28	3.10	12
50			(1,0.5,22.0)	48	2.97	11
100			(1,0.5,47.0)	98	2.88	11
20	1	5	(1,1.5,6.5)	18	4.17	<90
30			(1,1.5,11.5)	28	3.82	<80
50			(1,1.5,21.5)	48	3.59	<70
100			(1,1.5,46.5)	98	3.44	<60

Note: [1]Number of Bonferroni comparisons which can be performed without exceeding the experiment-wise error rate (α = .05)

Table 10. Comparison of Bonferroni and Roy-Bose Multiple Comparison Procedures

N	r	p	(s,m,n)	ν_E	*Roy-Bose* $\sqrt{\nu_E \lambda}$	*Bonferroni*[1] *Comparisons*
20	2	2	(2,−0.5,7.5)	18	3.37	15
30			(2,−0.5,12.5)	28	3.22	15
50			(2,−0.5,22.5)	48	3.08	15
100			(2,−0.5,47.5)	98	3.02	15
20	3	3	(3,−0.5,6.5)	17	4.56	<200
30			(3,−0.5,11.5)	27	4.20	<200
50			(3,−0.5,21.5)	47	3.96	<200
100			(3,−0.5,47.5)	97	3.72	<150
30	5	5	(5,−0.5,9.5)	25	6.06	>500
50			(5,−0.5,19.5)	45	5.36	>500
100			(5,−0.5,44.5)	95	4.95	>500

Note: [1]Number of Bonferroni comparisons which may be performed without exceeding the experiment-wise error rate (α = .05)

general, the Bonferroni procedure will result in narrower confidence intervals than the Roy-Bose procedure.

It should be noted that the Bonferroni procedure is not related to the union-intersection procedure of Roy. Hence using the Bonferroni procedure as a follow-up when the multivariate hypothesis is rejected may not be too meaningful. However, this procedure is often advocated as a protected procedure. The same caution against following up other multivariate tests with the Roy-Bose confidence bounds applies here. If combinations of the response variables have been planned, the k Bonferroni univariate tests could be carried out without carrying out the overall multivariate test.

Often it is desired to select and order response variables according to "importance." The procedures that have traditionally been employed for this purpose are: discriminant analysis, including step-wise discriminant analysis, and the Roy-Bargmann step-down procedure. In the strict sense these are not response-wise finite procedures.

The discriminant analysis procedure is well known and documented (e.g., Huberty, 1975, 1984). In the present context it suffices to note that the coefficients of the first discriminant function are the elements of the vector v that results in the largest test statistic for testing hypotheses of the type given by (35a, 35b) with M = I and, therefore, are related to the infinite intersection procedures. In fact, the discriminant functions are the logical by-products of Roy's union-intersection procedure. In the strict sense, if the overall multivariate hypothesis is not rejected, discriminant analysis should not be carried out.

The number of discriminant functions equals the parameter s. The discriminant function coefficients are loosely interpreted as providing information about the ordering of the response variables, an interpretation that is clearly not valid unless the response variables are uncorrelated. The discussions on this issue provided by Huberty (1975) are illuminating and hence are not repeated here. The step-down discriminant analysis is also fraught with problems and is not recommended. Since alternative procedures are described by Huberty elsewhere in this volume, we shall not discuss them here.

Discriminant analysis can provide a meaningful graphical description of group differences. A plot of the group means on the discriminant function space may clarify the dimensions on which the groups differ. Bock (1975) has provided illustrations of this approach. This graphical procedure, unfortunately, is not widely used.

In our example, s = 3, and hence there are three discriminant functions. Only the first of these is significant, as indicated by the significance of the eigenvalues. The first discriminant function is

$$\eta_1 = .262V1 - .105V2 + .037V3 - .290V4 + .009V5 - .162V6.$$

Although only the first discriminant function is significant, we shall include the second for discussion purposes. The second function is

$$\eta_2 = .069V1 + .080V2 + .233V3 - .277V4 + .059V5 - .002V6.$$

The coefficients of these functions do not indicate the relative importance of the variables. The first function, however, is the linear combination of the variables that led to rejection of the overall multivariate hypothesis. This function is the best predictor of group membership.

The mean deviation of each of the first three groups from the fourth on these two discriminant functions are given in Table 11. These mean deviations can be plotted in a two dimensional (η_1, η_2) space. An inspection of the plot may reveal which groups are most different. Alternatively, the Euclidean distance between the points may be computed to identify the most different groups. If we denote the distance between Group i and Group j by D_{ij}^2, and assume that Group 4 is at the origin, then, $D_{14}^2 = 3.096$, $D_{24}^2 = 6.362$, $D_{34}^2 = 1.109$, $D_{12}^2 = 2.302$, $D_{13}^2 = 5.487$, and $D_{23}^2 = 6.004$. It thus appears that Group 2 and Group 4 are farthest apart. Large differences also occur between Groups 1 and 3 and Groups

Table 11. Estimates of Effects for Discriminant Functions

Parameter	η_1	η_2
$\tau_1 - \tau_4$	−1.728	−.331
$\tau_2 - \tau_4$	−2.278	1.084
$\tau_3 - \tau_4$	.172	1.039

2 and 3. For further discussion of the use of discriminant analysis the reader is referred to Bock (1976) and Huberty (1975, 1984).

When the order of "importance" of the response variables is known, the contributions of each variable independent of the preceding one may be studied using the Roy-Bargmann step-down procedures (Roy & Bargmann, 1958). If y_{i+1} is the (i+1)th column of Y, that is, the observations on the (i+1)th response variable, then

$$\mathscr{E}(y_{i+1} | y_1, y_2, \ldots, y_i) = A\beta^*_{i+1} + Y_i\pi_i \qquad (42)$$

where β^*_{i+1} is the vector of regression coefficients corresponding to the group effects, Y_i is the matrix of observations on the first i response variables or "covariates", and π_i is the vector of coefficients on these i "covariates". The relevant hypothesis is H_{0i}: $C\beta^*_i = 0$, where C is the matrix defined in (26). This analysis is tantamount to a univariate analysis of covariance with the first i variables as the covariates with the property that

$$P\left[\bigcap_{i=1}^{P} (F_i \leq F_{\alpha i}|H_{0i})\right] = (1 - \alpha_1)(1 - \alpha_2) \ldots (1 - \alpha_p). \qquad (43)$$

It follows therefore that each of the p variables can be investigated independently in a step-wise manner. Since the p statistics are independent, the experiment-wise error rate can be specified exactly.

The above procedure is illustrated using the data from our example. Table 12 contains the results of several step-down analysis where different orders of the dependent variables are used. These orders produce markedly different results. Since the step-down tests are independent, each variable can be tested at .05/6 = .0083 level of significance so that the overall experiment-wise error rate is exactly .05. At this level, only Order 3 produces significant results for variable V3.

There are several problems inherent in the Roy-Bargmann procedure. The obvious one is that the order of the variables must be known since the order

Table 12. Step-down Analyses

Order 1	*F*	*Sig.*	*Order 2*	*F*	*Sig.*	*Order 3*	*F*	*Sig.*
V5	2.66	.067	V4	2.72	.064	V1	2.42	.087
V2	2.11	.122	V6	2.53	.078	V3	5.05	.007
V3	1.22	.323	V1	4.67	.009	V5	1.57	.220
V6	1.16	.345	V5	.77	.524	V6	.86	.474
V4	2.20	.114	V3	2.36	.097	V2	.75	.533
V1	4.12	.018	V2	.94	.438	V4	3.39	.035

affects the conclusions drawn. This is clearly not possible in an exploratory situation. However, in the present context, it can be argued that the procedure should only be used in a planned study, in which case the objection is not serious. The second problem is that although the step-down tests are statistically independent, the variables have an effect on each other. Since the response variables are used as covariates, the caveats that attend the analysis of covariance are applicable here. When the covariate means are different across the groups, as may be the case with the response variables, the covariate adjustment may result in the acceptance of the hypothesis of no group differences when without the covariate adjustment the hypothesis may have been rejected. This is the reverse of the usual analysis of covariance procedure, where with random assignment of subjects to groups the decrease in error variance results in a more powerful analysis. Thus the importance of a response variable may be masked by inappropriate covariate adjustments. In general, these problems limit the applicability of the step-down procedure.

Contrast-wise Finite and Response-wise Infinite Procedures

In this case, the planned comparisons are with respect to groups or the independent variables and not with respect to the response variables. An example of this is the Dunnett procedure in the univariate case where each treatment group is to be compared to a control group. In the multivariate case, each treatment group may be compared to a control group over all possible combinations of the response variables. The overall hypothesis is written as

$$H_o : \bigcap_j \{H_{oj} : CBMv_j = \underline{0}\} \tag{44}$$

Where the C matrix denotes the set of contrasts of interest. For this "partially planned" study, the acceptance region is defined as

$$\max T_j^2 \leqslant T^2_\alpha \tag{45}$$

where T_j^2 is the Hotelling's T^2 statistic. When all pairwise comparisons of the k groups are required, $\{\max T_j^2\}$ is the largest of the $k(k-1)/2$ correlated T^2s; when the $k-1$ groups are compared with a control group, $\{\max T_j^2\}$ is the largest of the $k-1$ correlated T^2s. When the T^2s are identically distributed, tables are available for the case of two response variables (Siotani, 1960; Roy, Gnanadesikan & Srivastava, 1971). For the general case, the joint distribution of the T_j^2s is not known. Krishnaiah (1979) has shown that when the sample size is large the joint distribution is approximated by the multivariate chi-square distribution. In addition, bounds for the critical values can be obtained through certain Poincare inequalities. Although this procedure is not in a readily usable form, the confidence intervals obtained are shorter than those resulting from the Roy-Bose method.

Returning to our example, we calculate all pairwise Hotelling's T^2 using the expression

$$T^2_{ij} = (\bar{y}_i - \bar{y}_j)'S^{-1}(\bar{y}_i - \bar{y}_j)\ n_in_j/(n_i+n_j)$$

where T^2_{ij} is the Hotelling's T^2 for the difference in the mean vectors between group i and group j, $\bar{y}_i$ is the mean vector of the ith group, S is the pooled within group variance-covariance matrix, and n_i is the number of observations in the ith group. The calculated values are as follows:

$$T^2_{12} = 8.164;\ T^2_{13} = 21.961;\ T^2_{14} = 16.263;$$
$$T^2_{23} = 26.149;\ T^2_{24} = 25.519;\ T^2_{34} = 8.391.$$

The maximum, $T^2_{max} = T^2_{23} = 26.149$. Now,

$$P[T^2_{max} \leqslant 26.149|H_0] = 1 - \Sigma P[A_i|H_0] + \Sigma P[A_i \cap A_j|H_0]$$
$$- \Sigma P[A_i \cap A_j \cap A_k|H_0] + \ldots + P[\cap_i A_i]$$

where A_1, A_2, A_3, A_4, A_5, A_5, A_6 are the events that T^2_{12}, T^2_{13}, . . . , T^2_{34} each exceeds 26.149. The probabilities given above cannot be computed easily. Hence, a lower bound for the required probability is obtained using the Bonferroni inequality:

$$P[T^2_{max} \leqslant 26.149|H_0] > 1 - \Sigma P[A_i|H_0]$$
$$= 1 - \Sigma P[T^2_{ij} > 26.149|H_0]$$
$$= 1 - 6P[T^2_{ij} > 26.149|H_0].$$

Since $F = T^2_{ij}\{(\nu_E - p+1)\}/\{p\nu_E\}$, $P[T^2_{max} \leqslant 26.149|H_0] > 1-6P[F > 3.58] =$ 1-6 (.012) = .93. Hence $P[T^2_{max} \geqslant 26.149]$ can be approximated as .07. Since this is not less than .05, the hypothesis cannot be rejected. We conclude, therefore, that the groups are not different.

The same conclusion can be arrived at by comparing the significance level obtained (from a computer printout, for instance) with the Bonferroni/Sidak adjusted α^*. Since there are 6 variables, using the Sidak procedure, we obtain $\alpha^* = (1-.05)^{1/6} = .0085$. Note that the Bonferroni procedure would have yielded $\alpha^* = .05/6 = .0083$. Since the obtained significance level, .012, is greater than .0085, the hypothesis of no group differences is accepted.

Response-wise Finite and Contrast-wise Finite Procedures

When only a finite number of hypothesis are of interest as in most confirmatory studies, overall procedures are not satisfactory. One approach is to use the Bonferroni/Sidak procedure to examine the planned contrasts of interest. An alternative approach is to use simultaneous procedures that allow the investigator to test only the hypotheses of interest and at the same time control the error rates precisely. Examples of these in univariate analysis are the Tukey and the Dunnett procedures. In general, the hypothesis to be tested is

$$H_o : \bigcap_{i}^{I} \bigcap_{j}^{J} \{H_{oij} : u_i{}'CBMv_j = 0\}. \tag{46}$$

Krishnaiah (1965a, 1965b, 1965c, 1969, 1979) has termed this the finite intersection procedure and has derived the appropriate joint distributions for testing hypotheses of the type given in (46). These simultaneous test procedures which include the Dunnett and the Tukey procedures as special cases require the evaluation of multivariate probability integrals. Although the procedure is difficult if not impossible to implement without a computer, it is mathematically and intuitively appealing. Tables of the percentage points of the joint distributions are available for special cases, as well as approximate procedures that are based on Poincare inequalities (Krishnaiah & Armitage, 1965). In these special cases, even with the approximations, the finite intersection procedures can be shown to yield confidence intervals that are shorter than the Bonferroni/Sidak intervals.

Graphical Techniques

Graphical techniques such as the half-normal plotting procedure and "gamma plots" (Roy et al., 1971) facilitate internal comparisons of a set of orthogonal single-degree-of-freedom contrasts. These procedures are visually appealing and offer the investigator an alternative procedure for the isolation of contrasts that are large relative to other contrasts.

The procedure described by Roy et al. (1971) requires an orthogonal transformation of the response matrix Y, a transformation that corresponds to meaningful orthogonal contrasts (such contrasts may be routinely obtained through a SPSS-X MANOVA procedure). Distances between the orthogonal contrast vectors x are computed in the metric of A as $x'A\,x$ where A is a suitably chosen positive definite matrix. The distances corresponding to the contrasts may be considered as random samples from a gamma distribution with unknown scale and shape parameters. Once these parameters are estimated, plots of the distances against the quantiles of the gamma distribution are obtained.

Under the null hypothesis of no effects, the points will lie on a straight line passing through the origin with slope given as the reciprocal of the scale parameter. Real effects will appear as deviations from the straight line.

The technique described above has been applied by Roy et al. (1971) to analyze multiresponse data arising in 2^N factorial designs. Orthogonal contrasts in such cases are readily interpreted. While this procedure is appealing, considerable work needs to be done before it is fully usable. The problem of choosing the matrix A must be solved since this greatly affects the outcomes.

SUMMARY

The interpretation of the results of multivariate analysis of variance involves several issues. The foremost is the nature of the overall test procedures. The overall test procedures commonly used are based on infinite intersection procedures. The rejection of the hypothesis guarantees that a bilinear combination of the response variables and group contrasts is responsible for the rejection but it may not necessarily be one of the combinations of interest. Since the experiment-wise error rate is controlled for an infinite number of contrasts, the simultaneous confidence interval procedures that are appropriate may be too conservative to yield meaningful results even in an exploratory situation.

Multiple comparison procedures other than the simultaneous confidence intervals based on the infinite intersection procedures can be classified as response-wise finite but contrast-wise infinite procedures, and response-wise finite and contrast-wise finite procedures. A summary of these procedures is given in Table 13.

Bonferroni/Sidak procedures are applicable to all these situations, are easy to implement, readily interpretable, and control for the experiment-wise error rate satisfactorily unless a great many comparisons are made. The critical value for the Bonferroni/Sidak procedure may be compared with the Roy-Bose critical value and the procedure that yields the shorter confidence intervals can be chosen as the appropriate procedure. Tests which are generally unrelated to the first stage overall test and which are used satisfactorily unless a great many comparisons are made. The critical value for the Bonferroni/Sidak procedure may be compared with the Roy-Bose critical value and the procedure that yields the shorter confidence intervals can be chosen. In general, when $s < 3$ and m is small, the Roy procedure is better than the Bonferroni procedure and should be employed.

Table 13. Classification of Multiple Comparison Procedures

		Response-wise	
		Infinite	*Finite*
Contrast-wise	Infinite	Roy's Procedure	Discriminant Analysis Step-down Discriminant Analysis Roy-Bargmann Step-down F Bonferroni/Sidak
	Finite	Max T^2 Bonferroni/Sidak	Finite Intersection Procedure Bonferroni/Sidak

The often advocated procedure of following up the rejection of the null hypothesis with a more powerful multiple comparison procedure should be discouraged. First, the overall rejection of the null hypothesis does not guarantee that any meaningful contrast among the means will be significant, as our example showed. Second, since the overall test and the follow up procedure are unrelated, significant contrasts may be found even when the null hypothesis would not have been rejected. Third, follow up multiple comparison procedures which are unrelated to the overall test result in an inflation of the experiment-wise error rate. If multiple comparisons are of primary interest, a suitable multiple comparison procedure can be used without first performing an overall test. For example, since the Bonferroni/Sidak procedure is unrelated to any of the four overall test procedures, it may be used to construct confidence intervals directly.

Discriminant analysis and step-down procedures as means of ordering variables according to importance are not satisfactory in general, since the order depends upon the intercorrelations among variables. In addition, step-down procedures may mask the presence of an important variable as a result of covariate adjustment that may not be appropriate. Furthermore, as was seen in our example, different orders of the variables can produce startlingly different outcomes. This introduces an undesirable level of subjectivity into the analysis.

Graphical techniques such as gamma plots provide interesting alternatives to currently available inferential procedures. However, they need considerable refinement before they can be routinely accepted.

When completely planned studies or confirmatory studies are undertaken, finite intersection procedures provide the ultimate flexibility. These procedures are not readily available and are computationally complex. However, finite intersection procedures hold the most promise for the analysis of completely planned studies.

REFERENCES

Anderson, T. W. (1984). *An introduction to multivariate statistical analysis* (2nd ed.). New York: John Wiley & Sons.

Bird, Kevin D., & Hadzi-Pavlovic, H. (1983). Simultaneous Test Procedures and the Choice of a Test Statistic in MANOVA. *Psychological Bulletin,* 167–178.

Bock, R. D. (1963). Programming univariate and multivariate analysis of variance. *Technometrics, 5,* 95–117.

Bock, R. D. (1975). *Multivariate statistical methods in behavioral research.* New York: McGraw-Hill.

Gabriel, K. R. (1968). Simultaneous test procedures in multivariate analysis of variance. *Biometrika, 55,* 489–504.

Huberty, C. J. (1975). Discriminant analysis. *Review of Educational Research, 45,* 543–598.

Huberty, C. J. (1984). Issues in the use and interpretation of discriminant analysis. *Psychological Bulletin, 95,* 156–171.

Krishnaiah, P. R. (1965). On the simultaneous ANOVA and MANOVA tests. *Annals of the Institute of Statistical Mathematics, 17,* 35–53.

Krishnaiah, P. R. (1965). On a multivariate generalization of the simultaneous analysis of variance. *Annals of the Institute of Statistical Mathematics, 17,* 167–173.

Krishnaiah, P. R. (1965). Multiple comparisons tests in multiresponse experiments. *Sankhya A. 27,* 65–72.

Krishnaiah, P. R. (1969). Simultaneous test procedures under general MANOVA models. In *Multivariate analysis II* (pp. 121–143). New York: Academic Press.

Krishnaiah, P. R. (1979). Some developments on simultaneous test procedures. In *Developments in statistics* (pp. 157–201). Academic Press, New York.

Krishnaiah, P. R., & Armitage, J. V. (1965). Percentage points of the multivariate t distribution. ARL Technical Report No. 65–199, Aerospace Research Laboratories, Wright-Patterson Air Force Base, Dayton, Ohio.

Morrison, D. F. (1976). *Multivariate statistical methods.* New York: McGraw-Hill.

Fisher, R. A. (1936). The use of multiple measurements in taxonomic problems. *Annals of Eugenics, 7,* 179–188.

Hotelling, H. (1931). The generalization of Student's ratio. *Annals of Mathematical Statistics, 2,* 360–378.

Olson, Chester L. (1974). Comparative robustness of six tests in multivariate analysis of variance. *Journal of the American Statistical Association, 69,* 894–908.

Roy, S. N. (1953). On a heuristic method of test construction and its use multivariate analysis. Annals of *Mathematical Statistics, 24,* 220–238.

Roy, S. N. (1957). *Some aspects of multivariate analysis.* New York: John Wiley and Sons.

Roy, S. N., & Bargmann, R. (1958). Tests of multiple independence and the associated confidence bounds. *Annals of Mathematical Statistics, 29,* 491–503.

Roy, S. N., & Bose, R. C. (1953). Simultaneous confidence interval estimation. *Annals of Mathematical Statistics, 24,* 513–536.

Roy, S. N., & Gnanadesikan, R., & Srivastava, J. N. (1971). *Analysis and design of certain quantitative multiresponse experiments.* Oxford: Pergamon Press.

Sidak, Z. (1967). Rectangular confidence regions for the means of multivariate normal distributions. *Journal of the American Statistical Association, 62,* 626–633.

Siotani, M. (1960). Notes on multivariate confidence bounds. *Annals of Institute of Statistical Mathematics, 11,* 167–182.

Swaminathan, H., & DeFriesse, F. (1979). Detecting significant contrasts in analysis of variance. *Educational and Psychological Measurement, 39,* 39–44.

Wilks, S. S. (1932). Certain generalizations in the analysis of variance. *Biometrika, 24,* 471–494.